Crossing the Threshold

Together As One

Clarence Benoit III

Copyright © 2018. Clarence Benoit III

Unless otherwise indicated, Bible quotations are taken from
the New International Version of the Bible.
Copyright © 1973, 1978, 1984 by the International Bible Society.
Used by permission of Zondervan Publishing House.
All rights reserved.

New Jerusalem Publishing LLC

Paperback ISBN
978-1-7324377-0-8

eBook ISBN
978-1-7324377-2-2

The man said, "This is now bone of my bones and flesh of my flesh; she shall be called 'woman,' for she was taken out of man."

For this reason a man will leave his father and mother and be united to his wife, and they will become one flesh.

(Genesis 2:23-24)

Table of Contents

Acknowledgments 6
Introduction 7
God's Expectations 23
   From Singleness & Dating 23
      Some Principles for Godly Dating 25
         Undivided Devotion 26
         Seek Advice 29
         Be Not Unequally Yoked 36
         Accept One Another 47
         Sexual Integrity 51
         #NoSpecificInstructions 122
      What About Testing the Water First? 124
      Cross-Gender Friendships 142
      What You Talkin' Bout Singleness Is A Blessing? ... 149
      Who You Really in Love With? 160
      Who Do I Marry? 172
      Why Do I Get Married? 192
      Imitating the Likeness of Christ 197
      Whatcha Marrying Into? 199
      Skeletons in the Closet 201
   Into Holy Matrimony 207
      Marriage by Design 208
         Covenant versus Contract 211
         Partnership 216
         Oneness of Marriage 220
         Divorce 235
         Honored By All 254

- Like Christ and the Church 255
- Dealing with Conflict 263
  - Battle of the Sexes 267
  - Two Lives Joining Into One 268
  - Environmental Products 275
  - Sins & Misunderstandings 279
    - Communication 281
    - Forgiveness 289
    - Grace & Mercy 299
- Roles of the Husband and Wife 303
  - Wives 305
  - Husbands 324
  - Husbands and Wives 352
- Personal Expectations 365
  - Having Realistic Expectations 365
- Conclusion of the Matter 373
  - Practical Application 373
- About the Author 379
  - A Jet Tour Through the Author's Life 379
  - Keeping Tabs on the Author 389
- Bibliography 391

Acknowledgments

First and foremost, I want to give glory to God and thank Him for putting this on my heart to write years ago. I thank Him for the experiences He's allowed me to have in order to bring this to fruition and put Him on display. And, as always, I thank Him for all of the amazing grace He's given me in abundance through His Son Jesus Christ for everything especially when I've totally blown it. People have no idea what they're missing out on in not knowing you. Thank you Lord Jesus!

I have a lot of gratitude and appreciation for those who took the time out of their busy schedules to assist in bringing this book to life. The combination of encouragement, questions posed to provoke thought to help me expound on particular areas, their reactions, feedback, and edits were invaluable. Thank you all so much. I love and appreciate you all from the bottom of my heart.

Barbara *"Momma J"* Joynes, I can't express enough gratitude to you for being as zealous as I am for the completion of this book and the confidence you've expressed in its potential. Thank you so much for being so forthright, for how you love and serve those around you. The way you care and nurture those around you is what makes you a mother in the faith. Hence, the affectionate moniker Momma J. Love you always!

Erin Dunivan, you are definitely one of those women who's raising her family, bringing home the bacon, and cooking it too. Keep on holding it down sis! You can do all things through Him who gives you strength (Philippians 4:13).

COVER DESIGN
JD Smith – Design
www.jdsmith-design.com

Image by Mikayla Herrick via Unsplash
www.mikaylaherrick.co
www.facebook.com/mikaylaherrickphoto

Introduction

The two of you may have been dating for a little while now or maybe you haven't been dating for that long at all. It's really irrelevant any way because all you know is that you've never, ever felt this way about anyone in your life before. When you're apart, you can't get your significant other off of your mind. Then, when you're together, the chemistry you share is so powerful that it's hard for others to determine if they're watching two people or last year's fireworks display. In an effort to enlighten you as to where you might be, see if any of the following statements sound familiar.

- "This is the most wonderful thing that has ever happened to me. I've never felt this way before; it feels so right, it must be love!"

- "I just know that Richard (you fill in the name) is the right one for me! He/she makes me feel so good."

If you've ever thought or said anything even remotely close to these phrases, you may be feeling that the stars and the planets are clearly lined up. This vibe that you're feeling between the two of you can't be wrong. The verdict is unanimous! You and your significant other are thinking about moving your relationship into something a bit more permanent. In other words, you're ready to tie the knot and get married! I'd be willing to bet a significant amount of money that you can already hear the wedding bells ringing.

Now, hold your horses for a minute. As Proverbs 19:2 says, "It's not good to have zeal without knowledge, nor to be hasty and miss the way," so let's look at this a bit more carefully. Before you rush off to get the engagement ring, pick your wedding colors, or compile that massive guest list, ask yourself a couple of very important questions. Are you **really** ready for marriage? Do you have any idea what to expect or what's expected of you? Most people have this naïve idea that marriage is absolutely blissful all the time. They have this idea that it's something you just do and everything will just work out. They have no idea of their roles or the work required behind the scenes in order to have a good marriage. I can conclude this without doing any research or performing a single study on the topic simply because of the attitude that the phrases I mentioned earlier conveys. The feelings that surround statements like those are the sole basis couples use for their decision to get married. Primarily for those who've never been married, this implies that some people think that marriage is always going to be like that – intense feelings of self-gratification. When in reality, marriage is better the more it resembles Jesus on the cross – death and self-sacrifice. Just as Christians find joy in Christ, first through His sacrifice on the cross, then the sacrifice of his or her life for Him, you find joy in marriage by the same means – the sacrifice of yourself for your spouse. Marriage is absolutely nothing like dating. Depending on your relationship, it can be like dating at different points in time. It doesn't come as easily as when you're dating. You have to work at it and it can get harder to facilitate as the years go by as you deal with hurts, complacency, and the challenges presented by the condition of the human heart. I also feel obligated to point out that those phrases are extremely selfish in nature. They only reflect how dating your significant other has made you feel. We know that emotions are very unreliable when it comes to decision making. When we make emotional decisions, they typically lead to trouble. Do you really want to base a life-long, important decision such as this on your emotions? Our feelings are usually selfishly motivated and when we're getting something that makes us feel good, we are likely to block everything else out except that which makes us feel good. Those phrases come across as though the other person is not taken into consideration or even exists. It's as though you're in love with being in love, which is exactly what's happening. This appropriately leads me to my next question. Is this person you're dating **really** the type of person you want to marry? Under the circumstances, think about the gravity of what you're saying here. You're saying that this is the person I want to spend the rest of my life with. Of course, this is obvious but let me pose a couple of simple questions to expound more of what this really means over the long haul of marriage. Is this the person you really want by your side supporting you during your greatest tragedies in life? Is this the person you want to share your greatest joys in life with? At this juncture, most people don't know anything of substance about the person that he or she is dating because neither of them has made any attempt to dig deeper into the other person or allowed the depth of his or her own character to be manifested to the other person. The couple can be so caught up in the emotional high of superficiality and the idea of dating or being "in love" that they neglect to extract anything of value out about the other person. This is not good as it is very shallow. What you know about them is primarily based on appearances or what you perceive that person to be. The dating relationship should be somewhat like shopping for a new car. You take the car out for a test spin and you push it. You want to see what it can do. You try to create as normal conditions as possible for you in that short amount of time because you want to see if the car is going to work for you. You pose questions to the salesman to find out those things about the car that lie beneath the surface that aren't so easily detectable. Although, you won't be able to come close to knowing all you can or need to about this car, which is perfectly acceptable, you want to get to know this car as much as possible before you make the purchase because it's going to be with you for the long haul. You can't easily get out of a major purchase like this, so you are committed to taking your time to compile as much pertinent information as possible. Now, if you've put this much effort into purchasing a car, a far less significant item, why wouldn't you at least replicate that effort into choosing your life partner? With this in mind, the exact same concept should be applied in a dating relationship. When you're dating, it is the test drive so to speak for marriage. You want to get acquainted with this person's character as much as possible. You know it won't be perfect as there will be problems with it along the way. The purpose is doing your homework so that you can make an informed decision that you can live with despite the difficulties that will inevitably come your way. You achieve this by taking notice of those visible traits.

Next, you dig a little deeper by asking questions in an effort to bring to light those things that aren't so easily visible. Question, not just the person of interest, but those close to him or her as well. This is important to do because you want to get an idea of how well the two of you will work together as a team. Also, what you are able to see during the dating period will definitely be present when you get married. Marriage doesn't all of a sudden erase the habits in your significant other, especially the bad ones. If anything, it'll seem to magnify them as you now realize that you're stuck with them for life. You will inherit and have to deal with them as you do your own. As with the car, you want to see what's pertinent in order to make a wise decision because, once married, this person will be with you for the long haul. I'm talking about the rest of your earthly life. If you see it won't work, then, just as you would do with a car that wouldn't work, you should move on. Maybe, he or she isn't the one or the time isn't right. Now, I'm not saying that you have to be like a robot or something, devoid of any emotions and be so analytical that you become extremely knit-picky. I'm just saying that you should have an appropriate balance between the two. How so? Well, having a balance between the two means bringing some logic and forethought into the process instead of assuming that simply because it makes you feel good that it must be right. Our emotions are always going to be involved; they are a natural part of this process. You'll see as you read throughout this book that it's designed to help provoke you to thoughtful insight in order to incorporate more wisdom and prudence into this process. It will help you to formulate precise questions to ask yourself, make a self-assessment, and have a bit of a game plan in mind. Remember Proverbs 19:2? Desire and wisdom must come together in order to avoid making major mistakes. Your emotions shouldn't be leading the way. We are not looking for perfection. We'd all be out of luck if that was the case. As with the car, there's going to be problems. But, is this person someone you want to live with, love, and grow together with despite his or her imperfections through the difficulties that life will throw your way. You can only make a decision like that by doing your homework, not jumping in unprepared. I want you to honor God, be happy, and feel good about your choice. That's all I'm trying to encourage.

At this point, what I'm curious about is whether or not I have your attention. Have your wheels started spinning expeditiously? I hope so. I wrote those things specifically with that purpose in mind. Sorry to bust your bubble, but somebody had to do it before you rushed off and potentially made the biggest mistake of your life.

So, what's this marriage thing all about anyway? If we observe what we see in the world around us, I'm afraid that the majority of what we see will be nothing more than a big disappointment. Marriage, as seen in the world, has been expanded into something it was never meant to be. To begin with, look at all the different types of marriages people engage in. There are open marriages, shotgun marriages, marriages of convenience, common law marriages, and now, there's a big push to legalize gay marriages. We have all of these different types now, but in the beginning, there was only one. If you take a look at what each of these 'marriages' consist of, you'll find that there's something very wrong with every one of these so-called marriages. Every one of them in some form or fashion is out of sync with God's original design for marriage. Anything not in line with God's original design then comes from man. This means that it does not glorify Him nor does it please Him. Although there are several things that destroy the sanctity of marriage such as infidelity (whether it's the physical act of adultery, the lustful thoughts that borne physical adultery, viewing pornography, and the like), I believe that its greatest predator is found in its dissolution. Of course, what I'm referring to here is divorce. The divorce rate in this country is staggering. You'd think with all of the love songs you hear on the radio with people boasting about what they're going to do for you, how they're going to treat you, and what type of man or woman they're going to be for you that the marriages in this country would reflect that attitude. Those songs get us all fired up; we get drawn into them, but obviously that's not the case when it comes to reality. We can talk a good game. But, when it comes time to man or woman up, the smoke clears and you realize there really wasn't much of a fire there after all. At a mind-blowing 47.9%, according to the National Center for Health Statistics, people divorce as though it's the latest fad sweeping across America to which I've made a significant share of contributions. Like a good friend of mine once said, "Anymore, marriage has become nothing more than a sprint to the divorce court. As soon as you cross the threshold, the race is on." It's no wonder that almost half of our marriages end in divorce. There are so many sources in the world that says it's okay. For example, listen to the poison that spews through the air waves of our radio and television stations.

> For you I gave my heart and turned my back against the world
> 'Cause you were my girl, girl, girl
> I done damn near lost my mama, I done been through so much drama
> I done turned into the man that I never thought I'd be
>
> I'm ready to sign them papers, papers, papers
> I done took all I can take, but you leave me no options, girl
> I can't deny how much I love you, I done gave up everything I had to
> As hard as it is, I'm afraid I gotta say
>
> I'm ready to sign them papers, papers, papers
> I done took all I can take, but you leave me no options, girl
> Oh, oh, oh papers
> Oh, oh, oh papers
>
> (Excerpt from *Papers* by Usher)

We live in a time where divorce is glorified; it has become the "solution" to the problem. On the contrary, it just causes more problems when you think about the strain caused by the grueling process of a divorce: the destruction of relationships, the long-term effects it has on the family (spouses, kids, and in-laws), and the spiritual implications. There are animals that stay together longer than we do! So, why do we divorce so doggone much? Some of the more popular reasons are falling out of love or irreconcilable differences. But, those are all lies. The answer to that question is found in Jesus' response. When the Pharisees tried to trap Jesus in Matthew 19 by questioning Him about Moses in regards to the appropriateness of divorce, Jesus fully captured the condition that serves as the sole catalyst for this social epidemic. Jesus said it was due to the hardness of our hearts. Our hearts can become so calloused, sometimes without much effort at all. It's like the calloused skin that accumulates at the base of our fingers. Due to the friction caused by the constant rubbing against something hard, the surface becomes dry, hard, and deadened. It can peel away with no pain at all. When this condition due to sin creeps into our hearts, we become deadened, unresponsive, and easily disconnected from one another.

Looking at marriage through the eyes of God, you'll quickly realize that it's drastically different from what we see in the world. Marriage is the most important relationship we'll ever engage in next to our relationship with Jesus. It is the only relationship that draws a comparison to Christ and the relationship He has with His church (Ephesians 5:22-33). This fact demonstrates the high importance placed upon this relationship within the realm of humanity. There's no other relationship whether it be mother, father, siblings, friends, or affairs with material objects that should come between or hinder this relationship. As with God, if something supersedes our relationship with Him; it's considered sin. In all cases, it may not be that cut throat, but if something disrupts the stability of the marriage, the issue needs to be worked out to restore the marriage back to good standing. Marriage is, also, the only human relationship where the two become one in the eyes of God. Something else you'll see about marriage is that it reflects the corporate nature of God. Let's think about a few characteristics of a corporation for a minute. A corporation is an entity that is made up of multiple individual entities that are unified and exist for the common good of the whole. Each of the individual entities does its part to fulfill its role within the corporation much like God, the Father, the Son, and the Holy Spirit, have been working since before the beginning of time to reconcile man back to Himself. Within the corporation, you can see and experience many of the attributes of God's corporate nature such as unity, teamwork, diversity, selflessness, fellowship, the denial of self for the greater good of the whole, and so on. One person cannot run a corporation alone – it is too much for one person much like life at times is too much for one person to handle on his or her own. I believe that these are reasons why God said that it was not good for man to be alone; he needed a suitable helper and at the time one wasn't yet available. This definitely dispels the old adage that a dog is man's best friend because the dog already existed at this point. In creating Adam's suitable helper, there's something very interesting to take notice of if you haven't done so already. Why didn't God create Eve from scratch? He created all of the other living creatures that way. Adam was raised directly out of the dust of the Earth. Why wasn't Eve created in the same fashion? Instead, God chose to take a piece of Adam to create Eve. What was this diversion from His previous method of creating the living, breathing creatures supposed to convey? I think Adam understood exactly what it meant.

> [23]The man said, "This is now bone of my bones and flesh of my flesh; she shall be called woman, for she was taken out of man." [24]For this reason a man will leave his father and mother and be united to his wife, and they will become one flesh.
> (Genesis 2:23-24)

Adam's relationship with Eve was meant to be unique; it would supersede all relationships Adam had with any other creature or person. It's reflective of our relationship to God in comparison to the rest of His creation. He made us in His likeness (Genesis 1:27) denoting our unique relationship with Him. We reflect His likeness spiritually, mentally, morally, and socially. This means that we were meant to bring Him glory like no other creature He had created. I believe if people would grasp and apply the concepts derived from just this passage alone; it would have a dramatic impact on the outcome of our marriages. Keep this passage in the back of your mind as you venture on throughout this book. You will see this passage again later on where you'll see it in a slightly different perspective.

Let's continue on with a couple of more thoughts about marriage. It is a way that we can begin to connect with God's unconditional love for us. Just think about it for a minute. You have two imperfect, sinful beings, despite knowing each other's flaws; they are helplessly in love and go to the ends of the Earth for the benefit of each other. Although on a much smaller scale, isn't this similar in some essential respects to God's love for us? Despite our wretchedness, which He knows to the fullest degree, contrasted with His holiness, He still chooses to love us. And, in order to have a relationship with us, He went to the ends of the Earth and beyond by sending His Son to die for us. So, in summary, marriage is a miracle by God where He reunites what He separated in the very beginning. Marriage is the most fulfilling relationship we will ever experience here on Earth if we strive to achieve God's standard for marriage. It is the most intimate relationship where you can experience a level of love, caring, sharing, and support you won't ever come close to in any other human relationship. Through the trials and challenges of marriage, you'll be pushed beyond your limits into a realm of strength and maturity you couldn't achieve on your own. Yet, with such great benefits, so many miss out on its blessings because they either gave up or simply allowed coexisting to be the culmination of their marriage. It is a relationship where the two constantly grow together to become better for the other person. The husband grows to become a better husband for his wife; the wife grows to become a better wife for her husband. So, essentially, what is marriage? It is at the very core of its existence a gift to us from God? Later, we'll see how this reflects Christ and the church.

So, what is the key to success and prosperity in such an important human relationship? My intent is to help you get on the right path to having a marriage that brings glory to God. That is the key to success and prosperity. The first step in achieving this goal is preparation. You prepare by educating yourself on what is God's design for marriage and the roles He determined for the husband and the wife. Of course, He's laid the standard for marriage in His Word, which I hope this book will spur you on to digging for answers there. The next step in achieving this goal is action. Begin now, as a single, to live the life that God wants you to live if you haven't committed to doing so already. Also, I hope that you will take steps in getting to know your potential future spouse a little more seriously and not just letting your emotions run rampant. But, most importantly, whether you're dating or not, I hope that you will get to know yourself a lot better because you're responsible for changing you and you only. I feel that I must emphasize this; you cannot change your partner; you can only change you. What you do does affect your marriage, which affects you and your spouse too. Your marriage is essentially the environment that you have to live in. Therefore, if someone feels that they're in a bad marriage, chances are they're partly responsible. In my marriages, my conscience intent was never to be a bad husband. But rest assured, I have my sins, made my share of mistakes, and have a skewed perspective of some things that have been influenced by the world and my past negative experiences. Like everyone else, I am a damaged good. So, I encourage you to get to know yourself because you bring all of your dents, scars, and rust marks into your marriage. Without God, preparation, and action on your part, along with the mess your partner will bring to the marriage colliding with yours, it will quickly turn your marriage into a colossal disaster.

God's Expectations

From Singleness & Dating

It's obvious that we have a need for the various forms of relationships that we can have in our lives. The most obvious reason being that I don't think God would have put us all here together if we weren't supposed to have some interaction with each other. Also, I see our need for relationships reflected in our design, creation, and the process. In regards to our design, remember we were modeled after our Creator's likeness, which consists of three separate, personal Beings that are completely united in perfect harmony with each other to form the One Triune God we worship. In regards to our creation, the partnership – the creation of Eve – stemmed out of the fact that it was not good for Adam to be alone (Genesis

2:18). The Bible is full of "one another" Scriptures that guide and direct us in relating to one another in harmony. It would be impossible to do those things by yourself. In regards to the process, we simply flourish when we have great relationships in our lives. In our relationships, we need people to share in our victories and be victorious with like David had with his mighty men. We need people who can look out for and help us through our trials and sufferings like David had with Jonathon. We need relationships in order to thrive in life. Therefore, relationships are a necessity and very healthy for us.

Dating relationships are no different but I believe that many people have the wrong perspective and or place too high a value on the dating relationship. Some people get their self-worth from being in a dating relationship so much so that they feel incomplete, insecure, or that they'll just die unless they're hugged up with somebody. Some are pressured by family and friends. Others have such low self-esteem that they stay in abusive relationships. Others are so insecure or vindictive that they use relationships to control others. While others yearn for one so much that they rush off and do something impetuous that they end up regretting later. Although we have this yearning, this love jones for relationships, we neglect to have the same attitude – an unquenchable thirst, this burning desire, or hunger that seems to never be satisfied – towards God. It's because of that broken relationship with Him that we died physically and spiritually. Although we still die physically, we can be revived spiritually (Ephesians 2:1-10).

Dating is really a relatively new concept. You will not find anything about dating in the Bible. With a few exceptions where God intervened, the wife was chosen early on for the man by his parents. She was groomed for him and when it was time for marriage – they got married. There was no testing of the merchandise or trying it out to see if it will work. In some parts of the world, that is still done to this day. In a fallen world, dating has really become more of an avenue for the rise of impurity, sexual immorality and improper relationships in the eyes of God. Although dating is not specifically addressed in the Bible, it does not mean that His Word can't be applied to dating in order to honor Him. Nothing in all creation is outside the power of His Word; it is relevant to and sufficient for every aspect of life (Hebrews 4:12).

Some Principles for Godly Dating

Therefore, I'd like to introduce some principles from God's Word, in case you're not already familiar with them that can be applied to your dating relationship. These principles are not a complete listing. They are, also, not meant to hinder you in any form or fashion. They are simply meant to help you be as successful as possible in honoring God, having a great relationship, and bringing some prosperity, not undo stress, to your life.

Undivided Devotion

The first principle that I want to introduce to you is by far the most important. It is living in undivided devotion to the Lord. Let's take a look at a passage of Scripture to begin the discussion.

> [32]I would like you to be free from concern. An unmarried man is concerned about the Lord's affairs – how he can please the Lord. [33]But a married man is concerned about the affairs of this world – how he can please his wife – [34]and his interests are divided. An unmarried woman or virgin is concerned about the Lord's affairs: Her aim is to be devoted to the Lord in both body and spirit. But a married woman is concerned about the affairs of this world – how she can please her husband. [35]I am saying this for your own good, not to restrict you, but that you may live in a right way in undivided devotion to the Lord.
> (I Corinthians 7:32-35)

Paul provides a warning in writing this to the disciples, namely the singles, in the church at Corinth. Marriage is the only situation where it's acceptable before God to have one's focus divided – but, even in this, God must remain the primary focus. When you're dating, you're not married. Some singles begin to date and they act as though they're already married. The focus or mark of an unmarried man or woman is to be how can I please the Lord with my life. What is it that the Lord desires? Love for and obedience to the Lord should be the foundation from which everything else in a single man or woman's life is built. Our call is to "love the Lord your God with all your heart and with all your soul and with all your mind and with all your strength (Mark 12:30)." Single individuals are the ones most free to live this lifestyle as we have no real distractions or hindrances. Yet, some singles act as though marriage is the goal of life and feel as though they will have arrived when they get married. Some of our married friends don't really help us with this either. They pose questions like, "When are you getting married?" or "What's wrong with you? You're not married yet." In feeling like this, we miss out on being single, which is a blessing because neither being single nor being married is above the other. We also miss out on properly preparing ourselves for marriage. It's our time to really grow and get closer to God. This is best done without the distraction of another person. You can't be responsible for or give to another person in a marital setting when you haven't taken care of and strengthened yourself. You'll be bringing absolutely nothing to the table. You won't be growing. You won't be equipped to help the other person grow. Thus, the marriage may suffer more and may end before it actually begins to prosper.

Our ultimate goal in life is to be closer to God and in the end, when it's all said and done, be in heaven with Him for eternity. Your spouse is your twenty-four by seven discipleship partner; you are responsible for helping each other spiritually. How does this principal come into play with a dating relationship? Well, ask yourself a couple of questions.

- Am I closer to God with or without this person?
- Is this person seeking to be closer to God?

I think these are two questions you should be asking yourself periodically throughout any dating relationship. As you contemplate and determine the answer to those questions for yourself, it can help you begin assessing your partner and the direction of the dating relationship. You want to make sure that the two of you are still moving towards God together. You absolutely don't want to become a stumbling block to each other. There is nothing that's supposed to come between you and your relationship with God.

So, on occasions, dating relationships will end for whatever reason. Some people become so devastated when it doesn't work out because they don't realize that the person they were dating may have only been there to season them for a while. It was never meant to be forever. Although it appears to be the end of the world – not to say there's not some hurt involved – there is good news as there always is with God no matter the situation. This is a time for reflection, a time for personal growth, and a time to be positive as the separation may only be temporary. The only purpose that person may have had in your life may have been to help you grow so that you may be better for God and possibly your future spouse.

In all of this, the best time to begin preparing for marriage is while you're single by committing yourself wholly to God. And don't forget to enjoy your singleness; it is a blessing from God. Let me say it again. Singleness is a blessing! In conclusion, think about this for a moment. What if you live your life longing to be married and being miserable because you're not? Then, all of a sudden, you end up on your death bed. What do you want to have said about your life as you lay there reflecting on it? Do you want to say that you didn't enjoy it because you were longing for something to happen that never did? As the Message version says, "God, not your marital status, defines your life." Be compelled by God and the love of Christ (II Corinthians 5:14).

Seek Advice

At the onset of a dating relationship and throughout, there can be so much excitement. It literally feels like ecstasy. It's so easy to become so enamored with each other. You've finally found someone you've connected with on a deeper level and that individual reciprocates those feelings right back to you. This is a person you probably share some important commonalities with and you're interested in learning more about each other. You can't deny. There's definitely some strong chemistry between the two of you. Have you ever found yourself in a crowded room knowing that he or she is in the vicinity? Suppose you're holding a conversation with someone, all the while in the back of your mind you're wondering where he or she is at. Being that he or she wasn't in your line of sight, you found yourself constantly looking for him or her no matter what you were doing in hopes of catching a glimpse. Then, with just a simple catching of each other's eye from across the room, a spark ignited causing your heart to palpitate rapidly, breathe more deeply, and smile from ear to ear with excitement. As studies have shown, this reaction is caused by the heightened level of adrenaline that's dumped into your body while dating. This spike in your adrenaline can rush through you like an F-16 fighter jet slicing its way through the atmosphere at six hundred miles per hour leaving behind an aftershock that can literally knock you off your feet when you least expect it. It'll have you dazed and confused wondering how in the world did I get here.

    I can remember so vividly, like yesterday, having these same feelings toward my first wife when she and I started dating back in 1995. We met while she was attending Kansas University in Lawrence, Kansas as a foreign exchange student. She was from Chalezeule, France. Prior to her first semester, I had just moved away from Lawrence to Kansas City. On the weekends, I frequently traveled back to Lawrence, which was about a forty-five minute drive from where I lived. All of my friends were there and I didn't know anybody in Kansas City at the time. When she and I really began getting to know each other, we took to one another like a fish to water. I soon began driving to Lawrence even more than just on the weekends. Rest assured it wasn't to spend more time with the boys either. In fact, they were seeing much less of me on the weekends. Spending time with her had me on a high that no drug in the world could duplicate. When we were apart, I literally couldn't get her off of my mind – not that I ever put forth any effort to do so. I knew that she felt the same way about me. One Sunday evening, after spending the weekend with her, I was leaving to go back home to Kansas City so that I could go to work Monday morning. While she was seeing me off at her apartment door, she asked me when I was coming back. No sooner than I responded with my answer, she exclaimed, "Wednesday!" and got a bit of an attitude with me. Later that evening, we talked on the phone and she apologized for getting upset with me, but she felt like three days was way too long to have to wait to see me again. Good Lord! Man, my heart just melted. After hearing that, I almost jumped in the car and drove back to Lawrence that night. As the end of the school year approached, we both began to feel the pressure of her having to leave to go back to France. We saw it in each other and had spoken briefly about it a few times before but elected to not be so concerned about it until the time comes. We just wanted to enjoy our remaining time together as much as possible. It hovered over us like a dark cloud and thickened as the time drew nearer. And, I think it may have been the cause of a little friction between us a few times. We had already spoken about her returning to the States and getting married. I had no doubt that I wanted to spend the rest of my life with her. Well, the inevitable eventually happened. One Monday, in the summer of 1996, I took her to the airport. She got on a plane and returned home to France. I had never felt so much pain and sickness in my life. Still, to this day, I haven't felt anything even remotely close to or comparable to what I felt those initial few months we were apart. We both knew we'd miss each other, but I don't think either of us expected it to have the impact that it had. During one of our conversations, a couple of days after she had left, we discussed the possibility of me going to stay the year with her in France, then we'd return to the States together. We'd take a couple of days to think about it and we'd discuss it on Friday when we talked again. Deep down inside, I knew it probably wasn't the best idea. With the way we both were feeling, I definitely gave it some serious consideration over the next couple of days. In addition to just flat out dropping everything, my primary concern was that I had just acquired my first job in my major field of study not more than two months before she left to return home. I had been out of school for three years at the time and it had been like pulling teeth trying to find a job in my field of study. I knew I just needed to get my foot in the door and all would be fine. If I had a nickel for every time an employer told me that I'd been out of school too long and that I should think about going back, I wouldn't have needed any of their jobs. Now, I was finally getting that foot-in-the-door opportunity. To drop that, go away for a year, then come back would have made things so hard for both of us. Intellectually, I knew without a shadow of a doubt that it would be best for me to stay here and continue getting established in my career. That way, I could have a good foundation ready for her to come back to. With us transitioning to a life together and her coming to a place literally foreign to all she had ever known, you want things to be stable and go as smoothly as possible. But, the pain of being separated from her, my emotions, and just hearing the pain in her voice over the phone kept fighting and preventing me from making the solid decision that I needed to. I was letting my emotions get the best of me. When I mentioned the idea to my mother, she went on an emotional tirade. She was mainly concerned about not seeing me as much. I'm thinking you had fifteen plus years already – what's the problem? Although, a couple of things she said could have held some water. That really didn't help any knowing that she was extremely biased in her thinking. What really helped me to make the decision that I needed was the unbiased advice that I got from a friend and his wife. They shared some thoughts that were already on my mind and a few that weren't. They really helped me to see this from multiple perspectives. This sound advice helped propel me to and be firm with the decision that I needed to make. On Friday, when she and I spoke, I shared that I didn't think it was a good idea and the reasons why. She agreed and although we didn't want to be apart for that long, we decided we'd stick it out together. I honestly think we both felt better about the decision even though we didn't like it. She even mentioned it to her parents and they thought it wasn't a good idea either. I owe a great deal of making that decision to the advice I received. If I hadn't received that advice, there's a slight chance that I would have dropped everything and gone to France.

Emotions can skyrocket at the slightest activity. They impact good judgment in the same fashion the iceberg did the Titanic and anyone even remotely involved will likely pay a price. In regards to dating, as with anything else in our life, it is beneficial for us to seek advice. The Bible makes its stand on the subject matter perfectly clear. Likewise, its benefits to us are perfectly clear.

There are two benefits that literally jump off the pages of Scripture that God obviously wants us to grasp from seeking out advice. Proverbs 11:14 and 15:22 says respectively, "For lack of guidance a nation falls, but many advisers make victory sure" and "Plans fail for lack of counsel, but with many advisers they succeed." In order to live victorious lives and be successful, we simply need to seek out advice. We all like to think that we achieved success on our own without any help from anyone else. You hear terms like self-made man or self-made millionaire. We even like to devour the success of others for our own glory by claiming that we taught them everything they know. It's pretty clear that we have a strong desire to be successful at whatever we do. But, no one who has any level of success in life got there alone. It's impossible and it just doesn't work that way. God didn't design it that way. Success is a community effort. The only thing you can achieve success in solely on your own is to reap the fruits of your laziness, which results in nothing.

The second thing we are so attracted to is wisdom. Who hasn't thought they were full of wisdom at some point in time? Man is so elated by his own mind, thoughts, and ideas that you'd think we assumed the role of creator instead of discoverer. That's what we're doing with our time in this world; we discover and learn things. But, Proverbs 13:10 and 19:20 says respectively, "Pride only breeds quarrels, but wisdom is found in those who take advice" and "Listen to advice and accept instruction, and in the end you will be wise." It is clearly seen that listening and accepting advice will make us wise in the end. This in no way means you are to blindly accept what someone tells you and to just do whatever you've been told as though you were a computer program. Simply put, no single one of us knows everything, so we should never assume that we have all of the answers or always know the outcome of situations. Seeking advice opens you up to hearing something you may not have thought of and may help you to avoid a catastrophe. It helps us make a better decision, even if it's by just a little bit. Even if you end up doing what you originally thought or end up not using any of the advice, you're all the wiser by listening and seeking. God wants us to learn the importance of seeking advice and to act accordingly, especially in regards to these concepts because we all desire success and wisdom; and in our pride always seem to think that we have it all together. We can't have success or wisdom without seeking advice; it's such an integral part of life that the Bible says that our preparation should consist of seeking advice (Proverbs 20:18).

Be Not Unequally Yoked

A yoke is a tool, a harness, used for connecting two animals together for the purpose of working the land. The yoke was such a beneficial tool because it allowed the workload to be evenly spread across both animals. They were able to work together to get more done with less effort contributed on the part of each one. Under the bind of the yoke, the animals were not easily broken from their connection to one another. This provided the ability to keep both animals in line, thus, maintaining their focus on the goal at hand. With this in mind, let's see what God's concern is in regards to being unequally yoked.

> [14]Do not be yoked together with unbelievers. For what do righteousness and wickedness have in common? Or what fellowship can light have with darkness? [15]What harmony is there between Christ and Belial? What does a believer have in common with an unbeliever? [16]What agreement is there between the temple of God and idols? For we are the temple of the living God. As God has said: "I will live with them and walk among them, and I will be their God, and they will be my people." [17]"Therefore come out from them and be separate, says the Lord. Touch no unclean thing, and I will receive you." [18]"I will be a Father to you, and you will be my sons and daughters, says the Lord Almighty." [1]Since we have these promises, dear friends, let us purify ourselves from everything that contaminates body and spirit, perfecting holiness out of reverence for God.
>
> (II Corinthians 6:14-7:1)

Although this is not just specifically for dating relationships, you can clearly see that God's expectation for His followers is that they pick a companion that will help them to live out God's standard. If you are a true Christian, God has called you out of the standard of the world. What being a true Christian means is that you are living as a disciple of Jesus…not the watered-down version you see in the world. He expects that we keep ourselves free from any influence of the world as it may impact our lives. In return, His promise is that He'll be with us. Let's face it! Why would you want to be in a relationship with someone who does not put God first and is striving to live out His standard for his or her life? That person will not have the same focus as you. It'll be like trying to plow the land using two oxen without the yoke. Both animals will be all over the place. The farmer would probably get very little if anything done at all. Being a Christian now and thinking back, it could be really scary getting into a relationship with someone because you really have no idea who they are. With Christ, you have a clear understanding of what they are striving for – not to say that they cannot revert. Without Christ, a person's focus may change at any given moment or they may have hidden agendas. You really have no idea of what's lurking just beneath the surface of an individual. I believe it's safe to say that the world really doesn't have any standards at all. It's pretty much a free-for-all, do-as-you-please, when it's convenient for you type of lifestyle that has no regard for anybody else no matter the situation. There will be challenges enough between two Christians. Why would any true Christian want to subject oneself to such a potentially horrific situation? As it says in the Scripture above, there's nothing in common between the two. There's no agreement, no harmony, no commonality. The two lifestyles are so far on the opposite ends of the spectrum from each other that they simply cannot coexist. Hence, the analogies of righteousness and wickedness, light and darkness, Christ and Belial. When one appears, the other totally disappears. Have you ever seen or heard of a room being half dark when you turn the lights on? Darkness always retreats to a location hidden from the light.

You may be thinking that this is just dating. What harm is there in dating? I'm not referring to the situation where you're just going out on dates with an individual. That is a different situation altogether, but the expectation of glorifying God in that situation is no different. What I have in mind is a dating relationship where your relationship turns monogamous in nature because you're emotionally involved and connected on a heart level to each other. Another way to look at a dating relationship is that it's the trial period for marriage like the 30-day trial period software companies provide for their products. Hopefully, your trial period lasts a lot longer than 30 days. In regards to marriage, God does not want you intermarrying with anyone from the world (I Corinthians 7:39).

> [1]When the LORD your God brings you into the land you are entering to possess and drives out before you many nations – the Hittites, Girgashites, Amorites, Canaanites, Perizzites, Hivites and Jebusites, seven nations larger and stronger than you – [2]and when the LORD your God had delivered them over to you and you have defeated them, then you must destroy them totally. Make no treaty with them, and show them no mercy. [3]Do not intermarry with them. Do not give your daughters to their sons or take their daughters for your sons, [4]for they will turn your

> sons away from following me to serve other gods, and the LORD's anger will burn against you and will quickly destroy you.
>
> (Deuteronomy 7:1-4)

God commanded His people not to intermarry with the other nations that He would drive out from them. His reasoning for this is far different from those of us that oppose interracial marriage. Some people oppose interracial marriage because of selfishness, hatred, and prejudice to name a few. But, God forbids this intermarriage with foreigners for the sole reason of the impact of sin in our lives. Just as those nations God would drive out were stronger than the Israelites, the power of sin is too strong in our lives. The influence of sin is so great that it would easily turn the Israelites from God, thus leading to their destruction. It's no different for us; the influence of sin is great in our lives. God calls all of His people to live a much higher standard than the rest of the world. It is far too easy to be brought down to living a lower standard than pulling someone else up to living a higher standard. Look at the examples of Samson, David, and Solomon, great men of God who were highly esteemed by Him. They each suffered detrimental consequences in their lives because they became yoked with an unbeliever. When you choose to be with an unbeliever; you are being unfaithful to God (Ezra 10:1-11). The message here is that we should pick a companion who is going to help us live out God's will for our lives and stay faithful to Him because they're trying to do the same for his or her life. Being that dating is the precursor to marriage and God has this expectation for your marriage partner, why wouldn't you apply this to finding a dating partner?

Besides, whether they know it or not, unbelievers want a companion who follows God, even though they may not want to follow God themselves. All of the qualities they want in a spouse is what God calls us to be for Him and for others. Women want men who step up and take charge (not implying dominate, controlling, or overbearing), lead the family, respect them, and are attentive and considerate of their thoughts and feelings. Men want women who are submissive, supportive, and respectful (no drama). In my opinion, marriage is the single most powerful tool God has given us to lead unbelievers to Him. We all have an innate desire for companionship. When you have a godly marriage, it's just so doggone attractive to the ungodly.

The act of going out on a date is very different from a dating relationship. You're not feeling the same things as you would in a dating relationship. There's no emotional or heartfelt connection. And, there's nothing monogamous about the relationship. In this situation, all you're doing is building a friendship with the intent of being friends. There is no preconceived notion or premise that this is going to be anything more than a friendship. At least that's the way it should be. At any moment that you begin to feel otherwise, the relationship ceases to being just a friendship for you. In regards to a Christian going out on a date with an unbeliever, I don't have any qualms about it – not that it matters what I think anyway. There's nothing wrong with it in a sense of the act itself. Just as Proverbs 4:23 – "Above all else, guard your heart, for it is the wellspring of life" – provides us with a critical warning to be careful in regards to what we expose our hearts to. I offer the same advice to the Christian adventuring into this situation. Be careful! Although it can be a tool to help lead someone to Christ, the situation can become a pitfall to the Christian. As a side note, evangelism is never a reason to expose oneself to a situation that's potentially harmful spiritually. Based on the proverb above, I would suggest that the Christian be wise and mature about the situation, always have in mind to set yourself up for success, and, at any cost, do not compromise your faith. Here are a few questions you may need to consider before going out on this date.

- Do you find the individual attractive?
- Do you think the individual finds you attractive?
- What type of environment are you going into?

All of these questions, as well as others that may pertain to your situation, are things that you need to consider beforehand because you don't want to get caught off guard. In dealing with the issue of attraction, you have to be real and honest with yourself. In your pride, don't be foolish and deny how you really feel, otherwise, you may find yourself in a predicament you never intended to be in. If you find this person attractive, there's nothing wrong with that. You're human. Just admit it and deal with it. It will help you to be wise and more cautious about what you need to do because you're not in denial about how you feel. This level of self-analysis and acting in accordance with your findings is simply an act of being mature. In this type of situation, for the Christian, I would suggest inviting the individual to church and getting out of the way. Who knows what God will do with such faithfulness? The person may come to Jesus. You may or may not develop a relationship down the road. You never know. But, always remember that it's not about you. It's about God. I say this knowing that this particular situation is really difficult because our hearts get involved. As deceitful as our hearts (Jeremiah 17:9) are, we can easily fool ourselves into thinking that our main goal is to bring them to God. When in reality, you're being drug away from your God. This is where seeking advice and generally having someone in your life that knows what's going on pays some high dividends.

Likewise, if you even remotely think that this person finds you attractive, this will be a great assistance in your preparations. You know that most unbelievers have no shame in their sin and have no problem whatsoever in carrying it out with boldness. It's our nature and we take to it like a fish to water. It may feel a little awkward, but you may have to be very up front about your convictions instead of letting them come out casually in conversation over the course of the night. In doing so, you may be able to ascertain whether or not they'll respect your boundaries. If at any point you feel uncomfortable with your spiritual well-being, then it may be wise not to pursue going out on a date with this individual.

Several years ago, a coworker approached me about going out on a date with a friend of hers. She thought that I was nice and that her friend and I would be good company for each other. At first, I was a bit surprised and caught off guard by the gesture and needed a brief moment to respond. I kind of had to figure out where she was coming from because I really don't like it when people take it upon themselves to play matchmaker – matching you up with someone they think you'd make a good couple with. During the brief pause, she explained her intentions which I was okay with and we set up a time for the three of us to get together. After initially meeting with our mutual friend present to facilitate, we decided to go out on a date. There was a movie that she had in mind that she wanted to see, so we decided to grab a bite to eat and see a movie. I shared with her that I didn't mind going to see a movie as long as it wasn't vulgar and sexually explicit. Yes, a little part of me did feel a little awkward in saying that to her as I'm no different from anybody else. I have my moments getting caught up in being more concerned about and afraid of what other people will think of me. I did brace myself a little for her response being that women, like men, are definitely not exempt from heaping abuse upon men when he's being righteous, respectful, and not following the normal patterns of men interacting with women. Well, I had nothing to worry about. She was very receptive and displayed no negative reactions. It ended up being an enjoyable experience – speaking for myself that is. I had a good time being in her presence and it was enjoyable getting to know a little bit about her.

Another important aspect to consider is the circumstances under which this date will occur. Think about these questions for a moment. Will it be just the two of you? Or, will you be part of a group? If part of a group, will you be the lone Christian? If so, what activities will this date consist of? And, where will the location be? Are you putting yourself in a situation to be dependent on this person? All of these questions will help you determine whether or not this is a good situation for you to be in. For example, let's think about the issue of dependency. Who will be driving whom? Depending on the circumstances, the ideal action would probably be to meet there separately. This would make it easier for you to leave if you ended up in a situation that you felt uncomfortable in. But, if you rode together, I would suggest that the Christian drive. This would still give you the ability to leave unexpectedly if you had to. You wouldn't be stuck or in a difficult situation if you rode with the individual and they didn't want to leave.

Before I whisk you away onto another topic of discussion, I wanted to briefly touch on a situation between Christians going out on dates with each other. Some churches make it mandatory, for the lack of a better word, for singles when going out on dates to go out on double dates. This is for the sake of accountability in maintaining purity and also it does help you get acquainted with more people in the process. I totally understand that. On the other hand, I don't think that you can treat people the same though. I can see this being more of a "mandatory" thing with teens and maybe people in their early twenties with the raging hormones and the lack of self-control. But, I don't think you can treat someone in their thirties, forties, or older the same way. Yes, a person's character does come into consideration in this too. Just as well, how a person is doing spiritually; and the circumstances does play a part in this too. For example, if two people are from two completely different churches, it may be wise to do a double date for the lack of familiarity. Otherwise, I do believe that if two singles wanted to meet up at a coffee shop for a bit to spend some time together and chat – the man and the woman are both comfortable with this – then I don't see a problem with it. I've gone out on solo dates for years. I led a singles bible talk for my church some years ago. For encouragement, I took each of the women in the group out on a solo date. I asked each prior to and they each were comfortable with it and I had an enjoyable time with each of them. The date I had with my co-worker's friend was a solo date as well. What I'm primarily saying here is that you can't treat everybody the same. It should be an option. And no, everybody isn't capable of doing this.

Accept One Another

Accepting one another is something that should be constantly at the forefront of our minds. In general, people have a hard time accepting each other. I'm not referring to attributes that we have in common, but in the areas where we are different. I'm not talking in regards to matters that are morally right or wrong. We have God's Word for that. I'm talking about inconsequential matters where we have legitimate freedom of choice. Matters of no significance in the grand scheme of it all have caused the best of friends and family members to part ways for years.

> [1]Accept him whose faith is weak, without passing judgment on disputable matters. [2]One man's faith allows him to eat everything, but another man, whose faith is weak, eats only vegetables. [3]The man who eats everything

> must not look down on him who does not, and the man who does not eat everything must not condemn the man who does, for God has accepted him. ⁴Who are you to judge someone else's servant? To his own master he stands or falls. And he will stand, for the Lord is able to make him stand. ⁵One man considers one day more sacred than another; another man considers every day alike. Each one should be fully convinced in his own mind. ⁶He who regards one day as special, does so to the Lord. He who eats meat, eats to the Lord, for he gives thanks to God; and he who abstains, does so to the Lord and gives thanks to God. ⁷For none of us lives to himself alone and none of us dies to himself alone. ⁸If we live, we live to the Lord; and if we die, we die to the Lord. So, whether we live or die, we belong to the Lord.
>
> (Romans 14:1-8)

Here, Paul addresses this issue of disputable matters that had been taking place amongst the disciples in Rome. The church in Rome had a considerable number of Jews as well as Gentiles. Can you imagine the ruckus in the church caused by these two groups coming together? They were so different in their nature. I'm willing to bet it was predominantly the Gentiles who were enjoying the freedom in Christ. They were under no observance whatsoever prior to their conversion. The Jews, on the other hand, were so rigid and constricted in their thinking. They were so deeply ingrained with strict observation of the Mosaic Law. It was a way of life passed down from generation to generation since the beginning so it wouldn't be something that would be disregarded so easily. Quite naturally, the lifestyles coming together are going to cause some conflict. I think that the mentioned issues of eating and distinction of days weren't the only issues at hand but were the ones that stirred up the most controversy. So, Paul probably uses these two to bring home his point in providing guidance on how to cope with all of their inconsequential differences. Just imagine how the Jews must have looked upon the Gentiles with contempt, judgment, and criticism as they pigged out on unclean meats. Or, how the Gentiles must have thought how pathetic the Jews must have been as they regarded days such as the Passover, Pentecost, and the Feast of Tabernacles better than any other day.

In today's time, we are not so different from the Jews and Gentiles in the early church. We are eager to judge, criticize, condemn, and look down on others who have different views and practices than us. Remember, God specifically designed each of us with our own personalities (Psalm 139:13) exactly the way He desired. God obviously likes variety and there's some significance in it or He wouldn't have made us with so many differences. We each have our varying degrees of likes, dislikes, political views, temperaments, thoughts, life experiences, perspectives, interests, and the list goes on. We are to be unified, not uniform. There is a place for our differences in regards to marriage. We will revisit this topic a little bit later.

Something for us to take in consideration in all of our relationships, but I'll convey it through dating since it's within the context of our discussion. Depending on a particular couple's maturity level, dating couples may follow different dating patterns. We are not to compare our dating relationship to another's or another's to our own and judge whether they are doing right or wrong. We are to compare our relationship to God's Word only. Many times, we are too eager to impress our opinions or convictions upon others. You must realize that what works for you may not work for someone else. I had my first introduction to this lesson as a young disciple. While dating, I don't believe in kissing on the mouth. The cheeks and forehead are fine, but the mouth is off limits even if it's just a peck on the lips. It's too personal and crosses boundaries. It leads to impurity and opens the door wide open to sexual temptations. Shortly after I was married, another couple started dating in the church I attend. After service, I caught a glimpse, from a distance, of them sharing a brief kiss on the lips. My first reaction was, "They shouldn't be doing that!" I mentioned to a good friend that was standing next to me that I wondered if I should go and speak to the brother about that. That's when he enlightened me to the fact that there was nothing wrong with it. There wasn't a Scripture that explicitly forbade it. It was their conviction and that I may actually cause them to struggle with impurity. Now, there necessarily wouldn't have been anything wrong if I would have gone and spoke to him. I think what would have been wrong was if I would have approached him enforcing my own personal convictions of what I thought instead of sharing, let's say, I Timothy 5:2 about treating women with absolute purity. That probably was the best way for me to learn that lesson instead of doing so by confronting them on the situation. Now, I try to be more careful of that and to some degree watchful of those who may approach me in that manner.

Sexual Integrity

Unlike no drug I've ever seen, this world has a powerful never-ending addiction to sexual sins. Cocaine, PCP, and methamphetamines don't even come close to touching the potency of pornography, adultery, fornication, lust, and the likes to addict, control, and destroy. The lack of sexual integrity is evident everywhere in our society. The world is an advertising agency for sexual sins and it maximizes the use of all its media and marketing schemes to get its product maximum exposure to the wide array of audiences. And, it does not discriminate. No matter where you go, you can see or hear something that takes you into the world of sensuality even if it's for a brief moment. If it's your first trip, it's willing to school you as well. This makes it incredibly hard for men to remain pure and maintain their sexual integrity. Of course, I'm speaking of Christian men when I say that. This type of behavior is atypical of the other group of men. The only way to truly avoid it is as Paul told the Corinthian church, you'd have to leave this world altogether.

So, who are the culprits, the players in this game? In most cases, it will always be put on the shoulders of the men as being the villains in this alone. And, rightly so, to some degree. Men are the brazenly obvious ones who are trying to have sex with pretty much anything that moves. Men are the ones more likely to openly initiate sex than women. For men, sex is how we experience intimacy. That's how we were designed by God. I will be talking from the viewpoint of a man and addressing men mostly on this. I can't help that; I'm a man. But, don't be fooled, women are willing participants as well. They just play the game a little differently than we do and usually aren't as brazen. Although, I've seen some who were. All of those men aren't being immoral by themselves you know. So, of course they're willing participants. As I've contemplated some of the interactions between men and women I've observed over the years, I have thought on many occasions that men are chasing after sex wherever they can get it; and women are trying to give it away. Have you seen the way some of these women dress? Oh my goodness! And, they have the nerve to get mad when men stare. How can you wear next to nothing showing all of your goodies and expect no one to look? Dressing like that, you have made yourself an advertisement for sex and sensuality. It's expected that men are going to look. These days women are looking too. Let me explain something to you for those who don't understand the simplicity of human curiosity. It's a natural impulse to look and want to see something that you don't see every day. Some women wear items so tight that it looks as though the outfit was sprayed on them. I remember watching this special recently on the life of Meagan Good, whom I happen to find extremely fine and attractive, which led me to begin referring to her as Meagan "Too Fine for Her Own" Good. Anyway, I think it was one of those shows like Unsung or something; I don't remember exactly what the show was. It told of her hardships in life and how she endured and bounced back. She had become a Christian and met a Christian man who I believe was a preacher, minister, or something like that if my memory serves me correctly. They eventually got married. Well, it came time for the 2013 BET Awards, which I did not see, but googled to see exactly what they were talking about. When she stepped on stage she had on a dress that was entirely way too revealing. It left nothing to the imagination. To be honest, we could have easily had another catastrophic event that would have easily surpassed Nipplegate if the slightest malfunction would have gone wrong with her dress. This sent the Christian community in an uproar. In her response, she said very defensively that men needed to check their hearts for lusting after her. I thought, "Are you serious? That's how you respond?" She's the one who really needed to do a heart check. What in the world is going on in her heart that would make her dress in such a way to reveal parts of her body that should remain covered and are only for her husband's eyes? Also, her Christian husband should have had something to say about that before she even left the house. Those men who are lusting after her are sinning, but they've received a great deal of help from her. She's sinning too because she's causing her fellow Christian brothers in Christ to stumble and struggle with sin. You see, in an effort to get attention, some women go too far and dress in order to be the desire of men's lust instead of their hearts. They know exactly what to do to get a man's attention. This is precisely what Paul was talking about when he instructed Timothy about the attire of the Ephesian women (I Timothy 2:9-10).

Exactly what does it mean to be sexually impure you ask? Sexual impurity is simply the act of receiving sexual gratification outside the context of marriage between a man and a woman from a source other than your spouse. Although the definition is simple, the way in which we can be impure is seemingly astronomical. Some ways in which we sin by being sexually impure are lust, adultery, fornication, petting, masturbation, pornography, same-sex unions, orgies, stripping – whether watching or performing, and anything that is like this where you're receiving or providing sexual gratification from a source or to an object other than your spouse. For singles, that means you're forbidden any type of sexual gratification in any form until you're married.

You may be wondering what's the problem. Everybody's doing it. Why is this so bad? Well, there's a pretty lengthy list as to why when you include all of the consequences that result from this. But, first thing's first. On a spiritual and moral level, it's just flat out wrong. I'm going to call it what it is. It is sin. God did not design sex to be used the way we have abused His precious gift. The way we casually have sex with one another without commitment, have one-night stands after meeting at a club for the first time, how we just live together and fornicate as though we were married to skim the surface with a few examples is way short of God's perfect standard for sex. This is what causes it to be sin. Jesus, in the Beatitudes says, "Blessed are the pure in heart for they will see God (Matthew 5:9)." Well, the inverse of that is that those who are impure of heart will never see God!

> [3]It is God's will that you should be sanctified: that you should avoid sexual immorality: [4]that each of you should learn to control his own body in a way that is holy and honorable, [5]not in passionate lust like the heathen, who do not know God; [6]and that in this matter no one should wrong his brother or take advantage of him. The Lord will punish men for all such sins, as we have already told you and warned you. [7]For God did not call us to be impure, but to live a holy life. [8]Therefore, he who

> rejects this instruction does not reject man but God, who gives you his Holy Spirit.
>
> (I Thessalonians 4:3-8)

You may have heard people express wonder as to what God's will is for their lives. I know over the course of my life, I've heard my share of people ask this question. Well, here it is explicitly in black and white – one of them. For most, I don't think they've ever looked here. It says that God's will is that you be sanctified. Sanctified means to be holy – separated from sin. Then, Paul adds context. The disciple of Jesus is to avoid sexual immorality and learn to control his or her body. Paul is reminding the Christian church in Thessalonica of this because Christians are susceptible to the temptation of sexual sins like anyone else. But we are not to live like that; we are to be chaste and control our bodies. Living in sexual immorality is to be out of control as one who is separated from and does not know God. The Message version of the passage uses the phrase "abusing it" in place of "not passionate lust". Consistently engaging in sexual immorality does not show honor for one's body. As the message version states, it's an act of abusing your body. Have you seen a woman who has been a prostitute for a while? I've seen my share and they get to the point where they literally look abused and their body looks like it's been run down and worn out.

Paul cites another reason I'm quite sure two people being sexually immoral with one another don't consider because they are only thinking of themselves. Prior to becoming a disciple, I know I didn't think about this and I really didn't care. Here is this woman before me that is as sexually attracted to me as I am to her and she's willing. That's all that mattered to me. So, it serves to say that reading this after I became a disciple of Jesus definitely enlightened me even more to the level of selfishness I had. When two people engage in sexual immorality, others are wronged (v6). You may think that this isn't true, but it is. When a married person commits adultery, his or her spouse is wronged. When an unmarried person has premarital sex, his or her future spouse is wronged because the virginity that should have been brought to the marriage is gone. That's something that's really unheard of these days. Bringing one's virginity to the marriage is something that is pretty much nonexistent in the world today. That's being lost so early these days in some cases before one leaves his or her teens; and in some cases before they even entered the teens. No matter what the circumstance is, when engaging in sexual immorality, you're stealing something that does not belong to you and you have now become a thief.

Lastly, Paul states that the Lord will punish all for such sins. If that isn't a reason for you to practice chastity, then I don't know what is. Then, he closes out with the fact that God calls us not to be impure but to be holy and anyone who decides to live an impure life is not rejecting man, but God Himself. It is stuff like this that validates that the Bible is from God and not man because man would not prohibit himself from doing the very things he desires to do, then eternally condemn himself for doing so.

We're going to be here for a while so let's switch gears for a moment and look at this topic from a practical perspective. I'm sure it's a perspective we all can relate to. I want to briefly look at impurity in the midst of a dating couple's relationship. This is not meant to be comprehensive in any fashion; it's just one avenue how things can start and fan out from there. Typically, a guy and a girl are drawn together by some degree of mutual physical attraction. This is definitely true from the guy's perspective and could be the only reason he'd like to get with her. Of course, there may be other factors involved. At some point, the two begin to have sex and indulge in other sensual pleasures. The couple has now crossed the line and has become impure. Once that boundary has been crossed, it is likely that they will continue to do so even at a greater frequency. Impurity brings two related obstacles into a dating relationship. The first obstacle is that the sexual part of the relationship becomes a distraction. It becomes a distraction in that it hinders you from really getting to know the character of the person you're dating. The sensuality of the relationship begins to take more of a focus.

You may even take notice of but completely glaze over traits that you know will be an issue for you. The second obstacle is that impurity masquerades as though it is love when in reality it's lust. It clouds your mind because your emotions will be so heightened that you will not be thinking as clearly as you should. You may feel like you're so in love with this person but it may only be an allusion. And, I'm not saying that some of it may not be genuine, but it's a fact that you can't love something you really don't know (I Peter 1:22). Lust will have you thinking that you're so in love with this person when you may just be more in love with the feeling from what you're getting in the sack. How can you really get to know someone if your focus is more of what they're giving you and how it makes you feel instead of who they are? Do not take this lightly or think this is a joke. This is real. Couples have married thinking they're so in love and made for each other only to realize shortly after they've married that they're really not in love with each other at all. And, to top it off, they don't really know each other as well as they thought. The question I would pose to them is, "Were you having premarital sex?" It's likely the couples were because this is an impact impurity can have on a relationship. No matter what point it enters the relationship, it will be an obstacle to overcome. And, has led to divorce.

In a dating relationship, maintaining purity and sexual integrity is a trust between the two involved in the relationship. Boundaries are set according to what each person can handle in order to stay as far as possible away from being impure or causing your boyfriend or girlfriend to struggle with sexual desires. Boundaries can be something like no kissing on the lips to not being alone together. Those boundaries may have to tighten up as the relationship progresses due to the couple's bond strengthening at the heart level.

Knowing that maintaining purity is a trust between the two in a dating relationship, you can get a good idea of one aspect of your partner's character. You will be able to see if this is someone who has your back or not. If your partner is constantly testing those boundaries and tempting you in this area, hear this and hear it well. He or she does not have your best interest at heart. That person is only thinking about his or her self. Your boyfriend or girlfriend may claim to love you so much all the while trying to get you to sleep with them. I'm sure some of the ladies are relating to this – guys do it to you all of the time even claiming if you loved him you'd do it. That's a guilt trip; don't fall for it! Rest assured that your boyfriend or girlfriend doesn't love you nor do they respect you. Love always protects (I Corinthians 13:7) and it is not self-seeking (I Corinthians 7:5). You see, the truth is that some sins are like wolves, in that they travel in packs; they're running buddies. Where there's any form of sexual sin, selfishness is right there driving the whole thing. And depending on the situation, similar to the one I described above, deceitfulness is hiding just around the corner. Many women face this on a daily basis from their boyfriends pressuring them to have sex, laying the guilt trip on them, trying their best to manipulate them to get what they want. My advice to you ladies is don't do it. Don't get involved. This is really for anyone male or female with a significant other that has pushed those boundaries. What would it be like to marry someone with those traits? Well consider this. He or she doesn't respect you now, what makes you think he or she will do so later after you're married. Probably won't or it'll definitely be a sore spot in the relationship. Also, think about the level of selfishness it takes to keep running someone in the ground like that. You may be marrying a level of selfishness you may not want to deal with. I know. My most recent marriage was just that. That'll make for a rough situation to be in when you're married. And you know, things tend to be magnified after you're married because you are now stuck with those very things on a day to day basis. That's why it's best to do your homework before hand.

    Now, I'm at a junction where I have to point out that it's not always the men. Women who have given into the consistent prodding from their boyfriends or just some men in general, even after saying no many times but stuck around in that situation and allowed it to continue until you eventually gave in. You have to ask yourself what was going on in your own heart. Did you think he was going to stop? If you did, I'm here to tell you that he won't. Anybody, male or female, that is pushing that issue won't stop until he or she gets what he or she wants or you cut the head off the snake the first time and cement it by leaving that situation. Or, did your no really mean no? Did you really want to give in, say yes, but threw up the front first not to seem so much like a you-know-what? Sometimes, some women already know they're going to give it up to a guy. I've overheard them. You play the cat and mouse game because it's exciting. You think he looks good and you like the "game" he's spitting at you. You sniggle and giggle at his flirtatious flattery. You're eating up all of the lines he's saying to you. This continues until finally the two of you are having sex. Then, all of a sudden – he's gone. You get angry but this is a chance for you to realize what's really going on in your heart and deal with your own wickedness. Men are not all to blame in every situation. And in actuality, there are even some women who push the issue just as well as the guys do.

Now, I understand that in many situations regarding couples, especially in this day and time, both will be enjoying the fruits of their sexual sin. So, it's time to get real and accept a heap of personal responsibility. Galatians 6:7-8 says, "Do not be deceived: God cannot be mocked. A man reaps what he sows. The one who sows to please his sinful nature, from that nature will reap destruction; the one who sows to please the Spirit, from the Spirit will reap eternal life." How does this apply to what we're talking about? The passage opens up with a solemn warning which essentially translates into don't be a fool; you can't make a fool out of God. What He designed to work a certain way will work that way or else there's consequences to suffer. They are built into the process. Paul made a very general statement about the grand scheme of the way things in the world function. For those of you who aren't farmers, essentially, your actions will get you what you fully deserve.

Sexual sins and impurity are the catalyst for (or in the mix of) an abundance of issues in our world and have been since the fall of man. From the multitude of single parents who were never married to their children's fathers to broken marriages due to adulterous relationships to men with so many children they can't visit them all or pay all of their child support; it touches so much more than can be discussed in one sitting. But let's take a different turn for a moment. Let's not look at the widespread issue of this sin but take a look at it on a much more personal level. What about the insecurities that are produced in us when we live like this? I think we argue about things some times without really knowing what's eating at us.

- Women: Have you ever started dating a man you knew was a "player", then wondered all of the time he was away from you who he was sleeping with? Why would you do this to yourself?

- Do you ever wonder who your significant other is going to cheat on you with when it was infidelity that brought you two together in the first place? Did this cross your mind in the beginning? If not, why wouldn't it?

- Men: Have you ever had a confrontation with your girlfriend's ex-boyfriend and he bragged in your face about what he used to do to your woman? Kind of pissed you off, huh?

- What about the natural ill-feelings you get from seeing your ex-boyfriend or ex-girlfriend with his or her new lover after your break-up? Did this sighting with the new beau or gal provoke you to spew out or think malicious things about them?

All of this and so much more could be avoided if we lived out God's intentions for sex which is only meant to be in the context of marriage between a man and a woman only. People try to have sex without having the relationship tie. You may know it by its other monikers like booty call, friends with benefits, and sidepiece. People have tried for years and probably will continue to do so. We can be so dumb sometimes. No matter how much people try, soon after the illegitimate sex begins, the drama and problems ensue. Why is that?

You may remember the episode of Seinfeld called *The Deal* where Jerry and Elaine make a pact to have sex with a set of ground rules in order to avoid all of the awkwardness and problems that arise when friends cross that sexual boundary. Well, of course, this blew up in their faces as it usually does at some point. Remember I said earlier that God cannot be mocked. You cannot go outside His original design without suffering the consequences whether they're immediate or delayed. The reason behind why this can't be avoided is this. What is it that consummates a marriage? It brings your union to completion, fulfillment, perfection, sort to speak. Of course, it's what we've been talking about. Sex. That's why when a married couple has an argument, sex always seems best after the argument. When a couple argues, it causes disharmony in the relationship. The sex after the argument brings the couple back together again into a state of harmony, if I may say, in a very major way. It kind of re-consummates the marriage relationship. When you have sex with someone you're not married to, you are uniting with that person on more than just a physical level and the more you do it, the more you're uniting with him or her. Once you engage in immorality, the relationship issues – the jealousy, the anger, the hurt, and the desire for commitment, or wanting more of a relationship – are right around the corner. The feelings may be suppressed for a little while, but they're there and they will come out soon. Why? Well, duh! The answer to that is simple. You have a broken relationship. Think about this for a minute.

What happens when you try to short cut, give a half-hearted effort if any at all, cut corners, or intentionally leave something out with pretty much anything you do in life? You have a mess. You try to build a house without first building a frame; you won't have much to live in. You try to get a degree but leave out some required courses. You end up with nothing more than an incomplete. You don't invest in and raise your kids; you end up with menaces to society. Likewise, sex is an integral part of a marital relationship. Let's say you hook up a little booty call with this woman. It doesn't matter if you're married or not, but you two decide that you're going to hook up whenever you want to have sex and you have no strings attached. Well, eventually she's going to want you to spend more time with her outside of the bed. You may even get a request to spend the holidays with her, meet the parents, the entire family maybe. You may be thinking, "Where in the heck is this coming from?" If you're married and she knows it, feelings of jealousy may be invoked. If you're not married but have an agreement that you both are just sleeping around, if she sees you with another woman that may invoke feelings of jealousy too. It's the other way around as well. A lot of men don't want to see a woman they're with being wooed by another man. That invokes feelings of jealousy too and feelings of competing may arise, heighten, and eventually go to an extreme. I was in a similar situation once where I was completely disrespected. And, you better believe I got with her afterwards too. She was with her "other" man who was passing through town. They were fishing at the pond in the apartment complex where she and I lived. As I passed by on my way to the mailbox, I waved at her when she looked my way. Contrary to what you may want to think, I wasn't trying to start trouble or was jealous in any way. In my days before Christ, that didn't bother me one bit as she and I weren't seriously dating. The way I saw it, everybody was sleeping around with everybody anyway, so I couldn't care less about that. Well anyway, she just turned around without speaking. I was pissed off because I felt disrespected. I didn't care that she was with him; I knew about the situation ahead of time although it wasn't conveyed to me initially exactly what was going on, but I figured it out. I'm thinking just speak to me like you would anyone else. When I spoke to her, she responded that she felt weird even though he knew what was up. And, I responded something to the affect if he knew what was up, then it shouldn't be a problem for you to wave. You see, this is the kind of foolish garbage you end up dealing with and worse. In another example, one that's more on the psychopathic side is from a couple of articles I read in Business Insider regarding Colin Firth and his wife, Livia Guiggioli. In the first article, the couple accused a man, Marco Brancaccia, who was a childhood friend of

Livia, of stalking them. In the second article released only hours later, Livia reveals that she had an affair with Marco while she and Colin were briefly separated years ago. You know this causes a lot of serious problems. I've seen guys really go at each other over some woman they both were getting together with. You cannot disassociate physical intimacy from marital relationships and expect everything to be okay. It just won't happen. God did not design it for purposes outside of a committed marital relationship.

Women and men each have to take some responsibility for what problems this has caused you. I was recently speaking to a good friend of mine who was confiding in me some problems he was having with his girlfriend. Some things that he didn't know about her that are now coming to light. She was dealing with some depression and a lot of emotional issues due to a previous marriage where she experienced physical and verbal abuse. She was putting a burden on him and expecting him to meet a need that he just cannot. During the conversation, it came out that they were being immoral. I shared with him that he wasn't helping her and wasn't being the man of God that he proclaimed to be. In fact, he was no better than her ex-husband as he was damaging her even more. Men have no idea how that plays on a woman's emotions being used by men like that. Some can become so broken down that they are driven to retaliation. How does this play out? Has your car ever been scratched? Have you ever awakened to find a brick in your windshield? What about the multiple obscene phone calls that seemingly took forever to stop? You must come to take responsibility for your actions. That's partly your fault playa.

Ladies, you're definitely not innocent in all of this either. You are not ignorant. As I was saying moments earlier, some of you play the game as well as or better than the guys. Guys who you know are players – they are there for one thing only. You play the role as though you're rejecting his advances. But, in reality, you're listening and entertaining the advances until he gets what he wants. Then, when he has nothing to do with you, you want to call all guys dogs and malign them. But, you too must take responsibility for your actions because you have chosen to consort with evil. You knew what you were doing. In Proverbs 11:22, the Bible says, "Like a gold ring in a pig's snout is a beautiful woman who shows no discretion." And, the truth is that in most cases you'll probably get the short end of the stick. By design and our sinful nature, men can just sleep with you and be done with it; there's nothing to it. Whereas, in most cases women don't function like that because of the way they're designed. I wonder how many decent guys you've dogged out and dismissed who would have treated you with dignity and respect. Tell me this. How many of you have how many children by how many different men? And, you want to tell me that all of that is the guy's fault. Think again!

Showing honor and reverence to God by using sex the way He intended, one could avoid all of the unnecessary insecurities and consequences that just adds undue stress and complications to a person's life. Furthermore, issues that plague our society would be minimized, if not extinguished altogether. Think about the reduction or elimination of sexually transmitted diseases or the number of single parents out there. A lot of kids these days would not have been born out of wedlock. I think this is a big contributor to the breakdown of the family. Children are more so the products of casual sex than they are of husband and wife these days. Statistics do show that's the going trend worldwide. In the United States alone, the percentage of out of wedlock births rose from less than 10% in 1964 to 40% in 2014. Amongst the three main races that dominate the United States during the same time frame, the figures rose from less than 25% for Blacks, less than 15% for Hispanics, and less than 5% for Whites to 72%, more than 50%, and 29% respectively. (Chamie) Doing it God's way is so much more beneficial. For instance, let's take a look at what the world ridicules and mocks. They mock a person who is saving him or herself for marriage. If a single individual has kept him or herself pure – avoided being sexually active out of being faithful to God, how do you think he or she is going to be with you? Do you think you'll have to worry about that person being unfaithful to you? No. He or she would have been faithful to God. That means no visible accountability whatsoever. You best believe that would not be something you'd have to concern yourself with. Doesn't this sound like it would be such a great relief? It is an absolutely wonderful feeling to be married into. Yet, the world ridicules and makes fun of this to no end because they don't understand. They are blind and darkened in their understanding. Then, in their foolishness, they run back to their immorality to suffer all of it worries, insecurities, and consequences. But, the very thing they ridicule is the thing they want most deep down inside. Just listen to their arguments, their complaints, and you'll hear what they're yearning for deep within. They want faithfulness.

There is a plethora of excuses people come up with to justify sexual immorality. Most are so ridiculous and asinine; it's not even worth wasting the breath to refute. My reasoning before I began following Jesus was as long as it was consensual, I'm single and she's single. I didn't lie, cheat, or steal to get it, so I didn't see what the problem was. Yeah, foolish thinking, I know. Human nature is so adept at excusing away its sin, so what else would we expect? This is especially true with the sexual sins as they are the ones that are extremely hard to let go of. Either way, no matter how we may reason its allowance, there's no reason for it. God has made it crystal clear that it is wrong no matter how you try and twist it. It should be avoided at all costs. There's a multitude of Scriptures that denounce sexual impurity in its many forms. Therefore, let's take a look at a few of the common reasons people use to excuse sexual immorality and knock 'em out the park with the truth of God's Word.

First on deck is the concept that it is love or making love. Some people feel that being in love with one's girlfriend or boyfriend makes having sex a normal response to that love. Mind you, these days, it doesn't have to be someone you're dating. It can be someone you just met at the club for the first time. It can be someone you're shacking up with, someone you consider a friend with the added benefit of sex. With the rise of social networking, these days, it can be someone you met in an app or on a website. No matter the situation between the two involved, it's considered love. And in their eyes, there's absolutely nothing wrong with it. Some couples figure that they're eventually going to get married anyway, so why not get a head start on enjoying the goodies now. Let's examine a true concept of love from God's Word.

> [1]Be imitators of God, therefore, as dearly loved children [2]and live a life of love, just as Christ loved us and gave himself up for us as a fragrant offering and sacrifice to God. [3]But among you there must not be even a hint of sexual immorality, or of any kind of impurity, or of greed, because these are improper for God's holy people.
>
> (Ephesians 5:1-3)

At this point in the letter to the church in Ephesus, Paul was admonishing the body of believers of the type of behavior they needed to leave behind. He also instructed them in the type of behavior they needed to adopt in Christ in order to replace the behavior they are to abandon. Here, he tells them to model themselves after God in His love. More specifically, they are to model themselves after the way God loved them in Christ Jesus. In doing so, he provides an important characteristic of love. That characteristic is self-sacrifice, which is the concept of being selfless or giving up oneself for the benefit of another. The way Christ lived His life for us climaxed by His death on the cross. Then, Paul seemingly takes a turn that contrasts what he was talking about in the first two verses. At least it seemed that way when I initially read this passage as a young disciple of Jesus. Paul begins telling them that sexual immorality, any kind of impurity, and greed must not be found amongst them. Not only that, but a hint of any of it. Do you have any idea how much a hint of anything is? When you give someone a hint about something you're keeping secret, how much information do you provide? You typically provide the most minuscule amount of information possible. Before you answer, you even think to make sure that there isn't a smaller amount of information you could provide than what you already have. Now, translate that over to your life in regards to sexual immorality, any kind of impurity, or greed. You should be above reproach in those areas of your life. People should be able to look at your life and have no cause to bring an accusation against you in those areas. In the process of becoming a disciple of Jesus, I was floored by this passage and I'm sure my facial expression showed it. In my life, I knew that I had bulldozed way past that boundary too many times to count. And, that passage alone probably had the most impact towards the deep convictions I had developed regarding purity as a disciple of Jesus. Anyway, why did Paul suddenly switch from love to talking about sexual immorality? The reason is because the two are stark opposites. You see, the church in Ephesus had a large population of Gentiles in the church, probably like most of the other churches did. In the opening verse of this section back in chapter 4 verse 17, Paul explicitly tells them to "no longer live as the Gentiles do, in the futility of their thinking." What was it that was popular amongst the Gentiles? The Gentiles indulged themselves in impurity all kinds of sexual revelry. Paul continued saying that the Gentiles had "given themselves over to sensuality so as to indulge in every kind of impurity with a continual lust for more (Ephesians 4:19)." The

Gentiles thought the same thing a lot of people do today – that sexual immorality equates to love. So, you see, that is not a new idea at all. The Bible is right again as there's nothing new under the sun. The Gentiles worshipped all kinds of gods of which many involved lascivious practices. One of those gods was Aphrodite, the goddess of love. There was a temple dedicated to her in the city of Corinth. In the service of this temple were hundreds of prostitutes where people could go to have sex openly as an act of worship or sacrifice to the goddess. In setting sexual immorality, any kind of sexual impurity and greed as a stark contrast to love, Paul makes it clear that these are rooted out of the exact same sin, which is selfishness. They are not equated with love, but with lust. Furthermore, Paul seals his statements in verse 5 with the fact that a person of such a nature is an idolater and has no association with the kingdom of Christ and God.

Next on deck is the excuse that sex is just a normal biological function. God created those parts with that specific purpose in mind. If He didn't want us doing that then He wouldn't have given us those parts to begin with. From this foundation, you get a bunch of other frivolous excuses such as if God didn't want us having sex, He wouldn't have made it feel so good. Or, God created men to have sex and that's just what men do. Well, the stupidity in that is that both, men and women alike are sexual beings. Creating sex for our enjoyment was one of God's purposes for sex but those excuses are taken way out of context to meet our own selfish desires. Let's briefly look at another Scripture on the topic.

> [12]"Everything is permissible for me" – but not everything is beneficial. "Everything is permissible for me" – but I will not be mastered by anything. [13]"Food for the stomach and the stomach for food" – but God will destroy them both. The body is not meant for sexual immorality, but for the Lord, and the Lord for the body.
> (I Corinthians 6:12-13)

Here we are in the letter Paul wrote to the believers in the city of Corinth. Remember, I just said the city of Corinth had a temple dedicated to Aphrodite, the goddess of love. And, Paul is addressing the exact same excuse for sexual immorality in the Corinthian church as we have here in our day and time. When those individuals responded with the statement that food is for the stomach and the stomach is for food, they were essentially saying that the human genitalia was made for sex. The implication was that the act had no impact or significance on spiritual matters or anything otherwise. Paul clearly states that it does by letting them know that the body was not made for sexual immorality, but for the Lord and vice versa. The body becomes the temple – the dwelling place of the Lord just as the temple was in the Old Testament. It should be treated with the utmost of dignity, honor, reverence, and respect. Also, something to think about. Being that as a disciple of Jesus, your body is the Lord's temple, you'd be dragging the

Lord into your filth every time you committed an act of sexual immorality.

Last on deck is the excuse that no one will know or its not hurting anybody. What immediately comes to mind for me hearing that excuse is every man's battle with lust. Of course, I'm speaking of Christian men again when I speak of men battling lust. As for worldly men, their lusts are like the conductor of the TGV, France's high-speed intercity rail service. They run toward sexual sins about as fast as the TGV speeds toward its destinations. I know it was that way with me once upon a time. The excuse that no one's hurt or knows is a flat out lie. The Bible says that the acts of the sinful nature are obvious and it's even clearer on the fact that sin hurts and destroys. How obvious you say? For starters, let's begin with men acting like a Kodak camera or a Sony camcorder with all of the second and third looks or just outright staring when an attractive woman passes by. How about those who exhibit no shame and stare with their significant other standing right there next to him. Then, add insult to injury by making foolish excuses when busted. Not obvious enough? Doesn't hurt? What about all the allegations of sexual misconduct that have surfaced in Hollywood as 2017 came to a close prompting the #MeToo movement? Harvey Weinstein? Kevin Spacey? Larry Nassar? There is a slew of other allegations that have surfaced against a variety of people since then. What about cases of rape?

What about men, married or not, ensnared by pornography? Men who frequent strip clubs? Men who are pedophiles? And the list goes on. Unchecked, these are the ways your lust comes out. You still want to try and tell me that no one will know or it isn't hurting anybody?

Let's look at an example from the Old Testament to see how damaging this can be. It contains all of the evidences associated with lust such as it has the appearance of love, it objectifies the object of desire, and it typically involves deceitfulness to come to fruition. The story is of the encounter of Amnon and Tamar. Instead of including the entire story, I'll only include the relevant parts, but if you want to read it in its entirety, you can read II Samuel 13:1-22.

> ¹In the course of time, Amnon son of David fell in love with Tamar, the beautiful sister of Absalom son of David. ²Amnon became frustrated to the point of illness on account of his sister Tamar, for she was a virgin, and it seemed impossible for him to do anything to her.
> (II Samuel 13:1-2)

The story opens up stating that Amnon, over the course of time, fell in love with his half-sister, Tamar. But, we see quickly in verse 2 that something is apparently wrong with Amnon's professed love for Tamar. He was so passionate for her that he made himself sick over it. This sounds a little suspicious. Then, to add to the suspicion, he wanted her, but wasn't able to because she was a virgin. Here's a brief history lesson to explain why he wasn't able to get to her. In those days the unmarried women (virgins) were kept in seclusion to keep them from being alone with men in order to protect them.

> ⁶So Amnon lay down and pretended to be ill. When the king came to see him, Amnon said to him, "I would like my sister Tamar to come and make some special bread in my sight, so I may eat from her hand."
> (II Samuel 13:6)

Since Amnon wasn't able to get at Tamar under normal circumstances, he took a little advice from a friend named Jonadab, who saw that something was upsetting Amnon. He advised him to pretend he was sick and have his father send for Tamar to prepare a meal and feed it to him. Here, we see Amnon resorting to deceit in order to get what he wants.

> ⁹Then she took the pan and served him the bread, but he refused to eat. "Send everyone out of here," Amnon said. So everyone left him. ¹⁰Then Amnon said to Tamar, "Bring the food here into my bedroom so I may eat from your hand." And Tamar took the bread she had prepared and brought it to her brother Amnon in his bedroom. ¹¹But when she took it to him to eat, he grabbed her and said, "Come to bed with me, my sister."
> (II Samuel 13:9-11)

As his plan begins to come together, we see Amnon requesting others in the room to leave so that he could be alone with Tamar to fulfill his desire. And soon as the opportunity presented itself, he did not hesitate. At this point, it is quite obvious that Amnon's love wasn't really love at all; it was lust. Reading further in verses 12-14, we see that Amnon was so consumed by his sinful lusts and completely bent on carrying it out at all costs. Despite

Tamar's pleading and appealing to the wickedness of the act and the disgrace it would bestow on them both, Amnon still raped Tamar.

> [15]Then Amnon hated her with intense hatred. In fact, he hated her more than he had loved her. Amnon said to her, "Get up and get out!" [16]"No!" she said to him. "Sending me away would be a greater wrong than what you have already done to me." But he refused to listen to her.
> (II Samuel 13:15-16)

No sooner than he completed his assault, Amnon despised Tamar even more than he had lusted for her. He immediately sent her away from his sight as he could not stand to see her anymore. What could have made Amnon so abhorrent towards Tamar all of a sudden? Was it because he got what he wanted from her and he no longer desired her? Could he be having feelings of guilt or remorse for the sin committed and she served as a reminder of that sin? Any of these or something similar could be true. That's the impact sin can have on us. You can trace that way back to Adam and Eve in the garden. Sin produces guilt (I done wrong) and shame (I am wrong) in us. It shows us our unworthiness. No matter how much we desire it in the beginning, afterwards, it makes us want to run and hide. You say, you don't feel that way after sleeping around. Then you have an even greater issue. You've become so calloused to your sin that you no longer feel guilt or shame for doing wrong. You've become debaucherous and are far worse off now than before. This is indicative of our world today – no sense of right or wrong.

> ¹⁸So his servant put her out and bolted the door after her. She was wearing a richly ornamented robe, for this was the kind of garment the virgin daughters of the king wore. ¹⁹Tamar put ashes on her head and tore the ornamented robe she was wearing. She put her hand on her head and went away, weeping aloud as she went.
>
> (II Samuel 13:18-19)

After being defiled and disgraced, Tamar's spirit was literally destroyed. She wasn't that radiant beam of beauty she once was. Contrary to our world in this day and time, taking your virginity into marriage was a way of life and honorable. Anyone to the contrary would be reviled. Tamar went into deep mourning and depression. Ultimately, she lived with her brother Absalom and remained unmarried and childless as a result of this violation.

Can't you see that sexual immorality leaves scars and impurity in any form is damaging. Here's a short laundry list of the damages of sexual impurity. There are sexually transmitted diseases, sexual assault, pedophilia, rape, adultery, emptiness, can be the cause of single parents (mostly women – sometimes with multiple children by different men), destroys families in a variety of ways, emotional wounds, unwanted pregnancies, performance degradation, devalues sexual intercourse in marriage, unhealthy cross-gender relationships, and skews negatively one's view of sex.

Most men just don't understand the impact this seemingly little culprit has on them. I know it sounds like I'm picking on men, but come on fellas, let's face the facts here. We are the ones primarily pushing this in most cases for as long as man has been in existence. Yes, women lust too. I know. I've heard them. Women are just as guilty of sexual sins as we are and they are sometimes the instigators as well in their own devilish, sneaky way. But aren't we supposed to be the leaders – the examples that they follow? So, I'm talking to us. On its own, lust un-blossomed into a more visible form affects two things right off. If you're a married man lusting after another woman, you're committing adultery with her. It's a sinful act against your wife and you're defiling your marriage bed. You're simply not loving your wife when you do that.

> [27]You have heard that it was said, "Do not commit adultery." [28]But I tell you that anyone who looks at a woman lustfully has already committed adultery with her in his heart.
> (Matthew 5:27-28)

In the Sermon on the Mount, Jesus was calling people to the higher, true standard of morality that God desired by dispelling the standards of the day. In the above passage, Jesus is equating lust to committing adultery even though it's just in the heart. This means that the consequences for lust in the heart are the same as committing adultery. You, in your heart, have defiled your marriage bed (Hebrews 13:4). Well, you might argue saying that it's just a thought; it's only in my heart and I didn't actually do anything. But, isn't the source of our actions, whether good or evil, doesn't it originate in the heart? Yes, it does. It starts with the thought then, it progresses from there. Sometimes the reason we haven't actually committed the act is simply because the opportunity hasn't presented itself. If it did and you could get away with it, would you? What it all boils down to is that you've given some of your heart to someone else. The affection, love, and desire that belong solely to your wife, you've become captivated by another or to keep it real, many others. You've cheated on your wife in your heart because you desire another. And, that is enough to hurt. Although you didn't physically do something, I'll bet she wondered if you would, given the opportunity. Don't you see how that can make your spouse mistrust you? Don't you see how that can make her feel unbeautiful to you and creates low self-esteem as though she doesn't captivate you anymore? You're driving a very big wedge between you and your wife lusting after other women.

Now, I did say that women lust too, but in a woman's world this is equivalent to an emotional affair which is what a woman is more likely to have. Have you seen the movie *Why Did I Get Married Too?* Remember Sharon Leal's character, Dianne? She was having an emotional affair with a guy at work named Phil. The night before, she would carefully pick out her some sexy clothes and primp herself in the mirror for this guy. She no longer made herself beautiful for her husband anymore. It was as if he didn't exist. And, what physical intimacy Tyler Perry's character, Terry, got from her, it was really meant for Phil because that's who Dianne was thinking of when they had sex. Although she didn't physically cheat on her husband yet, and you better believe that was the next step; she did cheat on him mentally and emotionally. It's just like I said for the men, the heart was given to someone other than your spouse. That's still adultery! There's a good book to read on this from the woman's perspective. The book is called *Every Woman's Battle* by Shannon Etheridge and Stephen Arterburn. Some years ago, I had a chance to read a very small portion of the book and it was really good. I wanted to confirm some thoughts I had on the matter. I intended to finish but haven't gotten the chance to do so. I still intend to as it would be very educational. For men, intending to marry, it would definitely be a good read because it would be helpful gaining insight into the female psyche so as to help you in meeting your wife's needs. That was another reason I began reading it. For the same reason, I feel that wives should read the male equivalent of that book with their husbands. The book is called *Every Man's Battle*.

  Okay, I have to take a bit of a detour here as I have to flip the script on this #MeToo movement in regards to some women taking responsibility for their part in this. Although I'm glad it happened in some form as it's a problem that needed to be addressed, it's not all that one-sided. Now, let me prefix what I'm about to say with these statements. What I'm about to say doesn't apply to all of those women. For those women who were actually raped, propositioned, or had to deal with unwanted constant sexual advances, my heart goes out to them. I am so sorry that they had to endure through such a horrific experience. They should not have been subjected to such crude and degrading behavior. Also, what I'm about to say does not mean that I'm relinquishing any responsibility from any of those men from their wrongdoing. Those who committed those offenses are wrong and are responsible for their actions. So now that I've gotten that out of the way. Some of those women who are complaining are not completely innocent and must take responsibility for their part. Some of those women eventually gave in because they didn't want it to hurt their careers. And, I'd be willing to bet that some of those women sought out those men and put it on the table because they knew it could help their careers. Now that a movement has struck out against these men for sexual harassment in Hollywood, they want to jump over the fence and play the total victim role now. You see, here's the thing. By jumping on the bandwagon of the movement, they're now proclaiming that their body is more important than their career and they shouldn't have been treated that way. In which, I totally agree. But in reality, their bodies should have been more important than their careers in the very beginning. If so, they would have never given in or sought the men out to advance their careers. But, that wasn't the case. Their careers were more important than their bodies and that is evident from the actions they took. If their bodies were more important to them then instead of their careers, they would have never slept with any of those men. And, here's another thing. If they would not have given in or put it on the table, it would not have given any power to those men because it would have communicated that sexual harassment wasn't okay. In contrast, giving in and putting it on the table communicated that it was okay and that's where a lot of its power came from. Sexual harassment would have never taken off as it did. After Matt Lauer was called out, he made an interesting statement. He said, "Some of what is being said about me is untrue or mischaracterized, but there is enough truth in these stories to make me feel embarrassed and ashamed." He didn't comment specifically on what was untrue or mischaracterized, but I feel to believe he was talking about women who possibly flirted with him and was more than a willing participant in the sexual misconduct. That stuff doesn't just happen in Hollywood you know. It happens in the "ordinary" world with "regular" people with a whole lot less at stake. Some women are attracted to powerful men (and funny ones too) with money and material possessions. I have seen women deliberately flirt, throw subtle hints, and flat out present themselves as an all-you-can eat buffet to men who have the best cars, money, and popularity. And, women know exactly what men want. They know how to get our attention in order to get what they want. We are not complicated beings in any sense of the word. For instance, Bill Cosby was found guilty on three counts of sexual assault in his retrial. Now again, don't misconstrue anything I'm saying here – wrong is wrong. If you do the crime, you must do the time. It's never too late for justice to be served. I know this simply to be true based on the fact that God will judge the world at its end and everyone who hasn't accepted Christ as Lord and Savior will do the time for eternity. Back when this first came to light, some of his accusers plainly said that they were invited up to his room – a hotel room mind you – at two o'clock in the morning. Alone. My question is this. What were you doing in a man's hotel room – a married one at that – at two in the morning? I can't see myself buying that you didn't know what was going on. This isn't anything new first of all. Oh, you were invited up for a friendly drink. Are you kidding me? Did this particular hotel not have a bar downstairs in the lobby? Are they not suitable for friendly drinks? I thought that was the primary reason they were created for. What other reasons can you come up with? No matter the reason, you can do that somewhere else and at a more reasonable time other than a man's hotel room at **two o'clock in the morning**. You know this. It's not a secret. It's common sense. Some of you are not the total victims like you portray. I know some of you are going to get pissed at me for what I said. But, you have to think about it though. Exactly, why are you pissed at me? Are you convicted of your guilt by my saying this? I'm not letting the men off the hook; I'm just calling the other side to the plate. You have to understand what the deeper issue is. You have an issue with being sexually pure and the lack of taking measures to maintain it. How some women dress to be the epitome of lewdness, therefore inciting men to lust. The stupid decisions some women make like going into a man's hotel room at two o'clock in the morning. You're failing at maintaining sexual purity. It may be a hint, but you're still guilty. Now, you see, men aren't solely to blame. We're all in the game together. Women just play it differently than men.

Secondly, back to the men now, lust has a negative effect on how you view women. It will have some degree of impact how you treat the women in your life namely your spouse, the women you date, and those you come across on a day to day basis. What this will cause you to do is objectify women. When you look at them, you will only see a mere object for satisfying your lustful desires and nothing more. Now, I admire a beautiful woman just as much as the next man especially one that's well-dressed and got herself together. What an amazing sight. In and of itself, there's nothing wrong with that. God made women with the intent of them being beautiful, gorgeous, and sexy. It's true that men and women are made in the image of God. There are passages that speak of God's beauty like Psalm 27 where the psalmist requests to dwell in the house of the Lord so that he may gaze upon His beauty. I believe that it's women who reflect, radiate, and are the embodiment of the beauty of God. Because of this, I also believe that when you lust after women, you're also showing contempt for the image of God. That's where the admiration of women turns to sin. In our hearts, we undress her with our eyes. We wonder what she looks like naked. And, wonder what she's like in bed. We see nothing more than a body for our own pleasures and care nothing for the soul or being within. Men see a beautiful woman and the thought of sex with her is automatically right there with it without so much as a conscious thought. It's so automatic. That's sin and it's wrong. Men think that's what makes a man a man, but that's wrong thinking too. When I became a disciple of Jesus, that's one of the things I had to unlearn. When I began the process of dealing with my lustful heart, I had to dissociate the thought of having sex with finding a woman attractive because those two do not go together. That's a desire of our fallen nature and what the sinful world system teaches us.

Being a disciple of Jesus and fighting the war of impurity is just that – a WAR! The enemy literally has you completely surrounded and is attacking you from every angle with every form of weaponry possible utilizing visual and audible cues to overwhelm your senses all with the goal of inciting you to salacious, lecherous, lewd acts of behavior. In this God-forsaken world, sensual temptations attack your senses on a daily basis all throughout the day whether it's a blatant up in your face image of graphic nudity or a subtle remark you see on a billboard as you pass by in your car that gets you thinking sensually. It's a difficult battle – one that takes an extreme amount of dedication, preparation, and moral support from fellow Christian men. At times you're doing well and others, not so well, but you keep on fighting. It is a battle you must keep fighting and I emphasize ***must***, whether fighting valiantly or fighting scantily, because the moment you stop fighting, you're defeated.

Like the title of the book by Stephen Arterburn and Fred Stoeker, it is every man's battle. It's that way because that's how we were designed by God. It's not that we're weird, but God designed us in such a way that we connect with our spouses through sexual intercourse. In our fallen nature, it's just like everything else, we use what God has given us for our own selfish desires. This means that we lust after women and sinfully desire to ravish and sleep with every woman we see who is attractive to us. It doesn't matter who we already have by our side, he will want another in his heart. A man can be married to the absolute finest woman on the face of the Earth. She could be satisfying him sexually leaving him nothing left to desire. Yet, in spite of this, the moment he sees another attractive woman cross his path – especially one he hasn't been with – he will immediately without a conscious thought or decision to do so lust after and desire to be with her sexually. And, if he has been with her previously and she was satisfactory, he will reminisce about being with her and more than likely wish he could hit it again.

In detailing this aspect about men, it brings me to the point that I want to convey here. The point is why is this such a battle for men other than the fact that it's a part of our sinful nature. Sexuality is such a battle for men because it has a strong appeal or force for us in two areas where we're most vulnerable. First, as I said above, it's our native language of intimacy. That's how God designed men to connect with their wives just like He designed women to connect emotionally. Secondly, our eyes are the other vulnerability. This is the one that gets us in trouble the most. Men can draw sexual gratification – almost as though they were actually having sex – simply from the things we see. Not only that, but sensual images men may have seen years ago can be mentally regurgitated and visualized as though we saw it only moments ago. This is because those images get burned into the male mind. Personally, I can attest to this fact. At the time of this writing, I am forty-seven years old; and to this very day, I still have sensual images pop into my mind suddenly that I saw twenty years or more ago whether it's an ex-girlfriend's nude body or something I saw in a movie or on television.

Because of these two vulnerabilities alone, it makes it so difficult. Then, add in the way it impacts us as men and you'll understand why it's so captivating to us. Fred Stoeker on an episode of Focus on the Family delves into this a bit deeper. He explains that there is a chemical side, dealing with the mind, an emotional side, and a physical side to the sin of sexual addiction. The very fact that men when we see something sensual we have pleasure chemicals released in the brain that are very addictive. Studies have shown that when a man receives sexual gratification from a sensual image, his brain is stimulated in the same way as if he was on heroin. Here's his statement. "In fact, in front of the U.S. Senate in 2006, Jefferey Satinover from King's College said this that modern science allows us that the chemical basis of pornographic addiction or the things that we kind of draw through our eyes is nearly identical in the human brain as a heroin addiction. What he was saying is that when we look at things that are sensual, there is a release of pleasure chemicals into the limbric center of the brain that is very addictive." (Stoeker) Now, you can probably understand why some men become so addicted to pornography, live in strip clubs, and become so enthralled with those sensual images. Don't get me wrong, I haven't changed my tune to this. It is still sin; it is wrong. I'm just saying you now have more of an idea surrounding what the appeal is.

Now, this is especially dangerous for men during times of dealing with emotional issues resulting from hurt, disappointments, failures, loneliness, and depression. When we're suffering emotionally, we become especially susceptible to the sexual sins as well as drugs and alcohol as a means to treat or medicate our pain. It gives us a feeling of conquering something – another trait God embedded within us – or a feeling of intimacy. Of course, in these situations, those feelings of intimacy are false and the impulse to conquer something is applied to the wrong things. Those things we do not conquer; they conquer us and get us into worse trouble than where we began. So, don't go down that road! Some situations where men are tempted to resort to this behavior of self-treatment are an unexpected loss of job or business, feelings of loneliness or depression, marital problems, or going through a divorce. This temptation can arise without notice even for a Christian man whose hope is in God alone. Back in 2010 when I was laid off from my job where I had spent the last thirteen and a half years, I found myself feeling like I wanted to flirt with some women when I went to the gym that day. Granted, I'm really not much of a flirter, so I was wondering why I was feeling like that was something I needed to do at the time. Even though I was rather jovial and in good spirits after the job loss, I surmised that it was probably due to the loss that I just experienced. The automatic response to this sense of loss that I may have been feeling deep down prompted me to want to conquer something in order to make myself feel better and increase my self-worth sort to speak. So, we must be careful to take notice of where we are after loss occurs. And, the answer is no…I did not end up flirting with a woman that day to make myself feel better. If you couldn't tell from the example, I realized and acknowledged the feelings and dealt with them appropriately.

Some Christian men have the misconception that this problem will disappear upon marrying the apple of their eyes. But lo and behold, you'll find out quickly that there was a snowball's chance in you know what for that coming true. Actually, you may come to find just the opposite happening to you for a while. You may end up lusting more frequently and intensely shortly after getting married. I know I did my first marriage as a Christian. I know a couple of my friends did too. I simply recognized that after not being sexually active as a single for so long and then all of a sudden getting married and reintroduced to it, it's on your mind a lot. We as men do not need any more help with that. For a while, I thought I was going to have to take what Jesus said in Matthew 5:29 literally because pretty much every woman I saw I was like, "Good gracious, not again!" I already had undressed her with my eyes and was ready to get busy. Fortunately, through the grace of God and continuing to resist, I was back to normal after a little while.

We know that changing our status is not going to assist with winning this battle over lust and sexual sins. We need to break out the heavy artillery for that and have a take-no-prisoner attitude about it. We must mercilessly guard and protect our two vulnerable areas in order to have a fighting chance. And, we must use the tool that God has provided us and apply it fiercely to fight this battle; and that is His Word!

> [1]Now for matters you wrote about: It is good for a man not to marry. [2]But since there is so much immorality, each man should have his own wife, and each woman her own husband. [3]The husband should fulfill his marital duty to his wife, and likewise the wife to her husband. [4]The wife's body does not belong to her alone but also to her husband. In the same way, the husband's body does not belong to him alone but also to his wife. [5]Do not deprive each other except by mutual consent and for a

time, so that you may devote yourselves to prayer. Then come together again so that Satan will not tempt you because of your lack of self-control.
(I Corinthians 7:1-5)

In this Scripture, Paul is beginning to answer a series of perplexing questions posed to him by the members of the Corinthian church. Judging by this chapter and the rest of the book, it seems that the majority of those questions centered on the variety of marital statuses of individuals in the church. After validating a question that seemed to have gone something like "Is it good for a man not to get married," he tells them the reason why a man should get married. Because there is so much immorality in the world, he says that each man should have his own wife and each woman her own husband. Here lies the solution to the world's problem of sexual immorality. Go get your own spouse! This is God's original design. If you know that the single celibate life is not going to work for you, then you clearly should be on the hunt for a husband or a wife. He further defines what this union is supposed to resemble. Essentially, each spouse is responsible sexually to fulfill and please each other. When you get married, your body does not belong to just you anymore, but to your spouse too. Is this beginning to sound like that oneness in marriage? This means you are to make yourself sexually available to your spouse and the only time you are to stay a part is by mutual consent for a specified amount of time. Afterwards, you two are to come together again. In marriages, sexual deprivation has been used as a weapon to get back at the other spouse, as a tool of manipulation, or because of unresolved conflict, it has simply become the norm. Sexual deprivation can cause your spouse to be given to temptation and stray. I'm not saying that your cheating spouse is justified for doing so under those circumstances. That's not what I'm saying. Let me let you hear me say this again. Your cheating spouse is wrong for making the decision to go and have sex with someone else. What I'm saying is that if you are starving your spouse sexually for any lengthy period of time, you are partly responsible for making his or her straying away a little easier. Lengthiness depends on your spouse. Everyone's sexual appetite is different. And, I'm sure that it doesn't take too long for spouses to figure out each other's sexual drive. So, you know your spouse and you know what's too long. In most cases, when a spouse has been cut off sexually, the length of time has more than likely grown to an extreme amount of time.

Here is another passage and its application to help you deal with lust and its temptations come from Proverbs 5. The entire chapter is dedicated to warning you against adultery, so go back and read it later on. I want you to focus on one particular part for the practical concept I want to share with you.

> [18]May your fountain be blessed, and may you rejoice in the wife of your youth. [19]A loving doe, a graceful deer – may her breasts satisfy you always, may you ever be captivated by her love. [20]Why be captivated, my son, by an adulteress? Why embrace the bosom of another man's wife?
> (Proverbs 5:18-20)

Now, this practical I'm about to share is specifically for married men when you're tempted to lust after and desire another woman. Remember, when you lust after a woman, you have become captivated by her in your heart. This takes a part of your heart away from the one who should have the complete devotion of your heart. The passage makes it clear that you should be captivated by the beauty (me widening the scope of breasts) and love of your wife. This dawned upon me towards the end of my first marriage as a Christian. I really wished I had thought of this one a lot sooner than I did as it gave me a place where I could channel all of that lustful energy in my mind and still be pleasing to God when I was tempted to go there with someone else. When you're tempted to lust after another woman, channel that energy into thinking "lustfully" about your wife. If morally you can have sex with her, surely you can lust after her. And technically, it's not lust because you're supposed to be thinking that way about her and her only. Remember the previous Scripture? Man, I tell you, I had fun with this one as I let my imagination run wild and there's absolutely no guilt involved whatsoever. If there's something your wife won't do for you for whatever reason, what's going to stop you now? You can do what you want; it's your mind. An example from my mental repertoire…you come home from work and she's sitting on the couch. You snatch her li'l butt up, ravish her, and treat her like the tawdry little woman you always wanted to. You're not feeling this? Why not? Aren't you going to do the exact same thing with the hot secretary in your office you been secretly eyeballing ever since she started working there? What about the scantily clad woman you saw jogging down the street yesterday on your way home from work? At the gym, what about the woman in the painted on outfit working out on the inner/outer thigh machine? I know you're pretending she's doing that just for you. You're lusting after these women for what reason? Is it something you're not getting at home, you and your wife are not experiencing harmony right now, or is it simply because you're enjoying your sinful desires?

Let's take a look at another passage now. I'm doing my best to try and equip you with some solid Scriptures that'll help you start fighting this battle if you don't already have an arsenal in mind. You can go back later and find more Scriptures to help you. This is a battle we have to fight together as Christian men and the sooner we start the better. Getting boys as early as possible and discussing the ramifications of this sin and putting them on the righteous path as early as possible will serve as a great benefit because trying to retrain your brain after it has been too far down the wrong path engulfed in the worldly ways only make it more difficult to overcome – not impossible, but extremely difficult.

> ¹⁸Flee from sexual immorality. All other sins a man commits are outside his body, but he who sins sexually sins against his own body.
> (I Corinthians 6:18)

Talk about cutting to the chase…Paul tells the Corinthian church to flat out flee from sexual immorality. This gives the impression of fear, running for one's own life. Because this was Corinth, I'm sure you can understand why Paul would phrase this in such a way. The church population was dominated if not consisted entirely of Gentiles who were well-known for their indulgence in sexual immorality. I don't need to remind you of that, but our world today isn't any different from the lascivious behavior that was going on in Corinth in Paul's day. I would say that the only difference is that today it is no longer done as an act of worship to a god, but it has become a god in and of itself. It is an idol that keeps people who live like that from being close to God. So, Paul's command to flee it stand as firm today as it did then; and no surprise as God's Word is always relevant regardless of what decade or century it is (Hebrews 4:12). After telling them to flee sexual immorality, Paul provides the reason why. The reason he provides is interesting as it alludes to the uniqueness of this sin over any of the other sins man commits. Paul says, "All other sins a man commits are outside his body, but he who sins sexually sins against his own body." When I first read this, I wasn't quite sure what this meant from a practical standpoint. I thought it may be a reference to the diseases and other consequences of being sexually immoral but I had a feeling that that wasn't quite it. It has a much deeper meaning than that. As you can see, I was thinking from a perspective of consequences we suffer as a result of sin committed. But, all sin has consequences that we suffer as a result of. Yet, this sin does have a unique quality than any of the others. Looking a little deeper, this has more of a reference to where the sin or the desire to do so will originate. Unbeknownst to me, I knew exactly what the practical application of this Scripture was referring to, but I just hadn't connected the dots until I heard Fred Stoeker reference it on the episode of Focus on the Family. What is meant by this is that the desire for this sin will come from within you; your body will crave it and you will feel it within your members. You can acquire this insatiable desire for immorality; and it can become habitual, addictive, and it can absolutely control you. This is why men must be diligent in this area of their life. This is a very strong force within us. Any kind of impurity will rob you of your joy and keep you from having a close relationship with God.

Are you ready for another passage along with a practical application?

This one comes from the book of Luke.

> ²⁴When an evil spirit comes out of a man, it goes through arid places seeking rest and does not find it. Then, it says, "I will return to the house I left." ²⁵When it arrives, it finds the house swept clean and put in order. ²⁶Then it goes and takes seven other spirits more wicked than itself, and they go in and live there. And the final condition of that man is worse than the first.
>
> (Luke 11:24-26)

These words of Jesus provide some great advice and insight in helping us in our battle against impurity. This is actually a concept of repentance so it is viable against any sin. Many times, we clean up our lives – rather Jesus does – and our focus is only to stay away from that which is wrong, but we don't fill that empty space up with anything else. It's kind of like going on a diet. We try to abstain from certain foods or overeating and that's where our focus lies, "I can't eat this, I can't eat that." Instead of staying focused on what we can't have, we need to replace it with something good. This is why getting rid of bad habits is so hard or we just flat out fail to begin with. We need to replace the negative with a positive that we can focus on. Our battle against impurity is no different. When you're tempted to lust after a woman, don't focus on her body or the fact that you can't look at her body; think about something else altogether different. If you have to look at her, look into her eyes. Pray to be more concerned about her spiritual condition than what she looks like underneath her clothes. Do whatever it takes to get your mind off of her body.

    This is a word specifically for the ladies. I know to some degree that you take this personally. I want you to know that this is a problem native to the heart of men. It has nothing to do with you, so if you catch your man, please do not feel like there's something wrong with you. There isn't. This is a battle that men have as sinful beings. We must fight it. For any guy that you're dating, here's something you should look for in his life. Do you see him fighting that battle of staying sexually pure? If you don't see it, don't let that slide because it's likely that'll be a problem in your marriage. It won't just magically disappear. I'd advise to reconsider the nuptials depending on how bad it is.

    One way you can be even a greater friend to him is to help him in his fight by not being a stumbling block. This also goes for any guys you're around on a daily basis. Don't wear inappropriate clothing. You have no idea how much this trigger and plays into our lustful thoughts. Clothing that is too revealing or so tight that it looks like you put it on with a brush is what I have in mind. Whether you like it or not, if you're revealing parts of your body that shouldn't be exposed to begin with, you're going to be looked upon sexually by men. You're advertising it. What do you think the purpose of advertising is? Companies run advertisements of their products as much as possible solely because they want you thinking about them as much as possible with the chance that you'll purchase them. When you expose too much of your flesh that should remain hidden, that is what are you doing? You're running an advertisement with the intent of wanting men to think and look at you in a sexual way. Don't wear inappropriate clothing if you don't want to be looked on that way. You may still get looked upon that way, but at least you're not inviting it and you will be justified in getting upset about it.

I suppose women who dress scantily or too revealing dress that way because they want to feel attractive or something, but in reality, it's a desire that seemingly comes from insecurities deep within. I see this as being similar to women who are already beautiful but are always getting face lifts because they don't feel like they're beautiful enough. Women who dress inappropriately usually don't feel good about themselves in some form or fashion. They feel that they have to put everything on display in order to get attention or feel beautiful. Well, as a man, here's an idea of what I see and am thinking when I see a sufficiently well-dressed woman versus a scantily-clad woman who is showing way too much. These thoughts may be specific to me, but they'll give you a general idea of how the male's mind is processing these two very different visions.

When I see a sufficiently well-dressed woman, I see a woman who is a vision of true beauty. I see a woman who is defined by class and elegance. As I'm drawn in by and admiring her beauty, this is a woman that I'd want to know more about. Who is she? Where is she from? Her likes and dislikes. You get the picture. This is a woman that I would definitely want by my side.

On the other hand, when I see a scantily-dressed woman, my thoughts of her are driven by what she's advertising. She's showing or emphasizing parts of herself that shouldn't be disclosed and remain a mystery except to the one whom she marries. My thoughts of her are only sensual in nature and she has assisted me in only viewing her as an object. Unfortunately, I probably won't be able to get past that. And, she is definitely not someone I want to get to know as I'm not even thinking about her character or personality. She has no discretion as she has laid herself bare before everyone.

Unfortunately, being a man, I may lust after the woman who is sufficiently dressed anyway. Personally, I don't always go there and I totally credit that to being a disciple of Jesus. But, I could. The difference is how each one is dressed and what that invokes within. One inclines to invoke an admiration of her beauty and have an interest in her and who she is whereas the other will only incline to invoke a desire to satisfy the sensual desires she aroused in me when I saw her. Unfortunately, we as people do judge a book by its cover. Because of the way you've scantily wrapped yourself, it does lead people to make assumptions about your character. You may be genuinely a sweet woman, but because of how you've clothed yourself, you may be thought of as a tramp or an easy lay. I'm not saying that it's right. I'm a black man. I've been judged by the color of my skin and I can't change that. However, you can change the style of your clothes.

Something else that's shameful is the one place where you'd figure it'd be a safe haven for men to go to get away from this but in some cases, it's not. It's the church! Sometimes I've gone to church and have had to divert my eyes and guard my heart because some teenager or grown woman had on an outfit that shouldn't be worn out to a club much less to church. They always want to put that back on the men like Meagan Good in the example I used earlier. But really, what kind of attention are you trying to attract with the too low shorts that has your bottom dropping out or so tight, they're cutting your inner thighs? And, you say you want men to respect you. Dressing like that, you can't be serious.

Also, ladies don't tempt or cross the boundaries that you and your boyfriend have decided. And, don't give in either. You both need to stay strong and help each other. Find out what he can and can't handle – you too

– and make sure you both stay as far away from what will cause him to struggle with this sin. It's not to find out how close you can come without going too far. Another thing to be aware of is the more you grow closer together in your dating relationship, you may have to adjust those boundaries to tighten them up. Believe me; the temptation will increase as you grow closer together and it will be hard. Finally, if you find yourself in an unintentional compromising situation all of a sudden, remove yourself the moment you realize it. After realizing it, the longer you stay in the situation, the harder it will be to move away from it.

In the summer of 2000 when I was studying the Bible and made the commitment to follow Jesus, one of the things God instilled in me was deep convictions about purity. As I mentioned earlier, I believe the passage in Ephesians 5:3 really set the tone for me when it was shared with me during my studies by those who were initially helping me begin this journey. Reflecting on the lifestyle I was leaving behind and my observation of others, I knew how easily it was to be tempted and become entangled with this sin. I know this reflection during the beginning of my journey helped in formulating my convictions in this area as well. As I continued my walk with Jesus and immersed myself in the Scriptures, it seemed to only strengthen my convictions and it became something I was known for amongst my fellow brothers and sisters in Christ. I had gotten married and transitioned back to singleness without a problem after my then wife filed for a divorce and it became final. On one occasion, a couple of years or so after the divorce, I found myself thinking about the transition and wondered how I was able to do it without any struggles. I concluded that as a disciple of Jesus, God's standard for purity was the standard for my life and His Spirit dwells within me, which was the only way I was able to do so. I maintained a high level of purity for a good twelve years until I met a woman that I began dating and would eventually marry. We met at a church conference. For a very brief moment, at the onset of the relationship, things were good and I will share an example from that time later on as it is something that can be beneficial to you. But things soured quickly. What I'm about to say to you is from one speaking from experience who wasn't very careful this particular time around. Pay attention to the dynamics of your relationship! There were obvious things that I missed. Take notice and consider what he or she is doing because that's a revelation of who that person really is. I'll give you a better idea of what to look for later on. Back to my example. Truthfully, I wouldn't be surprised if the dating relationship was probably the most pathetic spectacle of a dating relationship ever by two disciples of Christ. I can say this with absolute certainty for any relationship I've been a part of since following Christ. I was a foolish idiot at the time for tying the knot with this person. I'm now okay with saying that about myself because I've come to accept it although it took me awhile. I had been beating myself up over it all for quite some time because I knew better. What actually helped me get over the hump to accept my foolishness was the song *Everybody Plays the Fool* by the Main Ingredient. It came on the radio while I was driving one day. The words of the song soaked in after a few days or so of it playing over and over again in my mind. Jumping back to when we first met, we lived in different cities so after the conference was over our main interaction was through phone conversations. Those conversations were fine. For the most part, we were getting to know one another. But, there were things even in those conversations that were consistent enough that should have raised a red flag. Shortly after the conference, I did drive up to see her for the first visit. On that first visit, she attempted to cross a clearly defined boundary that we spoke about in one of our many phone conversations. It was after that first visit where things began taking a turn for the worst and my foolishness started blossoming. I went back for a second and third visit and it was the same outcome. She attempted to cross boundaries and I had to enforce them. In hindsight, I believe that I eventually began weakening in my convictions and I really didn't realize it at the time until it was too late. I began letting some things slide here and there that weren't good for me spiritually. My first mistake I believe was that I let my guard down way too soon and I believed the hype. I really believed that she was someone who had my back and I believed that she would stop pushing the boundaries I had set in place. I believed this in contrast to what her actions clearly dictated. Why would I think she would stop when there was no evidence indicating she would? This reminds me of some women who get in relationships with men who are absolutely no good for them. The guy may be extremely abusive to her, verbally and physically. He apologizes to her every time and swears up and down he won't do it again; and that he loves her. Yet, as always, he repeats the behavior. She believes his lies and believes that he loves her. The women think that they will change him or he'll just change on his own. And, she believes this without ever seeing any supporting evidence. That doesn't make any sense. No woman is going to change any man or vice versa. You see, what happens in situations like this is when we invest our hearts into something too quickly; it's hard to pull it back. When everything is showing you that you should get out of there, somewhere deep within your heart, you desire for things to work out. You maintain through all of the garbage no matter how bad it is simply because you're invested and you've progressed too far down that path. This is exactly where I was. It's not that I desired her so much that I thought she was the only one for me. That's ridiculous thinking. I was invested and, in my heart, I had already deemed her to be the one who had my back. Anything contrary to that would mean that I was wrong. As the Bible says, "Before his downfall a man's heart is proud" (Proverbs 18:12). In our hearts, sometimes it's hard to admit we were wrong about things like this. Well, back to my story. In reality, people bent on being impure and trying to have sex with you are not going to stop until they get what they want or you radically put a stop to it.

  Being that I was genuinely trying to get to know her, the time came where I moved from Kansas City to be closer to her to see how we'd work as a couple. Well, that move proved to be the breaking point for me. Spiritually speaking, it seemed like I just walked off the edge of a cliff and fell into an abyss. I left behind my church family in Kansas City where I had one heck of a support group, my closest and dearest friends. I went from that to a sister church where I wasn't received as though I was a fellow brother in Christ. I reached out to build friendships initially, but the sentiment wasn't really reciprocated. I think the change was a little more difficult than I expected and I became down and depressed. I know I became depressed because I lost my appetite and lost so much weight so fast that it scared me when I hopped on the scale one morning and saw my weight had dropped below what I weighed in college during basketball season. As I mentioned earlier, when men are dealing with emotional issues, we become susceptible to things that aren't good for us. It's already hard for a Christian man to resist the temptation of a woman trying to bait him. Considering the circumstances, I eventually jumped in with both feet and became a willing participant in the sexual sin therefore being a disgrace to God.

I did sinful stuff with her I had not done in well over twelve years; the lifestyle I gave up when I became a Christian. We did everything short of sexual intercourse; and that, we almost fulfilled about two or three weeks out from the wedding. We kissed on the mouth (something I stopped doing when I became a Christian and saved for my wedding day because it's too personal and for me it can take me there), to grinding, to touching each other in inappropriate places, to things that are too graphic and disgusting to detail. After spending time with her, I would drive back to my apartment feeling so guilty, low, and despicable because of the sin. I knew God was not pleased with me. I had quickly gone from being a man with high standards of sexual integrity to a man with absolutely no sexual integrity at all. But as soon as I could, where was I at again? I was back at her place the next day looking for the same thing. I remember on a few occasions while driving out there, my conscience telling me, "Clarence, you know you need to turn around and go back to your apartment." But I kept on going. I couldn't stop even though deep down inside I really wanted to. Looking back on that time, I realized that I had gone back to my old lifestyle before Christ. I was like a dog that returned to its vomit (Proverbs 26:11, II Peter 2:22). I had returned to living according to my sinful nature and not according to the Spirit of God. But, the sin didn't stop there with impurity. As I mentioned earlier, some sins are running buddies. I became so deceitful, which is the typical companion to sexual sins. I acted like everything was alright at various times. I presented this front to her as well as the couple that was doing our marriage counseling. I could not stand some things in her character but I don't think it was really obvious to me at the time. I wasn't focused on anything other than getting off with her. Some of you may want to say that I'm despicable or something for saying this. You probably want to ascribe all the blame to me and say, "Typical guy," or something like that. Unfortunately, in situations like this, it's always easier to blame the guy. But remember, this is how she presented herself to me. That wasn't my intentions in the beginning. Yeah, there were flags that went up in my mind at times about some things in her character, but I paid no real attention to them. Unfortunately, that's not where my focus was. My emotions had skyrocketed and supplanted logical thinking.

That's what happens with any kind of impurity before marriage. But don't worry; I paid the price for my sin. I ended up with someone I really didn't want to marry. It was a situation I never really wanted to find myself in. At my worst moment health wise, she was way more concerned about her needs than what was going on with me, thus making my condition worse. After we married, those red flags I didn't pay attention to before were flapping around in my mind like the American flag as it whips back and forth in a strong wind. That's usually how it goes though. Have you ever realized you made a humongous mistake the moment it was too late? This was definitely one of those times for me.

We eventually told the couple that was doing our marriage counseling in order to get some help and advice. Now, I was jumping back and forth over the gate in my convictions. On an occasion here and there, I would call her out, but by this time, I was right there mostly indulging. I figured like I did on other occasions that she would realize the importance of being pure and would stop after we spoke with the couple. But, she didn't. She persisted. I eventually had a moment where I so was fed up with it; I came close to calling the whole thing off. Something I should have done long before this point. This was about a month or two out from the wedding. I wished I had on so many occasions afterwards as that would have saved a lot of heartaches and problems for me and everyone involved or close to the situation. I just didn't give myself enough time. In all of that mess, one night to consider all that was going on wasn't enough. I needed more time to let the emotions settle, clear my head to think properly, but considering the circumstances, I was in a rush at that point. That is a typical mistake under those circumstances. Another one I made; I never should have based any part of my decision on her response. All of it should have come from the Bible and how being with her influenced my downfall spiritually. There was no genuine sorrow or repentance on her part. She said anything to get her way. Her response was reminiscent of a pleading child who hadn't come to terms with the severity of his or her actions and doesn't want to suffer the consequences. Of course, I didn't break it off and we continued in the sin. By this time, I had a complete loss of convictions. Now, the marrying in and of itself wasn't the problem. It's the condition under which we married that was beyond detestable. We married with a great deal of unrepentant sin on both parts. In a situation like that, the marriage should have been postponed until the sin was dealt with or it should have been called off altogether. Personally, I should have permanently broken that relationship off with a swiftness. She was far from what I was looking for in a spouse. At some point, my focus transitioned from genuinely trying to get to know her to just wanting to satisfy my lustful desires. I kept going back because of the sensual things we were doing not because of who she was.

So, why did I marry her despite all of this madness you ask? I've asked myself that question too many times to count throughout the marriage. I couldn't figure out for the life of me what the heck I was thinking. In my younger years, I heard people say they made a mistake marrying a particular person. I've even heard couples in agreement with this that they shouldn't have married each other. At the time, I couldn't wrap my head around how you could make a mistake like that, but I figured I'd do my best not to follow in those footsteps. Well, now I can understand. Over time, I concluded it was something similar to Moses' reaction at the waters of Meribah (Numbers 20:1-13). The people had quarreled with Moses as they had done so many times before. And, this time I think it had taken its toll. Again, they wanted water. The Lord told Moses to speak to a rock and He would cause water to flow out. Out of frustration with the people, Moses struck the rock twice with his staff instead, thus dishonoring God's holiness. Water still gushed out as God said it would, but Moses disobeyed God bringing judgment on himself. There's a valuable lesson to learn from this that we all can benefit from. When our emotions skyrocket whether it's due to frustration, panic, fear, or impurity, we are likely to make rash decisions. Moses fell into this predicament as well and it took his focus off of where it should have been – on God. This is what happens when we take our focus off of God. We blow it no matter how big or small. This is what happened to me. I made an extremely rash decision about something super important in the midst of heightened emotions. Along the way, my focus gradually turned away from God. This is why it is of extreme importance to always have our focus on God. When we don't, we blow it. Don't believe me? Then take a look at all of the evil things people do in this world today – from the most outrageous to the tiniest of things. That is the result of people who don't have their focus on God.

To my shame and in my foolishness, I became so blind to the obvious warning signs from a variety of sources like my very own conscience, her deliberate actions, and a parenthetical warning from a friend of hers that I received during my first visit. In the instant he said what he said, just enough of my pride surfaced so that I glazed over the most important part of what he said. It definitely should have gotten my attention. Under any other circumstances, it would have. He said it as we were walking back to his car and he plastered it in between two totally unrelated topics. He said, "I hope you're doing well in your purity because she's sure gonna try." Instantly, I thought out of my pride that I've always done well in my purity, which was true, and that I trusted her. I totally paid no attention to the last part, which was of value. I should have stopped him and asked him what about her character would make you say that about her. I called another friend of hers after I returned home to try and get the scoop on her, but she wouldn't give me anything. Then here, this morsel dropped right in my lap. I beat myself up for this one for a long time. Those words became so vividly etched in my mind; they practically haunted me. This is when my foolishness really ignited. Blinded by my own idolatry (which stems from strong selfish desires), I let so many things slide that I normally wouldn't have. I was not infatuated with her, but with my perception of her being the woman who would have my back and respect me for the man that I am. Overall, I saw how I failed at leading. It's not that I failed to provide direction, be the godly example, or led her into that sin. I'm the one who put up the boundaries, spoke of the importance of being pure utilizing the Scriptures, and shared my personal vulnerabilities thinking this was someone who would protect me (I Corinthians 13:7). I failed in leading by not radically suffocating her attempts to drag me into her sin as I should have. I should have mimicked what Joseph did with Potiphar's wife when she made advances at him. He broke out so fast that he left his cloak in her hands (Genesis 39:11-12). And, that's the way it is with some sins, you have to flat out run from them especially those that are sexual in nature. Consequently, my failure in not suffocating her advances conveyed the message to her that her actions – although, clearly wrong – were okay. The snowball effect comes into play big here because I also ended up not dealing with my own sin. Instead of guarding my sexual integrity like I always had, I gave my lusts and my sin an environment to thrive and flourish in.

After wrestling with the decision in my heart for several months or so, I moved out with the intention of not returning. One side of the conflict was not being disobedient to God and personally, I was supposed to have removed divorce from my arsenal. The other side of the conflict is that I really didn't want to wake up with my fallen past always before me. I was seriously hurt and felt deeply lacerated. I was enraged and frustrated from all of the pain I felt. This not only from her sins against me but my own sin and mistakes as well (I hurt myself too.). I felt confused as I tried to process and figure out how in the heck did I let all of this happen. After we were married, I felt like I needed to be restored back to God. Why? It's because I felt as though I could not repent of all that premarital impurity. True repentance is a change in your mind and heart that leads you away from sin back to righteousness. Well, I never repented of the impurity and in my mind I couldn't because we were now married. I could not reconcile that in my mind! These, along with the deeper things I was feeling, are the things that constantly ate at me and magnified as the days progressed. It was reminiscent to some of what Amnon probably felt after he was immoral with Tamar. Those were the two conflicting sides in my heart. The former option should have rightfully won out. The more I thought about the things that was stirring in my heart, I resorted to my sinfulness to get myself out of a situation with someone I really didn't want to be with. I'm not saying what I did is right. I'm just saying what I did.

So, I share my failures with you so you don't have to – fail. I want to equip you so that you have an idea ahead of time. Having knowledge is half the battle. The other half of the battle is turning that knowledge into wisdom through application of that knowledge so that you can strive to do better. That's another thing I realized. We may know better but we don't always do better. We only strive to do better and when we fail, in Christ, we get up, repent, and keep on going. Thank God Almighty for that. So many people rely on the superficial things this world teaches thinking that's going to make your marriage endure through the personal challenges, changes, and hardships of life. If they have a few things in common or if he or she makes me laugh every time we're together; they think that's good enough. Some people even believe if the sex is good, if he or she is good in bed, that's what's going to keep you together. There's a multitude of superficiality surrounding what makes a marriage last from a person's appearance to how big one's bank account is. But, considering the high divorce rate in this country, we know with certainty that this is not true. We are truly missing the boat in this area. Singles, when it comes to picking your potential future spouse, one's character should be of the utmost importance. Yes, you want someone you're attracted to. Yes, sex is an important component in a marriage relationship. But remember, you shouldn't even be concerned how that person will be in bed at this point. If you're thinking about that aspect of sex, you're sinning. That's something the two of you will grow together in satisfying each other over the course of your marriage. That's how it was meant to be by design. Those things have varying degrees of importance, but they shouldn't be your top priority for selecting your spouse. Character makes a world of difference during times of marital conflict, trials of life, and decision making. How good your spouse is in the bedroom skyrocketing you to ecstasy isn't going to make a bit of difference to you during those times. Do you see what I'm saying? I'm pleading with you! If all you can recite about your spouse is good things, then you're not ready to get married; and you desperately need a reality check. You should be able to name some of your potential spouse's weaknesses and shortcomings whether you saw them for yourself or your partner told you, then you identified the validity of them and how they manifest themselves. The difference between a predominantly prideful or humble spouse is what's going to make a difference during your times of conflict. A predominantly selfish or selfless spouse is what's going to make a difference during your times of need. If you can see these types of things and make some decision as to how they're going to play into your life, then you're approaching this with your eyes wide open and in the real world. You can consider if you can live with them for the rest of your life if it doesn't change because like I said before, they become yours when you two are married. That's the concept of oneness – the good as well as the bad. To take it a bit farther, you consider how you might help your potential spouse grow beyond that weakness or how you can help them through those moments of weakness. There's just going to be some things we're not going to get much better at and you have to learn to help your spouse lovingly through those times. That's just the way it is; we're human. A person like this is looking at marriage from the right perspective, not like some kind of fairy tale. You won't be shocked when it finally hits the fan.

#NoSpecificInstructions

God's Word doesn't speak to every specific situation we encounter. If it did, the Bible would be a very large multi-volume set of encyclopedias.

Many people a have hard enough time already reading the Bible as it is today. What do you do if you find yourself in a situation where the Bible hasn't spoken to specifically? The Bible is full of principles that are applicable to many situations in life. Another amazing quality about the Word of God!

> [17]And whatever you do, whether in word or deed, do it all in the name of the Lord Jesus, giving thanks to God the Father through him.
> (Colossians 3:17)

Does it glorify God? This one is pretty much a definite show stopper. There's a similar passage in I Corinthians 10:31 conveying the same message. If the activity doesn't bring glory to God, then there's no reason to go any further. Some variations on the same question are, "Is what I'm doing or how I'm doing something worthy of His Name?", "Would I be ashamed to associate Him with what I'm doing?", or "Can I appropriately give thanks to God for what I'm doing?"

> [12]"Everything is permissible for me" – but not everything is beneficial. "Everything is permissible for me" – but I will not be mastered by anything.
> (I Corinthians 6:12)

Does it hurt me spiritually, mentally, emotionally, physically, or does it bring me under its power? This is pretty self-explanatory. If there's a chance of you getting hurt in any way, then it may not be a good idea to participate. Or, if it may bring you under its power, it again wouldn't be wise to participate. I'm talking about addiction here. The activity doesn't necessarily have to be a bad thing in and of itself. Too much of a good thing can be bad for us as well. You really have to know what you can and cannot handle. For instance, taking a drink is not a bad thing, but if you've dealt with alcoholism in your past and taking a drink may bring you under its power again, then it wouldn't be wise for you to do so.

> [13]Therefore, if what I eat causes my brother to fall into sin, I will never eat meat again, so that I will not cause him to fall.
> (I Corinthians 8:13)

Is what I'm about to do going to hurt others? It's the exact same sentiment as the previous question but applied to others you're with. God calls us to care for others especially the family of believers. We can apply the example from the previous question in the same manner. If you're wanting to drink an alcoholic beverage but your companion has struggled with alcoholism in the past, then for your companion's sake, it would be wise not to do so in his or her presence. This may very well cause your companion to struggle and have a relapse. So, look out for the interest of those around you.

What About Testing the Water First?

Many couples decide to live together or cohabitate while dating. Anymore these days it has become the norm and some couples don't decide. They transition into living together. They're spending so much time with one another and one is usually at the other one's place so much that he or she eventually begins to bring clothes and other items over until the next thing you know, they're practically living together. Or, they just make it official since that's what's happening anyway. So, why do couples decide to live together before marriage? There are several reasons couples decide to cohabitate and the reasons vary from couple to couple. And, it's likely that the individuals in the relationship have some reasons that vary as well. A few reasons people provide for cohabitating are they want to spend more time with their significant other, sharing the financial burden only makes sense, they want to test the relationship out to see if it'll work, and they don't believe in the institution of marriage. Didn't I mention before that we can be so dumb sometimes? Here's a thought from the School of Asininity. How can you not believe in something that clearly exists? Now, if you don't want to have anything to do with it then just say that. Don't deny its existence when its right there and extremely prevalent. Now, I do understand that they are actually referring to the effectiveness of marriage. But, that's still ridiculous because marriage does work. It has for years and still does. The problem with marriage lies with the people involved, not the institution itself.

The only woman I can legitimately say that I lived with before marriage was my first wife, which was about five years before I became a disciple of Jesus. Since being a disciple of Jesus, I haven't done that or even thought about doing that. We weren't looking to live together although we weren't shying away from it either. The way it came about was that I was having some major financial difficulties because the car I had at the time literally broke down three weeks in a row. It was already killing a brother's pocket book, which had no thickness to begin with, from previous break downs it had. My lease had run out or was close to running out on the apartment I had on the east side of Kansas City off 87th Street where Bannister Mall once stood. If you remember earlier, she was from France attending school at Kansas University in Lawrence, Kansas. This all took place at the beginning of summer, so she and her friend had found an apartment on campus so they could go to summer school and then they'd be back off to France. Well, this seemed to work out perfectly. Instead of having to look for another apartment, clearly being under a financial strain, they invited me to stay with them for the summer. It would take a burden off of me for a while and I would get to have maximum time with my "Sexy", which is the nickname I gave her, before she left to go back to France for her last year of school. By that time, we wanted to get married, so she was actually my fiancée. So, I packed up my stuff and moved back to Lawrence to live with her and her friend. This is really the only time I've ever lived with someone I dated. The only other situation that came close to cohabitation was with a girlfriend who lived in Saint Joseph, MO. Quite often, I would pack clothes and go to stay the weekend with her and her children, then leave from there Monday morning to go to work in Kansas City. Or, she would have her mother babysit her children and come stay with me in Kansas City for the weekend. Although this wasn't really a habit of mine, as you can see, I didn't have a problem with it at all and was right there with everyone else. But now, unless something happens, God forbid, I turn back to following my sinful nature instead of Jesus, cohabitation is out of the question. I didn't cohabit prior to my two Christian marriages. It's wrong morally first of all. Practically, there's problems with it that are contrary to the health of a relationship.

Okay now, let's discuss what you're so anxious to talk about. What's the problem with cohabitating? First and foremost, it is a situation that is contrary to God's design because cohabitation always involves sexual immorality. The couple that cohabitates together will have sex together. And that is a no-no. We won't be spending any more time on that topic. If you've suddenly forgotten why this is a problem, then go back and reread the seventy plus pages on sexual integrity. This time better make it a bit slower though – give it some time to really sink in.

Another potential problem with cohabitation is that your relationship is starting out with an unstable foundation. What I mean is that living together causes insecurities and instabilities. Look at this quote from an article I read. It states, "Compared to married couples, cohabitating couples argue more, have more trouble resolving conflicts, are more insecure about their partners' feelings, and have more problems related to their future goals (Hsueh, Rhabar, Morrison, & Doss, 2009). These findings are concerning for couples considering pre-marital cohabitation, but a closer look shows a much more complicated picture." (DiDonato) Tell me what does this sound like? You know, marriage in one aspect is a partnership; it's a joining of two beings into one. How can you move forward, make plans for the future with someone when you don't even know if he or she is going to be around the next day let alone next year? In a way, you're kind of stuck in a hole and can't progress until the uncertainty is cleared up. Another potential instability is this. Do you really know your partner's motivation behind living together? I said earlier that the individuals cohabitating together can have very different reasons for living together. This is a situation that is easily driven by selfishness. Once your partner perceives that he or she is no longer getting what he or she wants, then your partner could decide on a whim that he or she has had enough and decide to leave. Something worse is that your partner may decide to simply withdraw from the relationship and just co-exist because you'll see later that it's not always easy to leave. Either way, you'll end up giving your best to someone without ever having a commitment.

For me personally, another downfall with living together is the messages that it sends and neither one is good at all. A primary reason for living together is to test the relationship out to see if the marriage will work. First of all, if you have to "test" it out, you clearly already have uncertainties about the relationship. It's usually a good sign to not even go there because it won't make anything better. Best to probably go your separate ways. Essentially, what's being communicated is the first thing I see in you that I don't like, I'm jetting out of here. This leads me to the second message that cohabitation is communicating. It says something along the line like "I'm not really going to commit to you" or "I don't value you enough to give you my all". I loved the way this one article posed it. It asked, "How can you practice committing to someone by not committing to them?" (Walsh) You either do or you don't; it's as simple as that. Cohabitation is not marriage. Cohabitation is missing key ingredients of marriage, which is commitment, oneness, and till death do you part. Those are not present when a couple decides to live together. The ingredients of cohabitation are conditionally, divided as two, and for an unspecified amount of time and these are proclaimed loudly deep within the statements couples use to seal the deal to cohabitate. Essentially, cohabitation always leaves the back door open. On top of this proclamation, if a couple who has lived together decides to finally tie the knot, they are in danger of living out their marriage in a cohabitating mindset. The same article so eloquently stated, "You leave the wedding reception and return to the apartment you already shared and the lives that were already intertwined in every practical way. The only difference – and it's a huge one, a defining one – is that now you've made a lifelong commitment to one another. But that's not what you've practiced. You haven't practiced commitment, you've practiced avoiding it. You've practiced living with this person tenuously and conditionally, and, whether you intend to or not, there's a good chance you'll continue on living exactly as you rehearsed." (Walsh) I don't know about you but this sounds like a drab to me. Living together kills the aura of a wedding. There should be celebration, excitement, and a lot of energy as the two begin to dream and imagine what their new life will be like together. But, there's literally nothing new. There's no looking forward to the adventure of living life together because you've already been doing that. You don't have that youthful energy that's present in a new marriage. Instead, you end up having that stale old married couple feel. I wouldn't want to be a part of that at all. Totally awkward!

Many people followed Jesus around. Quite often, you'd find thousands of people surrounding Him at times when He spoke. You couldn't find a rock musician or a band with a greater following of groupies than Jesus. All of those people followed Jesus around for a variety of reasons. Some wanted to be healed or have loved ones healed. Some had heard about Him and was super curious. Others wanted to get their fill of food as He fed many. And yet, others wanted to trap and kill Him. Like I said, there were a variety of reasons. Never said they were all good. He was always able to easily weed out those who weren't really committed to Him. Through His spiritual teachings, He would challenge them by taking them higher. People would literally turn around and walk away from Him by the droves much like groupies do when the popularity of their favorite rock band dissipates. Jesus knew right off the bat those who weren't committed to Him. The spiritual teachings only made it come to light. Let's take a look at a couple of Jesus' teachings that challenged His followers' commitment.

> [28]Suppose one of you wants to build a tower. Will he not first sit down and estimate the cost to see if he has enough money to complete it? [29]For if he lays the foundation and is not able to finish it, everyone who sees it will ridicule him, [30]saying, "This fellow began to build and was not able to finish."
>
> (Luke 14:28-30)

This is a small excerpt of a larger discourse Jesus gave the large crowds that were traveling with Him at the time about being His disciple. In this discourse, Jesus challenged an area of commitment that proceeds actually making the commitment. He provided information to those crowds of people as to what it would take to truly be committed to Him. Obviously, just following Him around everywhere He went and being visibly associated with Him wasn't enough. What Jesus laid out to the crowd had nothing to do with the emotions. What He laid out for them was bare facts and information. With that, they were able to make an informative decision about whether they could commit or not. As in the excerpt above, the builder will have to gather information on the total cost of building the tower and how much money he currently has or can realistically acquire towards building the tower. He wouldn't just jump into building the tower without that information. Yet, that's what many of us do with marriage. We date and are driven solely by our emotions. We pay no attention to the facts revealed in the other person's character, then we decide to marry without enough sensible information of the other person or any idea of what marriage really requires of us. I know this pretty much describes my very first marriage. Yes, I did genuinely love her. But, I had no clue of what marriage was about – the roles or responsibilities. And, I surely didn't ask the type of questions or take note of things that I should have like what I'm writing in this book to you. In going through this process, one must be wise enough to look more at the facts – not make it just an emotional ride – and count the cost to making that commitment of marriage to God, your partner, and yourself. This is the first step in making a commitment.

Another challenge on commitment comes from John 6. Once again for the sake of brevity, I'll only include excerpts, but I recommend you go back and read the entire chapter to get the full effect of Jesus' words. As usual, Jesus was surrounded by a massive crowd. It was about five thousand men – with the inclusion of women and children that number climbs to a much larger amount. Well, Jesus ends up performing a miraculous act here by feeding the crowd with only five loaves and two small fish. Everyone was able to get their fill – in other words no one suffered from missed meal cramps. And they ended up with way more left over than they started with. After feeding the crowd, Jesus was forced to withdraw from the crowd. Then, later that evening, His disciples got in a boat and headed for Capernaum. Then, Jesus, being Jesus, walked on water to go out to meet them. The next day the crowd that stayed behind on the opposite shore where Jesus performed the miraculous feeding went to find Jesus. Once they found Jesus, this is what He said to them.

> ²⁵When they found him on the other side of the lake, they asked him, "Rabbi, when did you get here?" ²⁶Jesus answered, "I tell you the truth, you are looking for me, not because you saw miraculous signs but because you ate the loaves and had your fill. ²⁷Do not work for food that spoils, but for food that endures to eternal life, which the Son of Man will give you. On him God the Father has placed his seal of approval." ²⁸Then they asked him, "What must we do to do the works God requires?"
> (John 6:25-28)

Here is where Jesus began to call the crowd to thinking higher to spiritual truths. This group of people were only concerned about getting their tummies filled again. That's why they worked so diligently to find Him. Jesus knew this right off the bat which is why He used this opportunity to introduce them to the everlasting food that He had for them. And get this, they weren't even impressed with the miracle Jesus performed to feed them. Good gracious, there were only five loaves of bread and two fish. Everyone ate and there were plenty left over. I guess it made no difference what was going on around them; all they wanted to do was eat. Know anyone like this? Well, Jesus' initial statement peaks their interest but it's obvious that they didn't exactly know what He was talking about or knew who He really was. They asked Him for a sign and referred to the manna that Moses gave their ancestors. Referencing the manna, it seems like they're still looking for food to eat. Jesus corrects them informing them that God is who actually supplied the manna to their ancestors and that God still does give bread from heaven. Still in confusion, they ask Him to give them the bread He's referring to from now on. Here is Jesus' response.

> ³⁵Then Jesus declared, "I am the bread of life. He who comes to me will never go hungry, and he who believes in me will never be thirsty. ³⁶But as I told you, you have seen me and still you do not believe. ³⁷All that the Father gives me will come to me, and whoever comes to me I will never drive away. ³⁸For I have come down from heaven not to do my will but to do the will of him who sent me. ³⁹And this is the will of him who sent me, that I shall lose none of all that he has given me, but raise them up at the last day. ⁴⁰For my Father's will is that everyone who looks to the Son and believes in him shall have eternal life, and I will raise him up at the last day."
>
> (John 6:35-40)

At this they began grumbling amongst themselves and questioning Jesus' identity. They absolutely could not believe Jesus was who He said He was. Then Jesus continues and goes even deeper on them. And in verse 52, you can see that they completely missed the point. They are still thinking in terms of feeding their faces. Jesus is clearly speaking figuratively here in order to bring home a critical spiritual point and they couldn't figure that out to save their lives - literally. Some people miss out on greater things simply because they can't see beyond the boundaries of their own desires. Jesus continues.

> ⁵³Jesus said to them, "I tell you the truth, unless you eat the flesh of the Son of Man and drink his blood, you have no life in you. ⁵⁴Whoever eats my flesh and drinks my blood has eternal life, and I will raise him up at the last day. ⁵⁵For my flesh is real food and my blood is real drink. ⁵⁶Whoever eats my flesh and drinks my blood remains in me, and I in him. ⁵⁷Just as the living Father sent me and I live because of the Father, so the one who feeds on me will live because of me. ⁵⁸This is the bread that came down from heaven. Your forefathers ate manna and died, but he who feeds on this bread will live forever."
>
> (John 6:53-58)

Now, I have to mention that there was a full course spiritual meal that was just served up – the meat, potatoes, vegetables, glass of wine, and even appetizers and desserts were served. But, it's beyond the scope of what I'm talking about. Along with the profound spiritual truths, Jesus was calling them to complete commitment to Him. With that commitment, they were guaranteed to receive what He promised, which was to be raised to eternal life. Here's their final response.

> [60]On hearing it, many of his disciples said, "This is a hard teaching. Who can accept it?" [61]Aware that his disciples were grumbling about this, Jesus said to them, "Does this offend you? [62]What if you see the Son of Man ascend to where he was before! [63]The Spirit gives life; the flesh counts for nothing. The words I have spoken to you are spirit and they are life. [64]Yet there are some of you who do not believe." For Jesus had known from the beginning which of them did not believe and who would betray him. [65]He went on to say, "This is why I told you that no one can come to me unless the Father has enabled him." [66]From this time many of his disciples turned back and no longer followed him.
>
> (John 6:60-66)

They were totally perplexed by what He said so they walked away. Jesus never enlightens them to His technique or simplified His teaching so they could understand. This is why He spoke in parables; it reveals people's heart. If they were really committed to Him, they would have hung in there until they figured it out, asked questions, or something. The group of people didn't understand Him because they didn't truly take the time to get to know Him. Quite naturally, they're not going to believe in Him or want to do what He asks. Just hanging around Him occasionally as they did wasn't enough.

Some people are no different today. They associate with Jesus because it's the "right" thing to do. But, they don't ever think about, follow, or love Jesus. Their lives don't show it. Now, as disciples, we still sin. I'm not talking about perfection; I'm talking about the direction of your life. Where is it heading? Does your life fit into the template that Jesus laid out in His word?

> ⁶⁷"You do not want to leave too, do you?" Jesus asked the Twelve. ⁶⁸Simon Peter answered him, "Lord, to whom shall we go? You have the words of eternal life. ⁶⁹We believe and know that you are the Holy One of God."
>
> (John 6:67-69)

Peter ended up speaking for the Twelve. His response revealed that they were committed to Jesus. They knew Him; they knew He was who He said He was. Unlike the others, even though they may not have understood everything He said to them over the years He was with them, they weren't going anywhere. The lesson here regarding commitment is simply this. Without commitment, you really have nothing at all. And, you shouldn't expect to acquire anything worthwhile over the long haul. This is the difference between cohabitation and marriage. In years past, if you just lived with someone and your partner died, you received nothing. You had to be married. Recently, society began to acknowledge partnerships, so there are some benefits in that now. But, it wasn't that way in the beginning. And, because there are benefits now doesn't mean that it's any more appropriate. It's just that the more life continues; the more mankind moves farther away from God.

What happens when you suddenly realize that this person is not the person you want to spend the rest of your life with? Well, you're only dating, so all you need to do is make a simple phone call and voilà, you're done. Simple isn't it? Oops! I forgot. You're living with this person. What should be simple is now a very complicated task. It's pretty much like you have to go through a divorce. Well, I guess you did say you wanted to see if it worked by playing marriage. Now, you get an opportunity to play divorce, but without the lawyers. That'll probably be the only good part of this process. This is another problem with cohabitation; it's not easy to just break up. You've conjoined your lives together by sharing bank accounts. You've either purchased a home together or you may just be renting. You've purchased furniture to fill up your home. You share the bills and you may even have acquired a pet or two. Some cohabitating couples even go so far as having children together. When you intertwine your life together like this you make something that should be simple an extremely difficult task. It's so difficult there are couples who have stayed together for years even though they couldn't stand each other. And some of them aren't shy about showing it. Why would you take a chance and do this to yourself? This woman posted a long comment to an article about cohabitation sharing her experience in a cohabitating relationship. She said that she lived with this guy for most of her twenties. If it wasn't for the two of them living together, this would have been a guy she would have broken up with inside of a year. This is real people and it can happen to you. Some people hate complications so much, they talk themselves into staying in a bad situation, convincing themselves that it's not that bad, even though it really is. Years go by; they finally leave and wish they would have done it much sooner. No matter how much you think this can't, won't happen to you, no one is immune from something like this happening to them. We all have our dumb moments no matter how smart we are. You can literally end up wasting some of the best years of your life in a situation like this.

As if the 49% chance of divorce for marrieds who cohabitated versus the 20% chance of divorce for those who didn't isn't enough, here's something that might explain the increase in divorce rate amongst cohabitators. I read something recently in an article that shed some light on an aspect I hadn't thought about regarding cohabitators. It's called the Inertia Effect. It states that once a couple begins to live together, that act actually drives them towards marriage. This is true for couples that otherwise would not have married at all. Marriage becomes somewhat inevitable; couples seem to slide right on into marriage from the momentum of moving in together. This certainly makes sense considering the previous fact that it can be sometimes hard to leave a cohabitating situation. This kind of reminds me of my childhood when I'd go to the park to slide down those super slides that went around and around in circles. I remember we used to stop right in the middle of sliding down by grabbing a hold of the sides real hard. As if this wasn't tough enough, we'd turn around and try to climb back to the top of the slide. What an arduous task that was? Trying to climb back up that slippery metal slide back around those curves against gravity and the momentum of all that was trying to pull you down. No wonder the success rate was minimal. And if someone came sliding down while you were trying to climb back up, you could pretty much forget it. Mission impossible. Down you went. So, I totally get the Inertia Effect as it applies to cohabitation. It may very well be the cause of the higher divorce rate for couples who live together first. When you start on the path, the momentum is sure to take you closer to marriage if not all the way. Even if you figure out along the way that you don't want to go all the way with this person, it may be hard to severe the relationship and move on. In reality, you can see all you need to know about a person without moving in with him or her. All you have to do is take notice of what they show you of themselves.

Finally, here's bit of logic from a summa cum laude graduate of A.U. – Asinine University. Some people are going to clearly look at all of this information against living together, the moral and practical aspects of it, and they'll pick and choose cafeteria style feeble pieces of supporting information and ride that against everything else that strongly suggests against cohabitation. There are statistics that say people who were engaged before living together fared better than those who weren't. Or, if you waited until you were older to cohabitate, then the risk goes down. Some people will take things like this and exclaim that they'll just wait until they're engaged or older before cohabitating being that those statistics are better. But remember, that's not the rule; it's the exception to the rule. And that's not a guarantee that any of those bad things or worse won't happen to you. Cohabitation is not what's in your or anyone's best interest. Don't you want what's best for yourself if nothing else? That's the problem with our sinful human nature. We shortcut everything God designed to get what we want, when we want, the way we want it. We think we know better than the Creator and our actions clearly show that. It's a lack of trust in God. And therein lies the real problem. People want to use science, statistics, and feelings as the ultimate authority to justify their desires instead of God, who **is** the Ultimate

Authority.

Cross-Gender Friendships

"Men and women can't be friends because the sex part always gets in the way." Remember this line made famous by Billy Crystal in *When Harry Met Sally*? Although it became a highly referenced phrase due to the movie, that mentality has been around for ages. This also reveals how long a lie can linger if someone doesn't call out the big white elephant in the room. Men and women can be platonic friends. I've had quite a few over the course of my life. And no, it wasn't because I fell in the friendship zone either. Sex is not something that just gets in the way of male and female relationships as it is made out to be. The reality is that sexual immorality is sin. Without Christ, people are slaves to sin; therefore, they are controlled by their sinful nature. That's what they are looking to gratify (Ephesians 2:3). So, now it becomes plain. If sexual immorality is a dominant part of a person's sinful nature, then that's what they are seeking after, not the friendship.

I believe that platonic friendships with members of the opposite sex are a very significant part of life. My belief in this is rooted from the simple truth of how God created us – man and woman. He created the two from one being. He divided the characteristics of the one between the two giving to each as they would need for their role in their relationship to each other and in creation. So, how does this support the importance of having friends of the opposite sex? As a man, I don't see or experience the world as completely as I should. And, there's absolutely nothing wrong with that. I can only do so with the attributes God equipped me with as a man. It benefits me to have the viewpoint of a woman. As I learn and understand my female companions more and how they see and experience the world, I can do so vicariously through them in a way that I could never do by myself as a man. The same thing holds true for women and their male companions. If you get married, do you realize that having these friendships prior to can be a great benefit as well? It helps you to be more sensitive and aware of the viewpoint of your spouse. Ever heard a guy who grew up in a household full of sisters say that he thinks that helped him be more sensitive to the needs of his wife?

In an effort to foster these friendships, some churches encourage singles to go out on dates. Now don't misconstrue what follows in to thinking that I have a problem with or something against going out on dates. That's so far from the truth. The push for men to take women out on friendly dates has seemingly become synonymous with the legalism of the Pharisees. I think that because I feel the heart has gotten away from what's really important – the friendships and encouragement. That's what we should hear about more from the pulpits. How you go about doing that within the moral boundaries of God's law shouldn't matter. As Christian men are urged to take Christian women out on dates, it sometimes comes across as though the salvation of the women depends on it. And some women act as though they are entitled to it. The Scriptures tell us to encourage one another but going out on dates was no longer encouraging for me as it was when I was a young disciple of Jesus. It was because the encouragement flew out the window when entitlement moved in. Some women were no longer appreciative of it. When you have one party feeling entitled to something on one end, rest assured, there's always a party on the other end that's feeling burdened due to that entitlement.

Allow me to divert to an example for a minute. At a regional conference back in 2010, a young single woman from another church within the region approached my table where I was selling and autographing copies of my first book. She was distraught that the single men in her church weren't taking her or the other single women out on dates. She said the men complained about the lack of having money to go out on dates because the economy was so bad. From the impression that I got, that really didn't seem to matter to her as she was visibly having a hard time because she wasn't being taken out. We exchanged words briefly back and forth as I was able to get a few in. I encouraged her to do something to encourage the men and reminded her that it wasn't and shouldn't be about the money at all. She eventually surrendered by commenting to the effect that she just better get used to the idea. The surrender was more out of self-pity instead of patience and understanding. She wasn't getting what she wanted and didn't have the power to change the situation. Due to attending my table, I wasn't able to get completely engaged in the conversation as I had liked because people were dropping in. She and I determined that we would chat about it later in more detail if possible. Unfortunately, we were never able to meet up afterwards. I really disliked how the conversation was left hanging in limbo because I wanted to share more in-depth thoughts with her and convey the importance of the friendships and that going out on dates is only a means to that. It's not the end in and of itself.

Yes, I know that Christian women are tempted by men of the world and I don't want any one of them to fall away from Him. But, remember, you're not here for dates in the first place. You're here because the love of Christ compelled you (II Corinthians 5:14-15). He is the only one that saved you. He is the only one that sustains you. Furthermore, I'm sure that's not the case with every woman. Has anyone ever considered that some Christian men are tempted by women of the world? Likewise, every Christian man is not tempted in that way either.

What about single women taking the initiative to encourage the single men? Lord knows, we sure do need it! The two or three times I heard single women were told to encourage the single men was in the form of a rebuke to their criticisms of the men not taking them out. This is something that should be preached as well. Why do the women just sit back and wait to be taken out? Scripture tells you to go and encourage someone (Hebrews 3:13, 10:24-25). This one-sidedness can carry on into marriage where the woman expects the man to do everything under the guise of leadership. This makes oneness in marriage virtually impossible to achieve. You can't accomplish oneness when the burden to do so is placed on one person. It takes the effort of two individuals. I can honestly say that I've seen some semblance of this in one of my marriages. And, I've definitely seen it in other cross-gender interactions.

Here's something else about this practice that's become a little irritating. Everything has been labeled a date when it really isn't. That word has just been tossed around and applied to seemingly every interaction between members of the opposite sex. What ever happened to just hanging out? I really appreciate the friendship I had with a young lady that I attend church with. She and I have gone out on friendly dates, but that hasn't been what's defined our friendship as in other situations I've seen or been in. What I mean by having your friendship defined by a date is if we're not going out on a date, then there's no interaction whatsoever. That's not much of a friendship at all. And yes, I do know that everyone is not going to be the best of friends or friends at all. I'm speaking from a perspective here where I've seen discrepancies. Not only has this particular lady and I gone out on dates, but we've talked on the phone. We've gone bike riding together. We've shot the basketball around in my driveway or church parking lot where I endured through her talking an enormous amount of trash to me (in regards to basketball). And by the way, she still does. Or, we'd just sit in my driveway and chat for a bit. In all of that, we came to have a great friendship which I appreciated a great deal. I'm not saying that every woman had to strap on a pair of sneakers and develop a patented Jordan-like turn-around fade away jumper. She did that because that's who she is. What I want you to get out of this is that there are more ways for men and women to interact with one another in order to have a very dynamic friendship.

Going out on dates amongst Christians and the safety of the environment that it provides is not an obligation; it's a blessing that we've been afforded in Jesus Christ. Simply put, having the friendship is what's most important and going out on friendly dates is merely one way to facilitate that.

Having cross gender friendships are extremely important. It helps us learn how to interact with members of the opposite sex and treat each other with dignity and respect. Although we're all human beings, there can still be this awkwardness for some being around members of the opposite sex. I think one thing that contributes to this is that we are so different and there's this kind of fear of the unknown. I remember a time when this was the norm. Growing up, you'd hear a variety of stories about the opposite sex before you really got a chance to hang around them. Those stories, whether true or false, influenced your thinking and when you began to hang around with members of the opposite sex, you kind of didn't know what to do because you was slightly confused. This is only one idea. And as I mentioned, this may not be the norm nowadays as this is a bit outdated and I may be showing my age here. This is more from my days of growing up and I'm long past those years. But some may still find themselves in this category at some point in their lives. Nowadays, the culture norm has swung to the other side of the pendulum and it's a more serious problem than when I was growing up. In this younger generation, things like sexting, sharing obscenities on social sites like Facebook and Twitter has become the norm.

And it goes both ways – boys and girls alike. I was reading an article on the NBC News website recently that talked about this from the perspective of how this is damaging to boys because we mostly hear about how it negatively affects the girls. It described one particular situation where a teen boy likes a girl sitting on the other side of his class. So, he texts her to find out if she's good at hooking up. She responds that she doesn't know because she hasn't given it a thought. He, then responds that he wants his genitalia (I chose to use a more appropriate word than he did) in her mouth and asks if she will at least be his girlfriend. Wow! That's a big switch from leaving a note in her desk saying, "I like you. Do you like me? Check yes or no" like when I was in school. And the big shocker is that those boys claim that their intent is not to be demeaning or hostile. They are only goofing around or joking. Boy, I'd hate to see when they're trying to be demeaning and hostile. To make matters worse, some of those girls don't even know if it's appropriate or feel empowered to tell those boys how those demeaning remarks made them feel. If this isn't a sign that the sexes need to learn how to relate to one another, I don't know what is.

What You Talkin' Bout Singleness Is A Blessing?

Adam and Eve were single before they were united in holy

matrimony. Did you ever wonder what it was like to literally be married by God Himself? Marrieds sometime look at singles as though we're diseased, pitiful, always scheming to run off with somebody, or just a millisecond away from stumbling into immorality. They seem to think that all of us are so hopeless and that we long to be where they are. I must admit though some singles do live like that. And, it has given the singles ministry a bad rap. To varying degrees of difficulty, whether it's a brief moment from time to time of desiring companionship or you're about ready to walk the plank, we all have our bouts with it. But I'm here to tell you something very different. You can accept it or continue to marinate in the hardness of your heart because you're still not married yet.

Singleness is not a weakness, but a sign of strength. Singleness is not less than marriage in any way, but on an equal playing field. Don't agree! Then, try convincing the apostle Paul of your point of view and we'll see how well that goes over. And more importantly, do you not realize that our Lord Jesus was a single too? God created them both, each with specific purposes in mind. Singleness is not a punishment, but a gift. Singleness is not a mistake, but full of intent and purposes. Singleness is not evil, but a tool for righteousness. Singleness is not something to be abhorred, but cherished. Singleness is not a disease, but a cure – and rest assured, that's true even in the mind of some marrieds whose marriage resembles a barren, dry, parched land. Singleness is not a stage of life to be passed through quickly on your way to marriage but embraced passionately. Singleness doesn't mean that something is wrong with you, but God has you right where He desires. He's walking with you, embracing you, and guiding you every step of the way without the distractions of marriage. Don't miss out on that!

  Singleness is a blessing. I'm happy with my singleness and I don't have the gift. You may be thinking how can I speak such blasphemy and are ready to stone me right on the spot. Don't get me wrong, I'm not expressing hatred towards marriage by any stretch of the imagination. To set the record straight, at the time of this writing, I do desire to be married again, but I'm not going to drive myself crazy about it. I'm enjoying my singleness. Has the Lord not made singleness as well as marriage? And, doesn't every good thing come from heaven above? Well, I understand that this may not be enough to convince you because if it were, you wouldn't be feeling this way to begin with. Here are a couple of biblical principles that may spur you on in appreciating your singleness more.

  One of the blessings of being single I think James makes very clear as he wrote to his audience in regards to how they should view life's trials and challenges.

> ²Consider it pure joy, my brothers, whenever you face trials of many kinds, ³because you know that the testing of your faith develops perseverance. ⁴Perseverance must finish its work so that you may be mature and complete, not lacking anything.
>
> (James 1:2-4)

As you endure through life's challenges as a single, you have no one to shield you from them; they hit you first and you have to deal with them as they come. Most youngsters have had the luxury of parents as a shield. Especially if you've been spoiled by them, they've done pretty much everything for you. Many parents don't realize the crippling damage they do when they spoil their children. Living life as a single for a while, you'll build and strengthen your character becoming a lot wiser and mature. It will help you develop perseverance and resiliency. If you have some life experiences under your belt as a single, it will help you be a better companion for your future spouse as you face life together. On the flip side, after living as a single, you'll appreciate more the benefits of having a spouse to go through life with as you'll have someone to reap the benefits of your labor as well as have a safe place to fall when things are down (Ecclesiastes 4:9-10).

Another blessing of being single is being free from concerns. First Corinthians 7:32 clearly states, "I would like you to be free from concern. An unmarried man is concerned about the Lord's affairs – how he can please the Lord." Paul reiterates the same truth for women. Being single, you don't have to worry about things that married people have to worry about. In other words, to be married adds excess burdens to your life.

The concern that Paul was specifically referring to when he wrote this letter to the Corinthians was persecution. During that time, the Christians were under heavy persecution. The opposition tried to force believers to denounce their Christianity. As punishment for noncompliance, they killed the family members of those they persecuted while they looked on. Can you imagine watching your spouse and or children being put to death? Now, you understand why Paul would write such a thing to Christians. Staying single under the circumstances was far better.

Depending on where we live, in today's times, most of us don't typically have those types of threats lingering over our heads, but there are concerns that are ever-present as a married. Quite naturally, you have to be concerned about your spouse and how a decision or something you do might impact your spouse. As a matter of fact, for that very reason, it is appropriate to consult with your spouse regarding major decisions. Typically, if you're married, you may have children, which adds another dimension to the mix. Being single, you don't have all of that on your plate. Especially when difficulty arises, it's just you. It makes life much easier to navigate through difficult times.

During the years of 2010 and 2011, I was in and out of jobs and there was a little uncertainty during those years that I hadn't experienced in a long time. God definitely took care of me during those years and made it very obvious that He was behind the scenes. My singleness afforded me the opportunity to consider some viable options that I would have avoided if I had not been single. Even though having a spouse, depending on his or her character, can and should help when navigating through difficult times, it still adds another dimension to the mix of things for you to consider and deal with.

Less concern means more freedom. It's a time to exercise your freedom, experience life, and do things you probably couldn't do if you had a spouse or family. As an example, I love to travel. More specifically, I love to take long road trips and will leave at the drop of a hat. The biggest trip that I've taken that some of my closest friends still tease me about to this day is a month-long road trip I took back in 2007. On this trip, I drove up to Niagara Falls and ended up in Fort Lauderdale, Florida about a week or so later after getting a small taste of New York, New York and Philadelphia, Pennsylvania. From there, I hit Orlando, Florida; Atlanta, Georgia; and Houston, Texas. About three and a half weeks later, I arrived back home in

Kansas City, Missouri. In each of the cities, I sampled a little of what the city had to offer. Believe me, I thoroughly enjoyed myself. So, what is it that you enjoy doing? Find yourself, enjoy thoroughly, and give glory to God. Besides, this will give you something to share over those initial years with your future spouse until the two of you make some memories of your own.

Next is a big misconception that must be addressed. Some singles think that marriage is going to solve all of their problems. If you think like this, then I've got a big surprise for you.

> [28]But if you do marry, you have not sinned; and if a virgin marries, she has not sinned. *But those who marry will face many troubles in this life*, and I want to spare you this [emphasis added].
>
> (I Corinthians 7:28)

This is not to give marriage a bad rap. Marriage is wonderful! However, this is the word of God; it's simply stating what's true. Marriage is not the answer to your problems. As a matter of fact, marriage is going to magnify and increase them. Guaranteed! Just as there's good individual qualities that a couple brings to a marriage to benefit the union; there's also sins, weaknesses, and the 'what in the world were you thinking when you did that' type of things colliding together to create a colossal disaster of epic proportions. You may have thought that your little tree was full of the fruit of the Spirit when you were single, but you'll soon come to realize that your tree was bare compared to what you'll need in marriage.

As a single, your life was primarily impacted by your sins only and that's all you had to deal with. Sure, people who cross your path during the daily course of life, your friends, relatives, and strangers, sin against you, but they don't have the same traumatic impact on your life as dealing with the sins of your spouse. You have united with them as you did your spouse; they are now yours to deal with as if they are your very own. Another thing to realize too is that as a single, some of your very own sin remains hidden or discreet due to the fact that we don't totally see ourselves. They are simply neglected or it's not really a problem since you're single. But as soon as you are married, those things that once were discreet will now be all up in your face as your partner will be pointing them out to you. Think that won't cause problems? Well, think again! All of a sudden, you now are being called to the plate with a character issue you either didn't see or merely wasn't a problem because you were single. Well, all I have to say is, "There goes the neighborhood!"

As I mentioned earlier, Adam and Eve wasn't always the hottest couple on the block; they were single for a brief moment. So, the natural thing to wonder is what can we learn from Adam and Eve during their singleness? God does give us a brief glimpse into their life back when they were a pair of swinging singles. And, as always, there's something we can learn from it.

> ¹⁵The LORD God took the man and put him in the Garden of Eden to work it and take care of it. ¹⁶And the LORD God commanded the man, "You are free to eat from any tree in the garden; ¹⁷but you must not eat from the tree of the knowledge of good and evil, for when you eat of it you will surely die." ¹⁸The LORD God said, "It is not good for the man to be alone. I will make a helper suitable for him." ¹⁹Now the LORD God had formed out of the ground all the beasts of the field and all the birds of the air. He brought them to the man to see what he would name them; and whatever the man called each living creature, that was its name. ²⁰So the man gave names to all the livestock, the birds of the air and all the beasts of the field. But for Adam no suitable helper was found. ²¹So the LORD God caused the man to fall into a deep sleep; and while he was sleeping, he took one of the man's ribs and closed up the place with flesh. ²²Then the LORD God made a woman from the rib he had taken out of the man, and he brought her to the man.
> (Genesis 2:15-22)

What can we learn from this snapshot of Adam and Eve's days as a single. Here are some thoughts I accumulated as I read through and pondered the given activity.

Once, I heard a man say that he couldn't really know who he was until he knew who his father was. If this is true, then how much more does this apply regarding man and God? In his singleness, Adam walked closely with God. This is the primary advantage of singleness – being able to walk closely with God. You may rationalize that Adam was in the pre-Fall state, so we can't have the type of relationship he had with God. Well, this is possible even after the Fall. Although we don't possess Adam's innocence in and of ourselves, it is through the Savior that we have been absolved of all guilt and can approach God with confidence as the Hebrews writer informs us. Man's greatest pursuit or life's accomplishment is to know his Creator (John 17:3).

As Adam interacted with and grew in his knowledge of God, there are a few critical attributes that Adam picked up along the way. These are qualities that would be vital in fulfilling his role in life. First, we see that Adam was led by the LORD, given tasks by the Lord, and given freedoms, restrictions, and their consequences – actually one restriction – that he had to adhere to (v15-17). In this sequence, Adam learned who had the real authority; he knew who was the boss and he submitted to his authority, otherwise there would be consequences to suffer.

Secondly, we see that Adam was given the specific task of working and taking care of the garden (v15). Here, Adam was learning about responsibility and providing. God provided for Adam. Consequently, he learned that God cared for him and would meet all of his needs. In working the garden, he learned how to appropriately manage God's abundant blessings and provisions.

Lastly, as they are brought to him by the LORD, we see Adam naming all of the creatures God created (v19). Here, he was learning about his God-given authority. He was learning to exert it under the close supervision of the One who gave it to him.

In all of this, I believe that God was preparing Adam for Eve's arrival. He was equipping him for their life together and his role as the man. He taught Adam how to be the authority figure, the provider, and how to lead Eve and the family they would bare together. Adam knew how to fulfill this role properly because he knew the One from which it came, and he saw the example as it was done to him. You see, it's really simple. A man can't properly fulfill the role of a man unless he is walking closely with the One from which it comes.

Although there is nothing specifically written regarding Eve and her time with God during her singleness, we can look to what God said about her in His reason for creating her and know for certain that he fulfilled His purpose in doing so. In Genesis 2:18, the Lord God said, "It is not good for man to be alone. I will make *a helper suitable* for him [emphasis added]." Considering that God made Eve as Adam's suitable helper, I have no doubt in my mind that He fashioned her specifically for him. He fashioned her to be his perfect complement, which is why I believe when He created her, He extracted her directly from Adam. He fashioned her so that she could be in tune with him, support him, be his ideal partner in subduing the Earth, to love and respect him, to encourage and make him feel like he can conquer the world even when he didn't feel much like a conqueror. Eve's singleness was her time with God to learn how to be the woman that Adam needed. She was designed by God to live with Adam in harmony and to bring him peace – and not the drama queen that some women excel in being – through complementing him, assisting him with God's intended purposes for mankind (Genesis 1:28, 2:8), submitting to his God-given authority, and being his most intimate companion in every sense of the word – spiritually, mentally, emotionally, and physically. Only after this divine fashioning was she ready and brought to Adam.

Who You Really in Love With?

There's a culprit out there that we must be aware of whilst in our dating relationships. I know many have fallen prey to its deceitful illusion of love. I'd be willing to bet that it played a major role in the marriage of couples who, now divorced, say that they got married too young or just really didn't know each other when they decided to tie the knot. The culprit I'm referring to is called infatuation. It masquerades itself to those under its influence as being "in love", but you couldn't be farther from the truth. With infatuation, the object of your desire is typically oneself – how your partner makes you feel or you're head over heels in love with the idea of being in love. This is what makes me pose the question, "Who are you really in love with?" Really, think about it and answer this question for yourself. Infatuation is strictly an emotional response, superficial, and temporary. It most likely stems from nothing more than a physical or sexual attraction, which is more appropriately described as lust than it is love. Its definition further reveals the true story behind its deceitful imagery. Infatuation means to inspire or possess with a foolish or unreasoning passion, as of love; to affect with folly; unreal or illusory. This is not the foundation you want to base decisions on. It doesn't mean that it can't lead to the real thing in due time, but infatuation alone is not real. You absolutely can't fall in love with something you don't know. I suspect that many of you will disagree, but that's probably just your emotions talking or your human reasoning kicking in. Let's take it to the word of God.

> [9]And this is my prayer: that your love may abound more and more in knowledge and depth of insight, [10]so that you may be able to discern what is best and may be pure and blameless until the day of Christ, [11]filled with the fruit of righteousness that comes through Jesus Christ – to the glory and praise of God.
> (Philippians 1:9-11)

In this passage, Paul is praying for the growth of the Philippians' love. He is praying specifically that their love increases from a deeply rooted knowledge and understanding of its object, which is Christ. Knowledge comes from the

Hebrew word yadà which is the verb 'to know'. It means to know by experience, to recognize, acknowledge, or become acquainted with. Thus, knowledge is the process of knowing through experience, which involves the physical; perception, which involves the mind; and the senses, which involves the emotions. Once again, we have genuine love expressed only through the knowledge of its object. This was especially important information to have because it has an effect on how one lived their life. Spiritually speaking, the more we come to know Christ, the more our love is expressed through obedience (John 14:15). So, what's the practical application for us? How does this translate to our relationships with our significant other? As you begin to know someone more and more, being enlightened of his or her strengths, weaknesses, and sins, you grow more in love with that person. How does that love manifest itself? Hopefully, you will turn that knowledge into wisdom by utilizing that knowledge to care for and meet the needs of your partner. It impacts your life because you know how to love them; you know how to meet his or her need. You don't take that information and use it to intentionally hurt or anger them (now that you know it) because you wouldn't be acting out of love. It is a show of respect, an act of obedience to his or her boundaries. It's like the concern Paul told the Roman church to have for one another (Romans 14:15).

From Singleness & Dating

Love is not a whimsical feeling or sentiment. Love is the process of growing and becoming more mature through the ever-increasing knowledge of its subject. The more you know; the more you can love. This is far from the superficial knowledge presented by infatuation. It means having a more well-rounded view of your potential partner. This means not only knowing the positive attributes of your partner's character, which is what we tend to emphasize while dating, but the negative attributes as well – those things that get on your nerves. You will have to deal with those things when you get married and love this person even through those times when they are not so lovable. It's funny, first, how we know nobody's perfect, but neglect to take notice of negative characteristics while dating in order to better know the person we're dating. With the things we do see, we don't take them seriously or even laugh them off as though they're cute, but once you're married, those are the very things you seem to complain and argue about the most. The intent is to know your partner and love them, appreciate them which mirrors God's love for us. He knows us through and through, every detail of our wretchedness, yet He chooses to love us anyway. His love wasn't left as just a thought or a feeling, but He showed His love by meeting our most dire need (Romans 5:8).

Here is what can happen when infatuation is the sole basis of your relationship. You'll find it's just the opposite of what I've been describing in regards to love having the foundation of knowledge and understanding of its object. Observing the life of Samson, it becomes extremely obvious that he had a weakness, and infatuation, a consuming lust for beautiful women unlike any man I've personally known. The extent of his weakness was evident in decisions like the following:

> ¹Samson went down to Timnah and saw there a young Philistine woman. ²When he returned, he said to his father and mother, "I have seen a Philistine woman in Timnah; now get her for me as my wife."
> (Judges 14:1-2)

Samson eventually married the unnamed woman later on in verse 8. Not only did he marry a woman outside his covenant people, but he also slept with prostitutes (Judges 16:1). Back to Samson's marriage in chapter 14, you'll find that later on in the chapter the woman betrays Samson. Unbeknownst to us how many times he repeated this type of behavior; it's quite obvious this is a pattern for Samson's life and eventually leads to his ruin. The most famous of Samson's women, Delilah, betrays him as well and is the one who ultimately brings him to utter ruin. In what had to have been very obvious to Samson, she coerced him to reveal the secret of his strength and told the Philistine rulers so that they may subdue and torture him. Although it doesn't specifically say, based on his track record, his desire for

Delilah was probably due solely to her intoxicating beauty.

Samson's primary reason for his marriage and relationship with Delilah was because they were very beautiful. That's a very superficial reason to have as the foundation of a relationship. Seemingly, there wasn't any attempt at pursuing a deeper relationship, therefore the relationship remained shallow. Both women easily betrayed him later with Delilah's betrayal starting pretty much at the onset. The take away is that when your relationship is based on superficiality, it's much easier for discord to occur in the relationship. It's easy to betray or be betrayed. It's easy to cheat or be cheated on. It's easy to leave or be left by your partner. The reason is that there's absolutely no mutual connection whatsoever. There's no mutual investment of oneself into the other. The relationship is devoid of true, genuine love. When there's no investment, there's nothing to lose.

Dr. James Dobson, Ph.D., founder and host of Focus on the Family from 1977 to 2003, captures this concept as he describes his love for his wife in a short article, *Love at First Sight*, which addresses the same issue. He said, "Genuine love, by contrast, is an expression of the deepest appreciation for another human being. It is an intense awareness of his or her needs and strengths and character. It shares the longings, hopes, and dreams of that other person. It is unselfish, giving, and caring. And believe me, these are not attitudes one 'falls into' at first sight, as though one were tumbling into a ditch. I have developed that kind of lifelong love for my wife, but it was not something I fell into. I grew into it and that process took time. I had to know her before I could appreciate the depth and stability of her character – to become acquainted with the nuances of her personality, which I now cherish. The familiarity from which love has blossomed simply could not be generated on 'some enchanted evening across a crowded room.' One cannot love an unknown object, regardless of how attractive or sexy or nubile it is!"

In order to help foster this knowledge seeking experience about your partner while you're dating and to just not accept the angel-like façade that we all tend to put up, I have four questions you can consider about your partner's character. They are: 1) what characteristics do you like about this person, 2) what characteristics do you not like about this person, 3) in what ways do his or her sins manifest themselves, and 4) in what areas do you think you can help this person grow closer to God? Hopefully, these questions will be a good starting point to help you assess your dating partner and your compatibility. When you answer these questions, write them down along with your answers. Doing so will cause you to take the time to really think and search your heart. Also, do this periodically over the course of your relationship. Do it once at the very beginning and yes it will be pretty shallow, but you will still have answers because it's obvious something attracted you to this person that made you want to date them. Then, continue to do it every three months or so, it's up to you. As you do it, you should see your answers expand, change, and become more profound as you get to know your boyfriend or girlfriend better. This should help you make an effective decision. As you consider these questions and others that may be important to you, you can even ask yourself why you like or feel a certain way about some of your partner's characteristics. This will give you some insight into yourself and may give you an idea of how you'll react to these traits over the long haul.

Now, I don't have the gift of prophecy, but I know you have a question formulating in your mind. Do you want to know how you can tell if you're in love or infatuation? Was I right? Whether I was or not, you're going to get the answer anyway! A good friend of mine forwarded a message he heard on the topic by Living on the Edge host Chip Ingram. The message was accompanied by a test that has criteria spanning across twelve different categories pertinent to distinguishing between a relationship based on love or infatuation. The twelve categories are as follows: Time, Knowledge, Focus, Singularity, Security, Work, Problem Solving, Distance, Physical Attraction & Involvement, Affection, Stability, and Delayed

Gratification. (Ingram) If you happen to take the test or any like it, be honest with yourself. We have a tendency when emotions are stirring to not want to hear anything that contradicts what we feel. But it may save you from making a grave mistake down the road. Here's a summary of what each of the topics are referring to.

- Time – refers to the fact that love grows over time whereas infatuation more than likely comes in an instant.

- Knowledge – pertains to the fact that love grows out of an appreciation of the multitude of characteristics of the other person, good and bad included. Infatuation sprouts out of a minimal amount of character traits that are most likely superficial in nature.

- Focus – refers to the fact that love is outward-focused (other person is the object) whereas infatuation is inward-focused (self is the object).

- Singularity – refers to the fact that love is focused on one person; infatuation may have many people as objects of desire at the same time.

- Security – refers to a person who is in love tends to be secure and have feelings of trust after consideration of his or her relationship with the other whereas an infatuated person has more of a false sense of security based upon what they wish his or her relationship to be with the other person, which may be expressed as jealousy.

- Work – refers to the fact that a person in love works primarily for the benefit of the other person or the benefit of them both. An infatuated person may lose his ambition or interest for daily affairs. He or she may daydream often and sometimes give themselves over to the dream rather than reality.

- Problem Solving – involves a couple in love faces problems head on and tries to resolve them in an intelligent manner. Infatuated

- Distance – pertains to the fact that love remains constant no matter the distance between the two; and infatuation is likely to vary in accordance with the distance between the two.

- Physical Attraction & Involvement – refers to the fact that for couples in love, physical attraction is a smaller part of the entire relationship. They are more focused on other aspects of the relationship that provide meaning. Any physical contact is a reflection of that meaning. For infatuated couples, physical attraction is the relationship or one of the greater parts of it.

- Affection – talks about couples in love usually have expressions of that love being delayed to later in the relationship whereas couples in infatuation, the expression of love comes much sooner or the relationship is rooted out of that expression.

- Stability – is simply that love endures and infatuation is subject to change at a moment's notice.

- Delayed Gratification – refers to a couple in love is not opposed to delaying the nuptials if it's wiser to do so. Infatuated couples see this as a deprivation and are in a hurry to do so.

Remember the woman I met at the church conference. After listening to the accompanying message, she and I took the test together discussing the particulars of our relationship. As most may perceive, things did happen quick for us, which nothing is wrong with that in and of itself. People do connect with some people quicker than they do others. Considering the context, I definitely do think you should take age and maturity level into consideration. I wouldn't recommend a young couple, in their teens or twenties, moving this quickly as there is a lack of maturity and probably a lot of raging hormones in the driver's seat. Although you can't put the same stipulations on a more mature couple as you would a young couple, even mature couples should be aware as they're not exempt from exhibiting qualities of infatuation. They could be heading into one of those situations where the relationship is intense in the beginning, and then fizzles out soon after and you realize there was really nothing there solid to begin with. When it comes to determining if a couple is moving too quickly, it's a little more to take into consideration. In all truth, it's best to take your time and move slowly anyway. No one is exempt from making mistakes, misreading situations, or glossing over things as I have learned. What I'm about to describe here is how we started off before taking a turn for the worse. During the first two months after the conference, we talked frequently on the phone. Although, we literally worked at getting to know each other; it seemed to come easy for us in some aspects. We were very vulnerable and very open with our lives. We seemed to bond and connect naturally. At the end of the two months, we found ourselves in a conversation expressing feelings for one another. What was of essence though is that we were not going to rush through anything. We were going to take our time getting to know one another more to see how it played out. As the weeks progressed, our mutual attraction only grew stronger, but we still had apprehensions as we wondered if we were really in love or just infatuation. And, how were we going to distinguish where we were between the two? My friend sending me this test was a Godsend! It had been sitting in my inbox for a few days or so as I hadn't gotten around to taking a look at it. Once I looked and figured out what it was, we decided to take the assessment. We found that we considered two or three categories as infatuation. For example, we deemed the Time category as infatuation being that it occurred in a short amount of time. On the other hand, we considered the category of Knowledge as love because we did have an extensive amount of information about each other than most would in that amount of time. This for us offset the infatuation we gave to the Time category. Our overall conclusion was that what we had was love. The test was informational, fun, and provided a means for a great discussion and insight into what the other person was thinking. I must admit though…at the very beginning of the test, I did have a fleeting thought of what if we are just totally infatuated with each other. As I said, it passed quickly. Basically, the test provided an answer to our question and in addition gave us a snapshot of where we were in relation to each individual category.

Who Do I Marry?

Has all of this gotten to be a bit more intense than you expected? Are you wondering who in the world do you marry? Well, that's not for me or anyone else to make that decision for you. People want you to hook up with someone because they think you two "look" good together. What is that about? It's all about your heart. No one else knows your heart but you and that's only a decision for you, your potential partner, and, of course, God to work out. Unless God has directly told you someone specific to marry in order to fulfill a specific purpose, which He has only done a couple of times or so, marry anyone you choose to keeping in mind that they must be willing to marry you as well. God intervened like that because He had a specific purpose in mind as He was writing out history. For instance, when He told Hosea to go back to his adulterous wife Gomer, He did that to illustrate to the adulterous nation of Israel how faithful He is to them despite their unfaithfulness to Him. Outside of these times, the only other instruction regarding who to marry comes from the first letter to the Corinthians. It reads, "A woman is bound to her husband as long as he lives. But if her husband dies, she is free to marry anyone she wishes, but he must belong to the Lord" (I Corinthians 7:39). As a Christian, a person is free to marry anyone he or she wishes with the only stipulation being that he or she must belong to the Lord. So, as I was saying, marry anyone you want, but use His principles as the standard for your relationship in getting along with each other, solving problems, communicating, satisfying the desires and needs of one another, and the like which glorifies Him and things will go well with you (Deuteronomy 6:1-3). I do think there are some things for you to take into consideration that will assist you when looking for your life partner.

Before I delve into providing some thoughts on what to look for, here are some very popular sayings to be aware of. Don't get sucked into believing myths such as "it was love at first sight," "we are soul mates," "there's one person out there for me," or "I'm waiting for the right person." These may be seemingly nice or intelligible things to say, but they are a bunch of fluff and have no substance or truth behind them at all. It's a trap and they condition and put you in the wrong mindset with the wrong expectations about marriage. I've bought into these ideas once upon a time, but over the years my perspective has changed.

You'll find that there are a lot of people that think there's one person out there for them. And, you'll find that they're sincerely waiting for them too. At this point, two questions come to mind. How do you really know if a particular person is **the one** for you, especially without checking everybody else on the planet first? Also, what exactly are you looking for? Many will answer with the 'I'll just know' response. But, what on Earth does that really mean? You'll just know – you'll just know what? With that response, you've told me absolutely nothing. Do you detect that something's wrong? Many have said this very thing, yet we have an excess of forty-seven percent divorce rate in this country. Check in with them about a year after the marriage and they'd swear up and down they've made a grave mistake. They have no idea who this person is they've married. Now, they're ready to sprint to the divorce court at world record speed that would make Usain Bolt extremely jealous. So, what happened? Let me shed some much needed light on the situation. The fact of the matter is that there isn't one person out there that's made specifically for you. Here is some insight as to who we were made for. In Genesis 1:17, it says, "So God created man in his own image, in the image of God he created him; male and female he created them." Being made in or modeled after God's image implicitly implies that we are unique to God than any of His other creations. This means that we are to bring Him glory unlike any of the other things He created. So, what exactly does this glorify Him mean? Men and women, as woman was created from man, is made in the likeness of God. Each reflect some attributes of God's character. Together, in marriage, they should reflect the total image of

God that is in mankind. It's not that we ever become His equals, but we reflect His likeness that's in us, which we don't do naturally in and of ourselves because of our sinfulness. It's just like children reflect some of the likeness of their parents. You can tell just by the way they look and act who their parents are. The same for us. We were made for Him. Let's solidify this point of being made for Him a little more with "…whatever you do, do it all for the glory of God (I Corinthians 10:31)." Thus, we were made to glorify Him, not each other. There is no one or any number of persons out there that was made just for you. So, stop looking for that! The Bible makes it clear that everything in heaven and on Earth was made for God. Proverbs 16:4 says, "The LORD works out everything for his own ends – even the wicked for a day of disaster." Everything was made for His glory. In one way or another, everything will give Him glory even if it is to receive His wrath. The reason we get along so bad is that we don't seek to glorify God; we seek glory for ourselves, which we don't deserve. Yes, there are some people we each get along with better than others. And, some we don't. There's just a wide assortment of personalities out there. That's just the way it is. But, that still doesn't mean that one more than another was made just for you. In fact, I think God's glory is displayed even more when two very different people come together in harmony by working out their differences.

You want to challenge this thought? Then, think about God and mankind. Then, remember how much we are not like Him and the relationship man is able to have forged through the blood Jesus shed on the cross. Now, tell me that doesn't glorify God. It's all Him, and He didn't have to do it. Or, what about the Scripture that speaks about the bond of peace that united the Jews and Gentiles into one being (Ephesians 2:14-17).

So, why do people look for a right person? What is the implication? That mentality is reflective of our prideful and selfish nature. We have this superficial list of attributes that we think we need or want in a mate which are typically self-centered. We feel that we deserve to have someone meet all of our expectations – to worship us sort to speak. We all have this expectation that there's someone who's magically going to meet all of your needs and every little desire you have. That's why some people – namely men, but women aren't exempt – hesitate to tie the knot because they feel they may be missing out on something 'better'. That's not true at all. You'll only be missing out on a different combination of attributes – no one has everything. That kind of thinking is detrimental to any relationship. As long as a person is thinking like that, he or she will never give his or her all toward the relationship because he or she will be too preoccupied wondering what else is out there instead of being grateful for what he or she has. It prevents you from committing your heart to what you have and your relationship won't ever be what you want it to be because you're not really invested in it. And just like the stock market, if you don't invest, you'll get no return.

This type of mentality poses a major threat. Take into consideration the fact that at some point in time your spouse is going to let you down. If you're the type of person who has the mentality that your spouse must meet your every need for you to be happy, then how do you think this is going to play out over the long haul when the inevitable happens? In my opinion, it's not going to play out very well. I foresee a snowball effect occurring in a myriad of arguments and a wealth of unhappiness in a relationship consisting of a partner with this mindset. Every time the partner either fails to meet a need, can't, or a perceived need is neglected is a wedge that will potentially push them apart. In a lot of marriages, the expectation is that we want our spouse to fill us up, but in reality, they can't. We're supposed to be filled up by God. Therefore, the obvious solution is to strive in getting your joy and satisfaction from God and using that to love your spouse unconditionally instead of trying to get your joy and satisfaction from your spouse and loving them according to how much joy and satisfaction he or she has brought you. When you figure that out and put it into action, things will go a lot smoothly for you. Edward T. Welsh lays this concept out in detail in his book, *When*

People Are Big and God Is Small. I think this book is a must read for the entire planet!

Obviously, we've established that looking for the 'right' person is not the appropriate perspective to have if you happen to be spouse hunting. Instead, why don't you try being the right person? Be the type of person that you want to attract. With the right perspective, God will work out bringing compatible prospects your direction. Remember in the days of the Old Testament, marriages were arranged at a very young age without any regards or foreknowledge by the involved parties as to whether even their personalities matched much less the superficial things we look for. And, guess what? The marriages worked! They simply honored God by being committed to each other and fulfilling their God-given roles in marriage. This should tell you something about the effectiveness of our methods today.

Another phrase that people seem to believe in is soul mates. In and of itself, I don't think that the term is wrong. It's just that if you're looking for a soul mate; don't bother because a soul mate is not something you find. It's something you become. People refer to themselves as soul mates only after, let's say for good measure, two years of dating. That's only a fraction of a relationship. Have you really bonded that much? What have you really gone through in life together in that short amount of time? That's unbelievable that we would even think such a thing after a short amount of time. This sounds more like another emotional response to me. Granted, it may be one of those 'nice things' to say about someone you're dating and getting along so well with. But, in reality, there are probably things about this person you have no clue about. And, there are more than likely situations that you haven't experienced in life with this person enough to know how he or she is going to respond.

I believe you become soul mates in marriage as your lives are progressively fused and intertwined together to become one. This is achieved through the long and on-going process of growing together, changing together, working together, and learning about and helping each other as you endure through the various stages and myriad of trials in life. This process develops character and maturity in them not only as a couple, but individuals as well. The couple becomes more connected and in tune with one another or more unified. Without this process, what do you really have to base it on? And, how can you become soul mates? You become soul mates over the long haul of marriage. You'll know you have reached that point, for example, when your spouse is away for an extended period of time and you just can't function without him or her. Your life is literally in shambles; you feel like you can't function because a part of you is missing.

It's not that you're incompetent, but you have a system now that includes your spouse. When your spouse is missing your system is disrupted; your team is temporarily handicapped. Now, you have to get acclimated to doing things your spouse did; things he or she probably did better than you, which is why your spouse did them to begin with. Then, you reminisce back many years ago to your life as a single and wonder how you ever managed to survive. Your life has now become so much more refined and enriched by what your spouse has brought to the table. You literally can't live without him or her. This is what Simon Green, Ashton Kutcher's character in *Guess Who*, was getting at when he told Bernie Mac in the tango scene, "You know the thing about meeting your other half is you're walking around, you think you're happy, you think you're whole, then you realize you ain't (expletive deleted) without her. Then, you can't go back to just being a half cause you know what it's like to be whole." My friend, when you get to this point in your marriage is when you know you have become soul mates. Now, it's mandatory that I clarify what I mean by the term whole as it may not be so easily inferred from the context. I'm not sure exactly what Simon Green meant when he said it, but I'm quite sure it's not the same as what I mean although the point is still relevant. Just so you know, there's not another person in the entire world that can actually complete you or anyone else or make anyone whole. Once again, that's something "nice" to say about your significant other. Jesus Christ is the only one who can make anyone whole, complete, or filled up (Colossians 2:9-10, I Peter 2:24). In Christ, is where a person can have all of his or her sins canceled and in return have the righteousness of Christ imputed to him or her. Our personal sin is what makes us broken and in dire need of healing. This healing, being made righteous before God, is only found in Jesus Christ. In order to find out what "whole" means in the context of a marital relationship, let's revisit a familiar Scripture and see what God said in His original design of marriage. In Genesis 2:24, He said, "For this reason a man will leave his father and mother and be united to his wife, and they will become one flesh." The key phrases you need to pay attention to in this verse are "be united to" and "will become one". In the Hebrew text, the word for "be united to" transliterates to *dabaq* pronounced daw-baq. It means to cling or adhere to. This easily gives the impression of glue – two separate items glued together that's supposed to stay together. The second phrase solidifies and adds to the meaning of the first. The Hebrew text for "will become one" transliterates to *'echad* pronounced ekh-awd. It simply means united or as one. Essentially, what I mean by whole is that oneness of marriage, the unity that married couples are called to have.

Do you know what you're looking for in a spouse? Have you even considered it? If not, now would be a good time to do so. I'm not talking about those superficial traits that you fantasize about. We deem that as having the perfect mate and we hold out for nothing less. Let's be sensible here. What I'm talking about is the real attributes of the heart and having the self-awareness to know what areas you are willing to give and take in. For example, being that I'm considerably older now, I really don't desire to marry someone that's much younger than I am. But, depending on where she is maturity wise, I might consider it. It appears that some people get in and out of dating relationships in hopes of something arbitrarily coming together.

We've determined that getting married is your choice; and we've determined that who you marry is your choice as long as he or she is a believer. That is, if you are a believer. So, here's where I think some people get stuck. Some people are waiting on God for a spouse and think He's just going to deliver the right person on their doorstep. Now, waiting on God isn't bad at all; that's excellent. But, who are you waiting for? Do you even know? The problem is that some people believe that when the person comes they'll just magically know. God doesn't work like that. How is He going to bring you someone who's a match for you when you don't even know yourself? You haven't asked for anything specific. You're just waiting and don't know what you're waiting for. That puts you in a passive mindset in your search for a spouse which potentially sets you up for failure. In light of Proverbs 31:10, which says, "A wife of noble character who can find? She is worth far more than rubies," and Proverbs 20:6 which says, "Many a man claims to have unfailing love, but a faithful man who can find," don't you think you should actively look for a spouse? These passages tell me that a spouse is worth far more than riches or material things of value. If this is the case, then you should be actively looking for a spouse because in this mindset you will have focus and will actually have specific things in mind of what you're looking for and what areas you're willing to give and take in. For example, I know when I'm looking for a job, I have focus. I typically have very specific characteristics in mind pertaining to the company, the environment, salary, type of work, and amount of vacation time I can get (anyone who knows me know I love me some vacation time). And, I know the areas where I'm willing to be a little flexible and where I'm not. For something that's of far greater value, shouldn't you have the same mindset instead of waiting for it to drop in your lap? Then, when you go to God and ask Him, it is through your prayers that He'll bring you the person you ask for.

In picking your life long partner, you – as I mentioned earlier – want someone who above everything else fears the Lord God. How can you recognize this quality in a person? They will live a life characterized by obedience to God's Word. In and of ourselves, people think they can treat another person well, but that's just not true without having Christ in your life. We are just so full of sin and conditions. No matter how good of a spouse you are, a relationship with Christ will expose your weaknesses and call you to another level in your relationship. It seems like if a person has God first in his or her life, everything else will fall into place. As Christians, we never become perfect nor do we all of a sudden get in line. Being made perfect, becoming holy is an on-going process. So, in searching for a partner, there's some responsibility on your part. Remember, you are the one who will have to live with this person for the rest of your life, so choose wisely.

Let me share a little from my perspective on what qualities I'm looking for and it may provide some food for thought for you. Here are some things that I consider when looking at a potential spouse in regards to my relationship with God. The essential question to ask yourself that'll pretty much solidify this is, "Am I closer to God with this person than I am as a single person?" If your answer is yes, then it's all good. In trying to answer this question, I consider the things she shares with me from her own personal walk with God. Am I encouraged and inspired by her personal experiences with God? Does her personal walk with God challenge me in areas where I need to grow in my own relationship with Him? Does she remind me of God's immense love for me during the times I feel disconnected from it? Does she help me comprehend or see God from a perspective outside of my own limitations? It's not to say that all of your questions will be hit, but you should see some of these questions being played out depending on your particular needs.

Another thing that's pretty important for me is that she has to be a life learner. Now, you may be saying to yourself, "What on Earth do you mean by that?" The premise for this came from an experience in a past marriage combined with a statement Jesus made to the Twelve. He said, "Truly I tell you, unless you change and become like little children, you will never enter the kingdom of heaven (Matthew 18:3)." I thought about the characteristics of children that fit into the context of the passage. Children are meek, unpretentious, and eager to learn. It's important to me to have someone that's willing to learn and change. I think this is essential in order to be successful. If you're a Christian, you definitely had to learn and change things about yourself to be a part of God's kingdom; otherwise, you weren't getting in no matter what you said. Look at all of the changes you go through in life. For starters, if you want to be married and expect to live together, you have to be willing to change in order to become unified – to achieve the oneness so essential to a successful marriage. There are changes as you navigate through the various stages of life – youth to middle age to old age or no children to having children to empty nesters. There are changes as you endure through the trials of life. And, as we go through the good and bad experiences of life, we naturally change as we are affected by them. You see all of the changes in life that we go through. I feel that it's important to have someone willing to adapt with and help me through all of those changes in life.

Something else that's pretty important for me in a spouse is that she has to be prone to having a calm, sensitive, and mature demeanor during times of conflict. She can't be prone to loud, rude, or disrespectful behavior. I have a tendency sometimes to talk through my emotions when I've been consistently hurt or disrespected in a certain situation. A woman who's prone to loud and rude behavior and can't calmly talk through times of disagreement and conflict will not be a benefit to me. See, I realize that I have a weakness in that area. Although the Lord has brought me a way and I have grown in my anger, I know that having a woman who's stronger than I am in that area and can really talk through disagreements will be an enormous benefit to help me grow even more in that area because I would be able to see it modeled and imitate that godliness in my spouse. That's the essential element of being a disciple – imitating Christ's likeness. This is putting something into practice that I'll touch on a bit here later. That's finding someone that complements you.

One last thing I wanted to share with you from my pool of characteristics I'm looking for is someone who has a sense of responsibility. This partly comes from the woman described in Proverbs 31. That was a woman who rolled up her sleeves and took care of business when she had to. Her husband had not one concern about her once he left the home. Personally, I admire that in a woman and find it very attractive. I want a partner in life that is responsible enough who can handle business; one that you can set and attain goals with. It's extremely rough being in a relationship where you feel like you have to handle everything and can't trust your partner to get the job done. They are careless and don't seem to have a sense of urgency about anything of importance. That can cause a great deal of frustration to be in a situation like that. I've seen it be the brunt of a lot of the arguments in a relationship.

A little something extra specifically for the guys to think about. Does she support and encourage you? Does she see the good in you when you don't see it yourself? Of course, she'll benefit from you doing well. That's a natural part of a marriage. But, that's not why she does it. She seeks to strengthen you because she loves you and wants you to be the best you can be. To me, there's something very uneasy about a woman who belittles her husband and tears him down when he's going through some trials and life has a foot on his throat. I'm sure many people may not feel the same way I do, but I love the Rocky movies. All of them, one through six. Creed too, but it's the next generation and it doesn't fit in with the point I'm about to make here. Every time any of the movies would come on and I knew about it, I was right there watching. A Rocky marathon was even better. Now, that I have all of the movies in my collection, I can watch anytime I want to. First, I love the Rocky movies because it's a great example of an underdog. Someone who definitely wasn't especially gifted by any stretch of the imagination but had a lot of heart and rose above his circumstances. The other reason why I love the Rocky movies is because of Rocky and Adrian's marriage. There wasn't anything exceptional about either one. He wasn't well-educated. She was so shy; she seemed scared of people. Neither was anywhere near glamorous in appearance. Both could have been considered outcasts. But, they came together and was great for each other and great together. In their marriage, they grew as individuals and as a couple over the years. One scene I really liked and is fitting here is from *Rocky III*. Rocky is seriously doubting himself as a boxer and as a man after finding out that Mickey has been protecting him over the course of his career. Running on the beach with Apollo, the doubts are hitting hard and seemingly takes its toll and Rocky finally gives up. Well, Adrian, knowing all along that something's not quite right with her husband, she strolls down to have a chat with him. After gently peeling back the layers, she digs deeper and gets him to reveal that he's scared, gets in his face a bit, and helps him get back on track. She does all of this without so much of a disrespectful or degrading remark. Now, that's what a woman is supposed to do. Because of what she did in that scene, that's one of my favorites in the whole series. There are definitely other things that are important for men and women alike. What is it that's important to you?

In an effort to get more acquainted with the heart and character of the person you are considering marrying, the words of Jesus ring loud and clear when speaking to the Pharisees. He said, "You brood of vipers, how can you who are evil say anything good? For out of the overflow of the heart the mouth speaks. The good man brings good things out of the good stored up in him, and the evil man brings evil things out of the evil stored up in him (Matthew 12:34-35)." Simply put, pay more attention to what the person talks about. It is a sure sign of what's in the individual's heart. Another potential indicator that's not as tried and true as the words coming out of his or her mouth, but to some degree can reveal some information about your potential spouse. "Do not be misled: 'Bad company corrupts good character (I Corinthians 15:33).'" Paul gave a solemn warning to the Christians in Corinth about hanging out with those who were preaching the lie that there wasn't a resurrection of the dead. Sometimes the company we keep are the people that have a great influence on parts of our character. Tell me if this sounds familiar. You have a woman who keeps company with embittered, man-hating women. You best believe that at some point in time, when the two of you have an argument, who do you think she's going to run to for consolation? Then, guess what she may bring home for you to deal with when it's time to reconcile. Boy, I don't envy or want to be you once she hits the front door.

In considering the character of someone you are thinking about marrying, here's something you'll probably want to take notice of. You may be wondering exactly what kind of things I should be looking for. We all do a wide array of things we shouldn't do. How do I go about determining what I really need to be concerned about? And yes, that is a good question. We all mess up in ways that aren't truly a part of our normal character. For instance, a person may not be someone who uses profanity on a regular basis, but on an occasion he or she may slip up and say a curse word. "Whoops, I don't know where that came from." Well, it came from you, but it's not a normal part of his or her character. Or, it just took the right situation to bring it out. It may take another ten years before you hear him or her slip again if ever. What you should be looking for in your potential spouse are patterns of character – positive as well as negative. Those are the things that are a normal part of his or her character. Those are the attributes that will provide the bigger picture of who this person really is. Do you get the gist of what I'm saying? When I warned you earlier to take notice and consider what's going on in your relationship and that I'd give you an idea of what to look for? This is what I was referring to. If you see serious negative patterns of behavior, you should sever the relationship immediately. Now you may be wondering where to look for these patterns. Okay now, you're stretching me a bit as I'm not a psychologist or have any expertise on the subject. But, from my observations and life experiences, I can share this with you. Patterns in people's character can be manifested in different ways. From what I've seen, you can observe patterns in different situations a person may be in, different moods, different people a person may hang around, or a person's everyday behavior. To kind of bring home what I'm talking about, here's an example. In situations where I'm in a strange place and in a crowd of people I don't know, I have a tendency to be on the quiet side and observe, but in a place of familiarity and with people I know, I can clown around, be extremely silly, and unleash that hysterical laugh of mine that has caused others to laugh simply because I was.

Why Do I Get Married?

Why do I get married? Now that's a very good question to ask as opposed to asking, like Tyler Perry's movie, *Why Did I Get Married?* because by then, it's a tad bit too late to analyze your motivation. Why do you want to get married? People decide to get married for a variety of different reasons. Some are good and to be honest with you, a lot of them are not good legitimate reasons to tie the knot. Some people marry for reasons that are centered on money and materialism. Some marry because they're giving into peer pressure, whether it's coming from within or from friends and family. For instance, a woman may be in her late thirties or early forties. She may have been a career-minded woman or may have just been patiently waiting for the right one, which we've already exposed that for what it is. She may be feeling the pressure that time may be passing her by, her biological clock is ticking, and more in a rush to get married. Another woman in the same situation may get married to fit in or feel accepted in society. She wants to avoid those "what's wrong with me" looks or feelings that surface from deep down inside or those 'why haven't you gotten married yet' questions from friends and family. Another woman may be trying to find the love from a husband that she didn't get from her father. We'll see how well that works out. A man seeking validation of his manhood may try to get that from a woman. Just remember, if she validates you that means she'll also be able to invalidate you. Others may marry because they feel that marriage will be the solution to their life's problems such as loneliness and issues with purity. Marriage definitely doesn't solve any of these problems as these are strictly heart issues and need to be dealt with on that level. A person can be married and still deal with issues of loneliness and purity just as much if not more than when they were single. Then, of course, you have the well-known cohabitating couples anthem – we've been together for so long and neither one of us is going anywhere, so we might as well get married. It just seems like the right thing to do. How many people have tied the knot under that pretense?

Understand this. I'm not here to say whether these marriages are going to fail or succeed based on the reasoning. That's not my place to say. No one has the ability or right to determine that. Besides, many marriages have survived more traumatic events than a bad reason for getting hitched.

I've seen it. What I'm trying to facilitate here is getting your expectations on the right track. If you're expecting something that's never going to happen, you're going to get the shock of your life once you start the process and it doesn't meet your expectations. You won't be able to handle it because you were completely caught off guard. You weren't prepared so now you don't know what to do. I believe this plays a role in the demise of a lot of marriages. The couple went in expecting one thing and was blind-sided. That's why I'm disclosing as much as I can from my experiences so that you can put more thought into it and use the word of God to find out what you should really expect. Here are some biblical reasons for getting married.

As mentioned earlier, people marry for many different reasons, but the primary reason of legitimacy for marrying your partner has got to be based on love for that individual. That love for him or her has to endure through the good and bad of it all – the strengths, the weaknesses, and the sins of his or her character. That model has been handed down from the example of God's love for us. We love because he first loved us (I John 4:19). He loved us even knowing how utterly wretched we are. Love is what really gets you through the toughest of times you'll experience between one another (I Peter 4:8).

> ¹If I speak in the tongues of men and of angels, but have not love, I am only a resounding gong or a clanging cymbal. ²If I have the gift of prophecy and can fathom all mysteries and all knowledge, and if I have a faith that can move mountains, but have not love, I am nothing. ³If I give all I possess to the poor and surrender my body to the flames, but have not love, I gain nothing.
>
> (I Corinthians 13:1-3)

This is what it all boils down to. This has to be at the core of your motivation. The truth of the matter is you have absolutely nothing if you don't have love. What of the people who have married solely for material reasons? Or, those who surmised they'd come to love this person in due time? You continue to feel empty and nothing gets better because you had nothing to build on from the very beginning. Tina asked, "What's love got to do with it?" Obviously, from Scripture, it has everything to do with it.

Here's something that dawned upon me regarding love while reading a page from *When People Are Big and God Is Small*. The author was discussing the fact that we don't love because we seek to have our need cups filled or to have our self-esteem bolstered. I began to think about the motivation of God's love for us. He didn't love us to bolster our self-esteem – there's nothing to bolster being that there's nothing good about us. He didn't need to or need anything from us. He simply did it because it was His good pleasure (Ephesians 1:7-10) and it was for His glory. In practice, in marriage, it's a pleasure or a gift to love your spouse. Also, it's a good reflection back on you but your motivation shouldn't be to look good. It's not a right that we must use to rectify if we don't get it in return so we can feel good about ourselves. God commands us to love each other because that's one of the times when we are most like and glorify Him. When we love each other is when things will go best and be most pleasurable for us as it is His pleasure to love us.

Other reasons for getting married are: procreation (Genesis 1:28) as some people naturally desire to build a family, which is appropriately done under the design of marriage having a father and mother in the home to provide the stability needed for the children and proper functioning of the home. Companionship and support (Ecclesiastes 4:8-12) is another reason. Life is just too hard to endure through all by yourself and companionship provides an even greater reward than you can achieve on your own. Also, if you know a celibate lifestyle is just not for you, then marriage definitely is (I Corinthians 7:2-3). Now, don't misunderstand. Marriage is not the solution for problems dealing with matters of impurity such as sexual addiction, pornography, and the like. It's the alternative to living a single life, which requires celibacy to remain pure before God. On the other hand, the married life is pure before God, but it provides the element of sexual intercourse. Which one is right for you?

Imitating the Likeness of Christ

I think what I'm about to share is something many singles probably haven't thought about doing as a part of their quest for marriage. This isn't specifically geared towards finding your potential partner, but more for you. There's a saying, "If you want to become a millionaire, then you hang out with millionaires." Actually, I think the saying is more general, but the first time I heard it, it was with millionaires, so that's what we're going with. The logic behind this is that you keep the company of like-minded individuals, people who are already where you want to be, and you'll learn things from them to help you on your journey to where you want to be. There is definitely truth to that as that is somewhat of the same in the saying, "Bad company corrupts good character," which is in the Bible. It means that the people you hang out with will have some kind of influence on you. The point I'm making is this. If you're single and you want to be married, then you should hang out with couples who have enduring godly marriages. There are some couples with amazing Christ-like marriages. If you only hang out with singles all the time, then you'll only know how to be single. Don't just hang out with only one of them but get a little time in with them both. Hanging out with some marrieds, you'll get an idea of some qualities to imitate in yours. You'll see them at their best and depending on how close you are to them, you may get to see them at their not-so-best or at least hear about it. Your advantage in this is that you can learn a lot from them as you see them interact with each other as well as the information they'll willingly provide you. You'll quickly see that a lot of marrieds enjoy talking about some of their married life with you – even a little banter about each other's nuisances that's appropriate to share. I have a married couple that I'm close friends with and they crack me up because I get to see them playfully go back and forth a lot. Of course, the husband is one of my very best friends and he's who I hang out with, but I do get some time in with them both on occasions. I do consider both of them my friends and I love them both dearly. It just so happens that I was around when they went through some of the early stages of marriage with some of its growing pains. Now, I get to see them as the mature couple that they are today. Of course, I only got the one-sided version of some of their growing pains as I was a safe place for my friend to vent frustrations. But, I know there's two sides to every story. I have been over to their house when things were great. I've been over when things were not-so-great. And, there were times when it was just not good to go over at all. Now, I'm not saying that you're going to see everything, if any, that goes on. Don't get me wrong, that's not at all what I'm getting at.

What you'll get is an idea of how they function and work together. Also, you'll quickly realize that their amazing godly marriage wasn't always amazing nor godly. As you get to know them better, you'll get stories of how they used to respond in certain situations early on in their marriage and how they've grown. It took work to get there and staying committed to God and one another. Couples are very different just like the personalities of each of the spouses are very different. That's what make couples so unique. Find a few married couples to build a friendship with and hang out with each of them from time to time. If and when you finally do jump the broom, those same couples may become some of your most valuable resources in helping you have a successful, enduring, and godly marriage. You simply cannot place a value on a resource like that!

Whatcha Marrying Into?

Unfortunately, every marriage situation isn't going to be the ideal one person marrying another with it being first marriages for both and neither of which has any children. With so many divorces and sexual immorality going on in the world, often you can find yourself marrying into a situation God never intended for us to have to deal with so frequently in the first place. I'm pretty much talking about blended familics. From a biblical perspective, the only cause of this should be where an individual remarries after the death of a spouse. Obviously, this is definitely not the case. There are a variety of situations that brings a variety of different challenges. There are single mothers with one to many children at various stages in life with a variety of personalities and challenges of their own. The children, if more than one, can all have the same father or all can have different fathers. You better believe that a mother raising a single boy is going to present different challenges than, let's say, a mother raising four girls. For women, there's also single men raising children. It's scarce, but they're out there. What women are more likely to run into is marrying a man that has one to many children by one to many different women. The men may or may not be in their children's lives (Ladies, what could this tell you about the man you're thinking of marrying?). The mothers may or may not be working closely with the fathers in raising their children. What type of relationship does the parents have with each other? How did they break up when they were together? These are questions you should be finding out the answer to whether you ask them directly or you infer them on your own. You can ask those questions in such a way so it doesn't raise offense. If you're around enough and insightful, some of those things will begin to come to light. Know this with almost absolute certainty, if the break up was bad and they haven't worked things out, you may be marrying into some unexpected drama. Situations like that not only have an impact on the parents, but the children as well. These are all things you must consider ahead of time. And, it would be very wise to seek out some advice from someone who has gone through a similar situation. If you're a guy about to marry a single mother who is raising a son, talk to someone who has married into the same situation to find out what it was like. Also, talk to your potential spouse about the dynamics of his or her relationship with the other parent. Also, it wouldn't hurt to ask your future spouse about his or her relationship with his or her children and how the children get along with each other. If you're planning on marrying someone with children already, I definitely recommend taking note of the dynamics of the relationships between the parent and children and the children themselves. You need to get an idea of how you're going to fit into the mix of things. The entire household will be undergoing a major transition.

Skeletons in the Closet

To me, a dating relationship is probably one of the most deceitful times than any other point in a relationship. Think about it for a minute. Most people are trying their best to put on their very best. The intent is to impress and some people tend to put on these façades or even lie about who they really are. In worse cases, it can be a deliberate game of manipulation. Now, think about all of the unknowns about each other that exist in a dating relationship compared to let's say a twenty-year marriage. Because of all of this, critical things don't get exposed or are purposely hidden during the dating relationship that should come out. Now, you know the truth is always going to come out; it's just a matter of when and how that makes all the difference. I've heard my share of stories regarding marriages where one spouse finally found out about something his or her spouse should have revealed before they got married and the stuff totally hit the fan. It made it very difficult to deal with. And, of course, the question that's always the first to come up is, "Why didn't you tell me this before we were married?" And the next is, "Didn't you think this was important enough for you to tell me ahead of time instead of letting me find out like this?" Maybe not verbatim but it'll be asked in some form or another. I even know a few people who, after being married, said they wished they would have asked the right questions after finding out something that was a little disturbing to them. These little hidden secrets are what I like to call the Deal Breakers because they would have had a major influence on whether the couple would have married had it been revealed ahead of time. These culprits could be anything from the least to the worse of possibilities. A big one that is not uncommon is financial debt. It never fails. Two people date, get engaged, then marry; and one of the spouses finds out that the other spouse has an enormous financial debt that is just way out of control. And, to top it off the spouse had no plans in place to eliminate the debt and continues to spend freely. Now, it's both of theirs to deal with. Depending on the severity, things like this can put a strain on a marriage once it comes to light. If nothing else, trust can be damaged in the relationship. The spouse who had this hidden secret dropped on them can feel as though he or she has been betrayed by not being informed of the hidden secret ahead of time. Once trust has been damaged or lost, it can be hard to build again. Since these things tend to come out when it's too late, do you know what I like to recommend? If there's anything that is imperative for you to know before crossing the threshold, the point of no return, you should make sure you ask those questions specifically to find out the information that you need to know. And, don't be shy. Ask! With what some people are into these days, you have to ask. And, if there's any hesitation or reluctancy in your potential spouse to answer the questions, then you can surmise that something may not be quite right. Depending on the nature of your questions, you may want to ask early on in the relationship as not to waste anyone's time. I have something that's an absolute deal breaker for me. Well, there's probably another, but the one I have in mind, I don't ask right off the bat. And fortunately, it's something that I can observe very easily, so nothing even gets kicked off if I see it beforehand. Otherwise, I'll definitely ask outright. I've been asked if I was one of those guys on the down low. I didn't get offended. I just snapped back with a very quick decisive, "Heck no! Are you crazy!" And we went on like nothing happened. Hey, I'm the one suggesting this so I totally understand. I also have something very personal about myself that I consider to be a deal breaker. So, when things start to get serious, I actually initiate the conversation to reveal this information. From the moment it occurred in my past, I felt that it was something I needed to be up front about so I can pretty much say that I've always revealed it. Another suggestion is to just have a time where the both of you have a "come clean" conversation. This is self-explanatory. Each of you tell the other about the garbage in your past that will have an impact on the other person if the two of you got married. This is what the couple did who was counseling my first Christian engagement. We were told in advance what was going to happen during that session. Once there and after receiving a few simple instructions, we were allowed to go into a separate room alone to discuss these personal matters. From that point, if there was anything that either one felt we didn't want to or couldn't deal with, we could call it off amicably. Probably the most important instruction we received in the beginning was that any personal information revealed in that room was not to leave that room if we decided to part. It's not that there wouldn't be any disappointments if one decided to call it quits. The fact of the matter is that it would be done with dignity, respect, and maturity without all of the unnecessary drama that can surround break ups, which only makes it worse than it needs to be. That was a first for me and I actually favored the way it was handled. I thought it was wonderful after I thought about it. Either way, my advice is to ask the right questions to find out the information you need to know. Don't assume that your partner is going to come clean. You know what they say when you assume things.

God's Expectations

Into Holy Matrimony

Marriage is one of the most exciting and special occasions in a person's life. There are various factors that contribute to that fact. One take on this that I've come to conclude over the years is that it's exciting because two people are giving each other one of the most precious gifts they have to give possibly without realizing the full extent of what they're giving to each other. This precious gift is simply, your time. We don't have a lot of it (James 4:14), and we have no guarantee to be around any certain amount of time or any assurance that we'll be around from one moment to the next. From the way we live our lives, you'd never really know that this was the situation. What little time we have here is valuable, and we shouldn't waste or take it lightly. As an example of how we may take this asset for granted, some people, despite the time crunch, have the bad habit of making rendezvouses for whatever reason. When the time comes to meet, they neglect to show up without so much as a call to inform the individual waiting of the circumstances. This is done without considering the fact that the other person has had his or her life on hold while waiting and has lost valuable time that won't ever be reclaimed. So, for someone to say that he or she wants to spend the rest of his or her life with you is truly words to be cherished. It's very different when we give money and material things. Those are good, but too easy. It's done and over in an instant and requires little involvement. But, giving your time encompasses so much more. You're giving your very self for the benefit of another. It requires commitment, sacrifice, an investment of oneself through the good and bad of it all. You make yourself vulnerable and there's risk involved because you are likely to experience situations that you wouldn't have on your own. Also, it takes a lot of humility and selflessness. But, as with any investment, the return can be so rewarding.

Marriage by Design

With a major life event that brings so much initial excitement as the two envision life together for the rest of their days and a relationship that presents so many possible rewards, I have one question to ask. Why are we drowning in a pool of staggering high divorce rates? I'll get to the heart of the matter a little later, but I believe most people have no idea of what marriage is about or, more appropriately, know God's intentions for marriage. Yes, His intentions were for fruitfulness, companionship, love, and reproduction (Genesis 1:28, 2:18), but there's a much more profound intention that's not so easily detectable to us. We miss it because we are so full of our own selfish desires.

As I think about this concept, I'm reminded of an episode of my favorite show, *The Closer*. In the episode, "Road Block," the police commissioner's wife, Gail Myers played by Elizabeth Perkins, tries to cover up the death of a college student which resulted from her uncontrollable drinking problem. When the truth finally comes to light and her husband decides that it's time to put a halt to catering to her problem. She very arrogantly responds, "You get me an attorney or I swear to God I will get my own and I will sue you. I have given my whole life for this marriage; I will not let you screw me on this."

Although her retaliation primarily consists of anger, manipulation, fear, and denial, I believe Gail captures the mentality a number of people have in marriage. Some people feel that because they've given so much of themselves to make their marriage work that their spouse owes them something in return, is indebted to them, or is at their mercy. Correct me if I'm wrong but isn't that the whole purpose of marriage – pleasing your spouse (1 Corinthians 7:33, 34). Marriage is about unconditional giving. Sometimes, you may be bearing the brunt of the load, other times your spouse. Thus, having a good marriage would be your reward. Essentially, you'd be reaping the benefits of what you have sown (Galatians 6:7).

In all of this, you have to ask yourself, "What is marriage primarily for?" Is it to make you happy or is it to make you holy? God's purposes for our lives are so far above our petty selfish desires. We chase after scraps of garbage lying around the trash bin and God wants to give us perfection. The purpose of marriage is not for your happiness, but its purpose is to make you holy. Its intent is to purify you from all that is ungodly – your selfishness, pride, anger, lustful desires, and the like. When Isaiah entered into the Presence and saw in full force the holiness – the extreme perfection – of God, he was brought to his knees extremely convicted of his incorrigible behavior. Likewise, in a marriage, you see firsthand the damage caused by your sin by seeing the immediate affect it has on your spouse. So, once your marriage is holy, then and only then will you attain happiness in your marriage. How foolish is it to think that your marriage is for your continual happiness? What about the happiness of your spouse? The purpose of your life is to glorify God no matter your circumstances. His intent is that you reflect the glory of His Son by being conformed to His likeness. You will know that you are being holy when you bear the fruit of the Spirit in your marriage with ever increasing glory (Galatians 5:22-23).

Covenant versus Contract

Have you ever entered into an agreement without fully understanding or knowing the specific terms involved? If you answered "no" then I have no choice but to assume you always read all of the terms and agreements before checking that little box claiming you've read and understood them before signing up for any contractual service. I always check the box without reading the terms thinking of course that it's just your standard mumbo jumbo present in any contract. Besides, who has time to read all of that anyway and I don't plan on doing anything illegal or breaching the contract. I just want the service. Those contracts are a little bit more serious than our actions dictate though. On occasions, I can't help but wonder what am I really agreeing to. Is this something that's going to come back and haunt me? Did someone put something in here as a scam to try and trap people? Who knows without reading it? In the same fashion, I believe most people have no understanding of the type of agreement they're entering into when they recite and commit themselves to those marriage vows. Without that understanding, they end up breaching the agreement. The type of agreement is seen even in the vows. Let's take a look at a couple of sample marriage vows before venturing on.

> I, ____ take you ____, to be my wedded wife. With deepest joy I receive you into my life that together we may be one. As is Christ to His body, the church, so I will be to you a loving and faithful husband. Always will I perform my headship over you even as Christ does over me, knowing that his Lordship is one of the holiest desires for my life. I promise you my deepest love, my fullest devotion, my tenderest care. I promise I will live first unto God rather than others or even you. I promise that I will lead our lives into a life of faith and hope in Christ Jesus. Ever honoring God's guidance by His Spirit through the Word. And so throughout life, no matter what may lie ahead of us, I pledge to you my life as a loving and faithful husband.
>
> (Male Vow)

> I, ____ take you ____, to be my wedded husband. With deepest joy I come into my new life with you. As you have pledged to me your life and love, so I too happily give you my life, and in confidence submit myself to your headship as to the Lord. As is the church in her relationship to Christ, so I will be to you. ____, I will live first unto our God and then unto you, loving you, obeying you, caring for you and ever seeking to please you. God has prepared me for you and so I will ever strengthen, help, comfort, and encourage you. Therefore, throughout life, no matter what may be ahead of us, I pledge to you my life as an obedient and faithful wife.
>
> (Female Vow)

As you very well know that marriage vows are promises each partner makes to the other during a wedding ceremony. They can be traditional or a couple can choose to write their own vows. What's missing from these vows though is what most couples spend the rest of their married lives bickering about. The conditionals! Nowhere to be found is a remark about the expectations of your partner in neither of the vows. People recite the covenantal vows but live it out as though its contractual. Couples spend the rest of the marriage focused on what they're not receiving from their spouse. Since they're not getting what they want, they conclude that they'll stop fulfilling their end of the marriage, stop giving their heart, and pull away. This is not the idea behind a marriage, but this is what so many couples do. I know. I'm guilty of this very thing. No wonder we have so many divorces; marriages simply cannot last under those conditions. Just imagine if God treated us this way. There'd be no salvation and nobody would be entering through any pearly gates. Marriage has got to be based on the agreement that God makes with His people.

> [14]You ask, "Why?" It is because the LORD is acting as the witness between you and the wife of your youth, because you have broken faith with her, though she is your partner, the wife of your marriage covenant.
> (Malachi 2:14)

As you can clearly see in the passage of Scripture above, marriage is a covenant, not a contract and there is clearly a difference between the two. A contract is a legally binding agreement between two (or more) parties where the parties are looking out only for themselves. It's all about what they can get out of the interaction while protecting themselves in the process.

Contracts are, also, limited in nature. They are valid only for a set duration in order to accomplish a specific purpose. Or, if any part of the contract is breached by any of the involved parties, the contract can be broken. Big business deals between large corporations come to mind when I think about contracts. But, contracts seem to have carved out a more regular place in our daily lives over the past years. We see contracts in services we consume such as cellular phones and cable television service. Providers of those services utilize contracts extensively in order to protect themselves to assure that they're making money. They try to hold you to the stipulations of the contract even if it doesn't make sense for them to. If a customer needs to break the contract before its termination date, there are substantial penalty fees to pay for early termination. Many people view marriage from a contractual perspective. What this says is that when things don't go my way or the situation ceases to benefit me, I'm getting out and getting as much as I can before I go. This mentality is why divorces are so terrible. Contracts are very selfish in nature.

On the other hand, a covenant is a binding agreement between two (or more) parties. The difference here though is clearly the beneficiary and the duration. A covenant is for the benefit of the other person involved, not you. Also, it has a timeframe of forever. Even if the covenant is breached; it is not broken but remains a permanent agreement between the parties. I am so grateful that God is not a god who makes contracts because I faltered on mine a long time ago. How do I know He doesn't make contracts? Well, let's take a look at His track record. With Abraham, God promised to make his name great and that his descendants will be as numerous as the stars. Abraham didn't trust God to keep him safe so he had his wife lie about who she really was to him. Also, too anxious to wait for God to deliver on His promise, he allowed his wife to convince him to sleep with her maidservant in order to have a child. Despite his shortcomings, God still fulfilled His side of the agreement. Through Moses, God promised the nation of Israel that He would be their god and they would be His chosen people if they would hold to His decrees. The nation of Israel couldn't be faithful to God's decrees; they quickly turned to idols on a whim and rejected God by requesting a human king like the surrounding nations. Despite their sins and faithlessness, God still fulfilled His end of the agreement. With David, God promised that his offspring would be successor to the throne. David committed adultery with Bathsheba, then in an effort to cover it up; he had her husband killed in battle. At one point in his life, David actually went to live with the pagans and sided with them in a battle against the Israelites. Despite the failings of David, God fulfilled His side of the agreement. Even to this day, in spite of the Christian's ability to adhere to his or her side of the agreement due to sin, God promises and will provide salvation through Christ Jesus. As you can clearly see from all of the agreements God has made with mankind, mankind is getting the better end of the bargain by far – God no doubt had our best interest in mind – and they expand over the course of time. Marriage has that same expectation; it's a covenant we're making on two fronts. First, it's a covenant agreement we are making with God because He had our interest in mind when He instituted marriage. It is a gift to us in the form of companionship, partnership, and intimacy. In return, we are to fulfill our roles of husband and wife. We are to honor marriage as the sacred union that it is that we may bring glory to God. Secondly, it's a covenant agreement that we're making with our spouse. The husband promises to be the best husband he can be to his wife in spite of her inability to fulfill her side of the agreement. And, the wife promises to be the best wife she can be for her husband in spite of his inability to fulfill his side of the agreement. In both cases, the expectation is meant to be for as long as the two shall live.

Partnership

Differences are an integral part of a relationship. Its importance reveals itself in the areas of dynamics, diversity, and experience. The impact on experience is two-fold as it relates to what one brings to the table from the past as well as what one will gain in the future.

Anyone familiar with the technology giant named after a popular fruit? Apple was founded by two extraordinary people who brought very different strengths and abilities to the company's humble beginnings. We all know that Steve Jobs had an extraordinary, uncanny knack for visualizing innovative, new products. Then, Steve Wozniak, who had the technological know-how to make them come to life, would make the products Jobs envisioned a reality. These very diverse set of strengths and abilities that each one of them brought to the table did two things. It allowed them to complement each other, thus making them better together; and it defined each of their roles in the partnership. This made them an effective team, which allowed them to achieve their goals. Today, Apple is a megalithic figure in the IT world whether you're a fan of its products or not. Just imagine if Steve squared were too similar in their strengths and abilities, how successful would they have been?

Marriage is a partnership. God established that in the very beginning when He said, "It is not good for the man to be alone. I will make a helper suitable for him (Genesis 2:18)." Then, when speaking to Adam and Eve, He told them both to "Be fruitful and increase in number; fill the earth and subdue it (Genesis 1:28)." When God created Eve, He created her to be the perfect complement to Adam for everything He commanded them to do.

As a bit of a side note, here's an obvious reason against same sex marriages and relationships. Two people of the same sex absolutely cannot complement each other in the way God designed. Two men can't complement each other because God designed men to lead. You can't have two leaders in a relationship; that won't work. Two women can't complement each other because God designed women to be led. You can't have two followers in a relationship; that won't work. So, how does the gay community resolve the problem? In a same sex relationship, one of the participants must step out of how he or she was designed and fulfill the missing role. One of the men must fulfill the role of the subordinate female and one of the women must fulfill the role of the authoritative male. Although these differences are significant enough to warrant rejection, the most obvious way in which same sex couples are uncomplimentary is in the area of increasing in number and filling the Earth. They have no means of procreating. They don't have the tools to complement each other to do so. So, what do they do? The couples adopt. But, this still doesn't resolve the problem of procreation. If we all were gay, our race would die out because we simply could not procreate like God designed. Then, the animals would rule the world!

We all have strengths and weaknesses. No one is perfect, so no one knows or is good at everything. We need someone to compensate for our weaknesses. You bet Eve complemented Adam; she was created directly from him. In marriages, a lot of criticizing each other's weaknesses and differences takes place, but that's not what should be taking place. I'm just as guilty as the next in doing this in my marriages, especially in my first and second marriages. We should be helping the other grow in his or her areas of weakness and in some situations; the burden is going to be placed on the spouse with that area of strength. As an example, in each of my marriages, I was the one that was better with paying bills and budgeting. So, I was the financial guy. In one marriage, I flat out did all the paying of bills; in another, I had a share of the bills that I paid and she had hers; and in another, I taught my wife to manage her money better and assisted her in budgeting when needed until she was comfortable doing it on her own. This is a significant component to consider when looking for a spouse. Look for someone where the two of you mutually complement each other in some areas of your life. Weaknesses and differences in abilities shouldn't cause criticisms; they should create diversity. So, figure out who is better at what and get with the program.

Oneness of Marriage

I previously mentioned that marriage is a partnership, but that is only in regards to the two of you bringing your talents and abilities together in order to work as a unit to attain your goals and day to day functioning. If a partnership pretty much describes the sum total of your marriage, then you're doing something really wrong. Your marriage should rightly be defined by the term oneness. With oneness, there should be an intimacy there that you can't get from any other relationship. An excerpt from an article I read, in my opinion, capture some of what keeps couples from really achieving that oneness in marriage. It states, "Some think of happiness as a glamorous life of ease, luxury, and constant thrills; but true marriage is based on a happiness which is more than that, one which comes from giving, serving, sharing, sacrificing, and selflessness. Two people coming from different backgrounds learn soon after the ceremony is performed that stark reality must be faced. There is no longer a life of fantasy or of make-believe; we must come out of the clouds and put our feet firmly on the earth. Responsibility must be assumed and new duties must be accepted. Some personal freedoms must be relinquished, and many adjustments, unselfish adjustments, must be made." (Kimball) There are definitely a lot of misconceptions floating around out there about what a happy marriage consists of. And, based on those misconceptions, people marry and eagerly wait in expectation. Romance is a big one that people like to state as to what makes a happy marriage. I mention one or two others throughout this book and romance is no different than those or any others. Here's some food for thought. Romance in the Old Testament played a very minor role in marriage or a couple's time before they married. Here's a shocker for us modern day people. People in Old Testament times didn't marry the one they "fell" in love with; they loved the person they married. You see, marriage in the Old Testament was in some aspects like a business deal. The parents chose the brides for their sons. This was because the bride became a part of their clan which means that they were still under the authority of the groom's father. Also, people married very young, so it's only logical that the parents would choose. Being that the bride became a part of the clan, the logic behind the parents' selection is that they wanted to choose a bride for their son that would fit well in the clan. In other words, she had to get along and work harmoniously with mother and sisters-in-law. The family the bride came from was losing a valuable worker, so the father of the groom typically had to pay the family for their loss of a worker. So, in many cases in Old Testament marriages, love actually started at marriage like Isaac and Rebekah (Genesis 24:67). And, these couples made their marriages work. This should be a wake-up call to everyone in today's time about our fallacies of marriage. Because of this, I believe that if we strip away all of the superficial things we look for in one another – appearances, materialism, race, what side of the tracks a person came from and the like – any man and woman can get married, put God first, obey Him, work at it, and they can have a great marriage. Over the years, customs have changed. We've been afforded the opportunity to be able to choose for ourselves who we marry. So, choose wisely because the standards for marriage hasn't changed.

Contrary to popular belief, selfishness, an unwillingness to sacrifice, and a refusal to deal with one's own sins will destroy your marriage faster than a fire engulfing a house that's been doused with gasoline. You must, and I repeat, you must become better at being selfless, sacrificial, and crucifying your sins. Both parties must make a conscience effort and work tirelessly towards these characteristics in the early stages of their marriage. These three characteristics are of extreme importance because they all are traits that are exemplified in the cross of Christ and a covenant relationship, which are important concepts of marriage. These three traits are easily seen in the crucifixion of the Lord. He died for the sins of the world that those who would choose to look to Him and trust in Him wholly would be forgiven, saved, and become a part of the church, His bride. In doing this,

Jesus exemplified selflessness and was sacrificial. For those who decide to make Him Lord and Savior of their lives, we are called to be selfless, sacrificial, and to carry our cross daily in order to follow Him. Carrying one's own cross is just another way of saying get rid of or deal with the sin in your life. As I discussed earlier about a marriage being a covenant relationship and not a contractual one, that is you're looking out more for the betterment of your spouse than you are for yourself, you can easily see that a covenant relationship calls you to be selfless and sacrificial. On the other hand, you may not be able to easily see the call to crucify your sins. So, let's look at a few examples of the establishing of a covenant relationship by God in the Old Testament.

> [17]"I am going to bring floodwaters on the earth to destroy all life under the heavens, every creature that has the breath of life in it. Everything on earth will perish. [18]But I will establish my covenant with you, and you will enter the ark – you and your sons and your wife and your sons' wives with you. [19]You are to bring into the ark two of all living creatures, male and female, to keep them alive with you. [20]Two of every kind of bird, of every kind of animal and of every kind of creature that moves along the ground will come to you to be kept alive. [21]You are to take every kind of food that is to be eaten and store it away as food for you and for them." [22]Noah did everything just as God commanded him.
> (Genesis 6:17-22)

Here, God is telling Noah about the flood to come because of the wickedness of man that had filled the Earth. In verse 18, God told Noah that He is going to establish a covenant with him but there were instructions provided to Noah by God that he must fulfill. And, you see in verse 22 that

Noah did everything God commanded him without delay. Then, in the first seventeen verses of Genesis 9, we see God establishing His covenant with Noah. Of course, we see the evidence of that covenant to this very day – the rainbow which is the sign of God's promise to Noah to never again destroy all life and the Earth by a flood. What I want you to see in this is the fact that every time God established a covenant with someone or a group of people, there was a call to obedience. No matter what you were doing or where you were going, you were to stop and obey. If you did anything else, you would be guilty of sin. It was no different with the covenant God made with Abraham. God told him that he would be the father of many nations and that he would be very fruitful. Here's what Abraham was called to do.

> [10]"This is my covenant with you and your descendants after you, the covenant you are to keep: Every male among you shall be circumcised. [11]You are to undergo circumcision, and it will be the sign of the covenant between me and you. [12]For the generations to come every male among you who is eight days old must be circumcised, including those born in your household or bought with money from a foreigner – those who are not your offspring. [13]Whether born in your household or bought with your money, they must be circumcised. My covenant in your flesh is to be an everlasting covenant. [14]Any uncircumcised male, who had not been circumcised in the flesh, will be cut off from his people: he has broken my covenant."
>
> (Genesis 17:10-14)

Abraham wasted no time in fulfilling his end of the covenant either. You see him in Genesis 17:23-27 getting circumcised at the age of ninety-nine. Ouch, I can imagine he was pretty sore for quite a while after that. He also circumcised his son and every male in his household that fit the criteria. And, what about the Israelites? The covenant He made with them.

> ¹In the third month after the Israelites left Egypt – on the very day – they came to the Desert of Sinai. ²After they set out from Rephidim, they entered the Desert of Sinai, and Israel camped there in the desert in front of the mountain. ³Then Moses went up to God, and the LORD called to him from the mountain and said, "This is what you are to say to the house of Jacob and what you are to tell the people of Israel: ⁴"You yourselves have seen what I did to Egypt, and how I carried you on eagles' wings and brought you to myself. ⁵Now if you obey me fully and keep my covenant, then out of all nations you will be my treasured possession. Although the whole earth is mine, ⁶you will be for me a kingdom of priests and a holy nation.' These are the words you are to speak to the Israelites." ⁷So Moses went back and summoned the elders of the people and set before them all the words the LORD had commanded him to speak. ⁸The people all responded together, "We will do everything the LORD has said." So Moses brought their answer back to the LORD.
> (Exodus 19:1-8)

If you know anything about the history of the Israelites, you know that this was their problem all throughout their history. They were unable to keep up their end of the covenant. They couldn't even wait until they reached the promised land before they began to fail. They constantly sinned therefore they stayed in trouble. Their kingdom split into two separate nations. They were taken over by other nations, some killed and others taken into exile. They suffered many trials because of their sin. When they did well, things went well as God promised (Leviticus 26). You have to understand that God's call to obedience is a call to live righteously. In other words, flee from your sinful ways. The call is no different for us today in Jesus Christ. Many people today call themselves Christians, followers of Jesus, but have no idea of the stipulations of the covenant. They sin profusely and even stand in defense of their sin to no benefit of themselves. And they don't even know it. I speak of these three qualities of selflessness, sacrifice, and crucifying your sin because they help you to achieve oneness more so than anything else I can think of. Their stark opposites cause separation and division. Think about it. Selfishness is pretty self-explanatory. You can't bond with anyone when you're solely thinking about yourself. If you're not being sacrificial, that goes right along with selfishness. Finally, if you're not willing to deal with your own sin, well sin by its very nature causes separation and destroys relationships. Just look at what it did to mankind's relationship with God. It is very hard to live with someone who is unwilling to deal with his or her own sin. So, please try to incorporate these qualities into your life in increasing measure.

Other than having God rule over your marriage, oneness is the single most important quality for a successful marriage. After all, it was God who ordained that the two shall become one (Genesis 2:24). So, that makes it pretty important if you ask me. Although you can find bits and pieces of things that contribute to oneness throughout this book, I wanted to provide the main areas for connecting in to achieve oneness along with a brief synopsis of what that may look like. It's definitely not all inclusive by any means. Obviously, I haven't been married long enough to anyone to achieve oneness with anybody, but I can provide some general direction from what I've gleaned over the years from my experiences, observations, and just plain old listening. The areas are the same areas where we have to have our most basic needs met. I mentioned them earlier when talking about Adam and Eve. They are spiritual, mental, emotional, and physical. To achieve oneness in your marriage, you must be intentional and work at it diligently. It's not something you're going to stumble into or have occur all of a sudden out of nowhere. It must be the intent and purpose of both the husband and the wife to connect with each other. It will never take off if only one person is working at it, and it will cease and begin to sink the moment one or both decide to stop working at it. It will never be an overnight success story. It is a process that will occur and grow over the course of the marriage as the husband and wife continue to connect to one another. It will not always be such a strenuous process. I see that being more so true in the early stages of the marriage and declining as the husband and wife's relationship matures or when one or more children are born.

    I said earlier that the most important question you can ask yourself about someone you're dating is, "Am I closer to God with this person than I am as a single?" This is important because nothing or no one should come between or distance you from God. And, let me say this right now. If you don't have a relationship with God or not sure, which translates to you don't, then you better find out how. Just because you believe in Him doesn't mean you are right with Him (John 8:31-32). Belief isn't enough. Now, back to what I was saying. Just this morning at a singles men's devotional held at my home, the leader said that he wouldn't be where he is today in his walk with God if it wasn't for his wife. She has helped him to become the man of God that he is today. And, she'd probably say the same about him. I have another friend who regularly praises his wife from the pulpit for helping him to stay spiritually focused during those times when he loses his focus. You see, this is extremely important and beneficial too. A husband and wife should want to see each other get to heaven. Of course, the husband is called to a higher degree in that than the wife. When I think of growing closer to God and being more Christ-like, I think of the fruit of the Spirit in Galatians 5:22-23. Growing in love, joy, peace, patience, kindness, goodness, faithfulness, gentleness, and self-control. I see this in couples who have been married for a while, have weathered the storms, and overcome. They exhibit it to a degree that I cannot fathom. This is what marriage is supposed to do for you. It helps you to grow closer to God and become more Christ-like.

This is an aspect of becoming holy – growing in the fruit of the Spirit. I believe that Christian people who are married and have reached this point in their marriages have grown in the fruit of the Spirit in ways you just can't as a single person. It's not that a single can't grow more in those; it's just that you can't do so as you would if you were married. Living with a spouse, you get challenged, buttons get pushed in ways you probably couldn't have imagined. And, in order to succeed, you have to grow in those areas and you have to intentionally focus more on those areas in order to do so. As a single, you just don't have to focus on them quite so much or have the ability to be pushed by another like a spouse could. On another note, you can help each other get closer to God by being Christ-like with one another. You do this by helping each other see God's grace for one another by showing grace, love, compassion, mercy, and forgiveness. This is completely awesome because you not only help draw each other closer to God through these qualities, but you draw closer to each other too. These are the very same qualities God uses to draw us closer to Him.

Connecting mentally involves sharing dreams, goals, thoughts, ideas, and the like with each other. In order to do this, you must be speaking with each other on a regular basis. More so these days, you have to schedule or set aside time daily for you to connect as husband and wife. It's just not going to happen. Life can easily get so busy if we're not intentional about preventing it. I remember when I worked at DST, I asked one of my colleagues how his weekend went. He said that he and his wife were so busy running their kids and others around to their sporting events that they didn't get to see each other the entire weekend. I got the impression that that was a usual thing for them. I couldn't help but to think when in the world do you have time for each other. Now, I realize that I didn't know the ins and outs of their situation and all but I couldn't help but think that. In reality, there are a lot of married couples that are like that; they don't spend any quality time together. They go to work and back home again. They may be in completely different rooms the entire time they're home or they may sit and watch television together. That's really not considered quality time. Although you're together, may make a few comments about the show, or laugh at it together, your focus is the show and not each other. You need time together where there are no distractions and your focus is one another. You have to make time to spend together where you are the object of each other's attention. That's why you hear a lot of couples say they feel like they don't know each other. They've never spent any quality time together or they eventually stopped doing it over the course of time. This is critical to having a successful marriage.

Connecting emotionally is just that. It's that how do you feel question that sends some of us into a frenzy. This is a call for you to explore your primary and secondary emotions. Are you angry, sad, happy, fearful, shameful, or anxious? Of course, the next question is why. I'm not a psychologist by any stretch of the imagination but I do know from having to do this myself that dealing with your emotions, especially those secondary ones, can help you to learn a lot about yourself. Figuring out why you feel a certain way about a particular situation or action can help you trace back to events in your past, for instance, traumatic events that has left you emotionally wounded. If you don't connect with those emotional wounds from those traumatic events and deal with them appropriately, you can become emotionally stuck or as I like to say, emotionally constipated. You'll need a little help to get those emotions flowing correctly again so that you can move on. For couples to connect emotionally, I have found that it takes vulnerability and trust. It takes you having a willingness to be open with your spouse and you creating an environment where your spouse feels safe to be open with you. There can be no judgment, statements or responses that make your spouse feel singled out or isolated. This doesn't mean you can't speak the truth in love. And, this must be a two-way street. Your partner may have trouble trusting you and it may not have anything to do with you.

Together As One

It may be totally on their end as we all have baggage that causes us not to trust in some way or another. But, you do what you have to do to make sure you are trustworthy with your spouse's deepest secrets. I believe that men are more likely to have trouble with this than women. For one, men tend to struggle with getting in touch with their emotions and expressing them – that is if they even put forth the effort to do so. There are some "emotional guys" out there who are more adept at this than most. I'm pretty sure that I fit into that category of guys. I think being raised by a single mother had a hand in that as well as a traumatic event that happened early in my childhood. I have a friend who was raised by his mother too who happens to be the same way. So, we can relate to each other a bit. Two, society doesn't afford men the opportunity to be vulnerable. It's viewed as a sign of weakness and not considered to be a part of masculinity. But that is wrong! God feels. He feels every one of those emotions I named earlier. And, He expresses when He's feeling each and every one of them. We were made in His image. So, why would we expect to feel nothing? If you've ever read the Psalms, you'd know that King David was a man who was in touch with his emotions. He went from one end of the spectrum to the other and he was proficient in expressing all of them too. And, David certainly was a man's man. Men need to take the risk and have the willingness to be more open and vulnerable. You have to tap into those emotions and talk to someone about what's going on with you on the inside. I'm not asking you to become effeminate; and it doesn't mean you're gay. By the way, some of you all need to grow the heck up too! And get rid of all that foolish thinking! I'm merely asking you to be human. That's why so many men throughout the years have been like a volcano. They're boiling inside with anger, rage, and malice and they don't even know why. Then, without notice; they erupt. They are easily recognized. They are the ones who look like they're always mad and you never know the reason. Like I said, "Emotionally constipated."

It's no secret what we're talking about when it comes to connecting physically. We're talking about sex baby! One on one! Flesh to flesh! Husband and wife gettin' their freak on! Work it out, work it out! Just the way God intended it to be experienced. And, that's one reason why I expressed so much excitement about it because it's in this context where there are really no restrictions or limitations in place. There's no guilt. There are no emotional scars or any of the other consequences associated with sex outside of God's original context. God ordained it for our pleasure – within the context of marriage between a man and a woman. Contrary to what many want to believe, sex is so much more than flesh on flesh; it's so much more than a bodily function. Sex bonds and joins the two people involved into one. That's why Paul warns in I Corinthians 6:16, "Do you not know that he who unites himself with a prostitute is one with her in body?" I have come to see God's allowance for remarriage from a different perspective when adultery occurs in a marriage. As a young follower of Jesus, I used to think it was simply due to the fact that being cheated on in a marriage caused so much devastation, hurt, the loss of trust and all the other things that one may feel. But now, I conclude that God's allowance for remarriage for the spouse adultery was committed against is because the fact that adultery breaks the oneness that a couple shares in marriage. The act breaks the oneness – uniting the adulterer with the one he or she slept with – so divorce and remarriage is allowed for the spouse it was committed against if he or she chooses to. How does it bond the two you ask? Well, I really haven't researched it myself so I'm not going to sit here and act like I have the answer to any degree of specificity. I've heard several theories here and there over the years of my life. Honestly, I think it's one of those things that's a bit of a mystery. Like many other things that God set in place when He created the world, the intricate details are so profound that it's simply beyond the full reach of human comprehension. As of now, I just know that the Bible says it and it doesn't go into details about the specifics of it. God says it's true, then that means it's true. That's all I need. Sex binds you spiritually, mentally, and emotionally to the other person. I know this to be true because when it's abused, that's where you see the damage occurring. It's obvious there's something more profound than just bodily functions. I spoke of it earlier when I discussed people trying to have sex without the relationship. It always blows up in their faces and causes some of the most volatile situations. Such a wonderful gift God has given us, yet it's probably what we abuse the most and is responsible for so many of the problems we experience in our society.

Divorce

There's only one way I can think of to appropriately open up this topic. It is by saying that divorce was never a part of God's plan for marriage. Divorce is hated by God, thus making it a sin (Malachi 2:16). There's something about divorce that I just don't get. The couple involved typically does not take responsibility for it. Usually, the blame is placed on everything else from falling out of love to irreconcilable differences to we just grew apart. Nobody steps up and takes responsibility for their actions. Now, get this! We have these categories that I've seen referenced in multiple places now which are supposed to decrease a person's chances of divorce. Yes, you read correctly. The categories are having an annual income over fifty thousand dollars, having a baby at least seven months or more after marriage, marrying over twenty-five years of age, parents are not divorced, religious affiliation, or level of education. (Wright) Supposedly, if any of these categories apply to your life, then your chance of divorce decreases by a certain amount of percentage points.

Now, let me see if I got this straight. If you are a reasonably well-educated person with a decent income, your family is intact, have a religious background, marry after twenty-five years of age without having a baby first, then your chance of divorce is slim or none. In applying this to myself, I feel safe to say that I'm a pretty well-educated individual being that I have a Master's in Business Administration and a Graduate Certificate in Information Systems Management. As far as salary, I've been in Information Technology as a software developer for over twenty-two years of which thirteen was spent at one company; I made a pretty decent salary that was well over the fifty thousand per year mark. I miss the mark with my parents as they were divorced when I was very young. As far as being religious, how do you really define that for this situation? Is belief in God enough? Then, how does this apply? Sometimes religious people are the worse people to know. Well, let's just say that I believed in God and that'll be the extent of that. My first marriage was on May 24, 1997, which means I was fifteen days shy of my twenty-seventh birthday. And, of course, I don't have any children. By the looks of it, you would think I had a pretty good chance, but all of my marriages ended in divorce. There are people out there that exceed those categories far more than I do and have more divorces under their belt than they do waistline.

There are some people out there who are so scared to get married due to these chances. "Well, my parents got divorced, so there's a good chance that it's going to happen to me." They make it sound like it's the Twilight Zone or some place you end up without any control or say so about it. Enough with all the pitiful talk, I'm going to lay it out there plain and simple. The fact of the matter is people choose to divorce. In November of 2011, when I began working on the manuscript for this book, I had two divorces under my belt. Now in July 2017, returning back to writing after an unexpected hiatus, I've added another. Let me tell you, my circumstances or that of my spouses had nothing to do with the divorces. They had no impact whatsoever. My first marriage, which was prior to my becoming a disciple of Jesus, I chose to divorce from my wife. My second marriage, I was the first to request a divorce, but with some encouragement from church leadership, chose not to shortly afterwards. Then, after a year and a half separation, she chose to divorce me. My third marriage, as I detailed earlier, I chose to divorce her. Marriage is work; it can be tough work at times. But, it takes commitment and effort. And, therein lies the problem – commitment, the lack of it that is. There's absolutely no chance or magic involved in it whatsoever.

The issue of divorce and remarriage is not something to play with or to be taken lightly. To divorce and remarry outside of the three explicit reasons (death, Romans 7:2; marital unfaithfulness, Matthew 19:9, Mark 10:11-12; unbelieving spouse choosing to leave, I Corinthians 7:15) expressed by God is adultery. Now, I don't know about you, but I can't help but think about the myriad upon myriad of divorces filed stating irreconcilable differences which is just a cover up for someone just got tired of his or her spouse, fell out of love, or lusting after someone much younger than his or her spouse. These are not legitimate reasons for divorce. Then, these people run off to get married to someone else, which in most cases, they do multiple times. Some people have been married well in excess of seven times. Every single one of these remarriages is considered to be an act of adultery in the eyes of God. That is, unless you waited to remarry after your ex died or remarried. Take a moment to ponder the magnitude of it all.

Unfortunately, this is a problem for disciples when it really shouldn't be. Why does this remain an issue amongst God's people? The truth of the matter is that we are still sinful, but this doesn't justify it. Another reason I believe is that we truly aren't prepared or equipped. We have no idea of what we're getting into or what is required of us. This is what I'm doing here; I'm trying to give you an idea. And, to delve deeper, the reason as I mentioned I would reveal earlier is, "It was because your hearts were hard that Moses wrote you this law," Jesus replied (Mark 10:5). Our hearts become hardened due to sin. In marriages, as with any relationship, when issues arise and are left unresolved and allowed to linger in our hearts, we become unresponsive and our hearts deadened. We may think that it's the end of the road or we just want to get out, but that's never the case. Just as there's skin that's alive beneath those callouses at the base of our fingers, there's life below the hardness of our hearts. We **can** feel again. We are still human and wicked as long as we are in the flesh, but we must fight for moral integrity. We must allow God's Word to rule our hearts.

I want to share briefly an experience of enduring through a divorce as a disciple. I shared this same story in my previous book, *Enduring Through the Storms*, except I shared it from the perspective of suffering. Just as we mustn't make His word more lenient, we mustn't make it stricter than what it is either. In both cases, you're usurping the authority of God by saying that we know better than He does. That's not good. So, as ugly as it is, like I previously stated, God does allow for divorce in certain situations for very specific reasons. Also, if you are of God's family and find yourself or someone you're close to going through a similar situation. Be especially careful and remember that the heart is deceitful above all things (Jeremiah 17:9). Don't look at another disciple who has gone through a divorce and say if so and so did it, then I can too. You must compare your specific situation to the details of God's Word, not what someone else did. You probably don't know the specific details of another person's situation or what they went through to get where they're at. You committed yourself to following God's Word as the standard of your life and it should be your desire to please Him.

This particular wife and I had initially separated in June of 2006 after a dispute we had which resulted in her leaving with some friends who were visiting. About a week later, I asked for a divorce. During a meeting with the church leader and elders, it was decided that it would be good to separate for a while to work on our own characters. We eventually came back together again – socializing, but not living together – in December of 2006, then separated again which ended up being the final one in February of 2007. We were separated for approximately a year and a half before she filed for a divorce.

During the year and a half, a few people that I know of tried to contact her regarding the situation, but to no avail. Once we figured out early on that she wasn't going to respond, it was time to figure out the real matter at hand. As with any divorce that involves a member of God's household, the matter of concern is whether or not the person is able to remarry in the eyes of God. We, being the church leader at the time, an elder, and I, decided to study through God's Word on the subject of divorce and remarriage to have it fresh on our minds in order to determine my options if she decided to file for a divorce. Although I wanted the freedom to remarry, my primary concern was to honor God. I felt a bit intimidated at times at the thought that I might find out that I couldn't remarry. So, I consistently prayed to God for discernment and to have an open and submissive heart to the conclusive matter of not being able to remarry if she filed for a divorce. I was very diligent about the matter at hand. I studied the Scriptures, sought advice and discussed with the elders and fellow disciples, listened to messages on the topic by John MacArthur and others, and read some books as well, one of which is called *The Divorce Dilemma – God's Last Word on Lasting Commitment* by John MacArthur. This was not something we came to a conclusion on in a matter of minutes. It took some searching and digging. When you're seeking as profoundly as I was, many things tend to go through your mind. I felt my heart wanting to alter the situation to fit what I wanted. I remember on one occasion I found myself thinking that she wasn't acting very Christian-like nor was a Christian if she filed divorce thus allowing me to qualify for one of the situations in First Corinthians that allowed me to remarry. I had to quickly wipe that from my mind though. I had to contradict that with the fact that she was a disciple when I married her or I definitely wouldn't have done so as my convictions were to marry a disciple of Jesus. I also reminded myself that it wasn't my place, but God's, to determine where she was at with Him. And, I also had to remember that I was in the same place only months prior to.

An element that was briefly looked at was the possibility of infidelity. I knew from when we started back to socializing again in December of 2006 that she was leaving church early because she was going to another man's house alone to do music. That is what actually caused the argument that brought about our second and final separation. With proof, it would have given me the option of filing for a divorce and the option to remarry, but there wasn't any proof of infidelity. And, I wasn't going to stoop to the level of snooping around looking for proof either. My intent wasn't focused on getting out of my marriage as my heart had changed since requesting a divorce back in June of 2006. It had gotten back on track seeking to bring honor to God. Being that things were beyond me, I had to wait patiently on

God and trust in Him through my circumstances (Exodus 14:10-14). In reality, that is always the best option anyway.

What added yet another element to the mix is that deep down inside, I didn't want to continue being married to her. My heart still desired to be out. But, as a disciple of Jesus, I understood the fact that He had made that decision for me. If she still wanted to work on the marriage, then I was in. For God, I was willing to put my will aside and allow His perfect will to prevail. I openly shared this information with those who were helping me through the separation and divorce. In case the situation aroused, they would know just how to proceed to help me. Also, being that I tend to wear my emotions on my sleeve, they'd know otherwise right off the bat.

What seemed to prompt her filing divorce at least from my perspective as I'm not sure if she already had something planned or in motion prior to and it just happened to play out this way. But, when I returned from a month-long road trip at the beginning of October 2007, I decided to write her a letter, which consisted of three sentences. The whole gist of the letter asked what she planned on doing regarding the situation and conveyed the point that this can't go on forever and something has to be done. On Halloween, I returned home from work with a courier waiting to serve me with divorce papers. That year and a half was a long ride and I had some down moments as I endured through the process. But, one thing I can definitely say is that I was at peace through the entire thing. I had probably grown spiritually the most during that time. Thanks, and all glory to God for that. At the serving of those divorce papers, I felt a great sense of closure. I wasn't going to be stuck in the mud much longer, but my life was finally beginning to move on.

After much deliberation, prayer, and searching the Scriptures, we concluded that if she filed for a divorce, I could remarry on the basis of spousal abandonment. When she finally did return one of the many calls, it was conveyed to me that she was convinced in her mind that everything was okay and seemingly didn't even acknowledge the fact that she was still married. So, there definitely wasn't any intention to reconcile on her part.

But, looking back now, I don't think the basis we concluded for remarriage was correct in its entirety. Thank God that I still had that option at the time, but it wasn't available to me as initially expected. I believe something else had to happen before I got that option. Remarriage on the basis of spousal abandonment only applies scripturally to a believer with an unbelieving spouse (I Corinthians 7:15). My ex-wife and I were both believers, which means our only options were to either stay unmarried permanently until either one dies or reconcile (I Corinthians 7:10-11). In case anyone has any questions as to whom Paul was specifically speaking about, he wasn't talking to a Christian who has an unbelieving spouse as he clearly addresses them in the next paragraph. He definitely wasn't speaking to an unbelieving couple, so the only viable option here is a Christian couple. For my ex-wife and I, the reason that we only had those two options is that the only way God allows a divorce where He sees the marital bond being broken is death (Romans 7:2) and marital unfaithfulness (Matthew 5:32, 19:9).

I feel compelled to define what is actually meant by marital unfaithfulness being that people can and will misconstrue that into a multitude of meanings in order to justify their own selfish means when they don't want to work through difficult situations. To find out what was really intended by the term marital unfaithfulness, we have to venture to the original word used in the Greek. Terms such as fornication (KJV), sexual immorality (ESV), and immorality (NASB) from other versions of the Bible gives us a better idea of what was meant and a better term to use for searching for the Greek word. The word that Jesus used for marital unfaithfulness is the Greek word, porneia. It is the word which pornography is derived from. It means illicit sexual intercourse which includes adultery, fornication, homosexuality, lesbianism, bestiality, close relatives, and sex with a divorced man or woman. So, marital unfaithfulness is not just something that is displeasing or indecent, but actually refers to an act of sexual intercourse outside of the marriage context.

Since neither of these were the case, once she filed for divorce, the only available options were for both of us to remain unmarried or reconcile, otherwise adultery is committed. Our marital bond in God's eyes still existed. Contrary to what was originally determined, I wasn't free to marry again until after she decided to marry again, which led to marital unfaithfulness. If God allowed death and marital unfaithfulness to break the bond while a couple is married, it is surmised that the bond is broken while the couple is divorced.

Now, I get the feeling that there's a big question coming on or there may be a little confusion being that the divorcee is not allowed to remarry even though they didn't file for the divorce. They may not have even wanted the divorce. Does this seem like God is punishing an individual for the sin of another? Well, we know from Ezekiel 18:20 that the soul who sins is the soul that dies. God does not punish one person for any sin committed by another. You have to look at this from sin's destructive, infectious nature. It's not that God is punishing you for someone else's sin; you're suffering from the consequences of someone else's sin. Yes, the sin of one person can and does affect another individual. I bet you can understand now why singleness is a blessing. This is precisely the type of situation I was thinking of. I'm sure the Twelve felt that when Jesus explained it to them (Matthew 19:10). There are times back in the Old Testament when this was demonstrated. The entire Israelite camp suffered due to the sin of one or a group of individuals. One occasion that comes to mind is Achan when he sinned against the Lord (Joshua 6:18, 7:1-15). The whole nation ended up being defiled on account of him. When Adam and Eve sinned, the whole entire creation suffers. Also, you have to remember God's original intention for marriage. Divorce was never part of the plan. So, as Christians, He calls you back to His original design. For Him to permit us to divorce for marital unfaithfulness breaking the marital bond conveys the point of how severe of an issue it is to Him. I think it's synonymous with mankind's ever-increasing unfaithfulness to Him throughout history.

I remember when someone first told me that my ex-wife had remarried. You know how you have those automatic thoughts that pop into your mind without really thinking, right? While they were telling me, the first thing that came to mind was, "Why do you think I need to know this?" I really didn't care and that was not meant to be taken maliciously. People have just walked right up out of the clear blue and told me things about her as though I had hired them to keep tabs on her for me. I simply smiled and responded, "That's nice," and continued about my business. My second thought immediately after they completed the statement was, "She's not supposed to remarry," but I immediately caught myself in that critical thought and said to myself, "I hope that God gives her as much grace as He has given me," and believe me, that's a lot. Remember, at that time, I was under the assumption that I was able to remarry. Well, I guess, as it turns out, it was a good thing to hear that. There was a little bit of good news in it for me as well as some insight gained.

Here's a way in which our hearts become hardened in marriage before we even get off to a good start. It comes from an explanation I stumbled across regarding the story of Jacob, Rachel, and Leah. This explanation cleared up a long-standing loose end that just didn't make sense to me in the way I've heard that story preached all my years as a disciple of Jesus. There's also a critical message for us to keep in mind when entering the union of marriage. Here's the Scripture reference along with a summary of the article.

> [21]Then Jacob said to Laban, "Give me my wife. My time is completed, and I want to lie with her." [22]So Laban brought together all the people of the place and gave a feast. [23]But when evening came, he took his daughter Leah and gave her to Jacob, and Jacob lay with her. [24]And Laban gave his servant girl Zilpah to his daughter as her maidservant. [25]When morning came, there was Leah! So Jacob said to Laban, "What is

> this you have done to me? I served you for Rachel, didn't I? Why have you deceived me?" ²⁶Laban replied, "It is not our custom here to give the younger daughter in marriage before the older one. ²⁷Finish this daughter's bridal week; then we will give you the younger one also, in return for another seven years of work." ²⁸And Jacob did so. He finished the week with Leah, and then Laban gave him his daughter Rachel to be his wife.
>
> (Genesis 29:21-28)

In messages I've heard preached or referencing this passage, it has been made to seem as though Jacob was bamboozled into marrying Leah. I've even seen some Bible footnotes trying to explain how this could have possibly happened. I just couldn't ever see it going that way. But, is that what really happened? Did Jacob not know he was marrying the wrong woman? If so, how would that have played out? They weren't twins. To get to the bottom of this, we have to look more closely at exactly what happened and also answer an obvious question we may have overlooked. First, let's tackle the obvious question as it's the simplest to do. Do you think Jacob, a single man, lived in that community for as long as he did without knowing that the custom was that the older sister always marries first? That's not very likely especially since he had his eye on marrying Rachel to begin with. Now, let's look at what actually took place between Laban and Jacob. In the morning, after Jacob made love to Leah, what exactly did he ask Laban? He said, "I served you for Rachel didn't I? Why have you deceived me?" Jacob made no mention of Leah whatsoever. Surely, if he was mad at the fact that he was given Leah to marry when he shouldn't have, he would have mentioned something regarding why he was given Leah instead of Rachel. I know I would have. But, he didn't. He complained about the fact that he hadn't married Rachel. Then, once Laban told him he would marry Rachel upon rightfully completing his bridal week with Leah, Jacob was completely satisfied and finished the week with Leah without any other complaints or further explanations. You see the thing is that Jacob knew all along that he would have to marry Leah in order to marry Rachel. So, that wasn't a problem for him. The story of Jacob, Leah, and Rachel is exemplary of the mindset to have when you're approaching the marriage threshold because it provides an invaluable lesson for both men and women to keep abreast of. Whenever you get married, you always marry both women, Rachel, your choice, and Leah, your fate. "You choose your spouse, but that choice includes the future of your spouse which you don't yet know – your fate. And to succeed in love, you have to commit to both – Rachel and Leah, your choice and your fate, the revealed and the unrevealed. Most people don't enter a marriage with this attitude. Most people, when they wake up to find Leah lying next to them, complain that Leah was not their choice. Most people become frustrated with their spouse and their marriage when they discover character flaws, problems, and differences. Most people feel so duped into marrying Leah that they divorce Rachel. But it's not possible to marry one without the other. Leah always appears. The key to success in love and marriage is to know what to do when 'she' does." (Fertel)

Surprisingly, can you believe that the divorce rate at one time was under 10%? In 1867, when they started keeping track of divorce statistics, the divorce rate was at 3%. It didn't reach the 10% mark until somewhere between 1914 and 1915. The rate climbed at a steady pace and even declined some over the years. There were major events that occurred throughout history such as WWII and women entering the workforce that may have contributed to the increase in divorce rates. Divorce rates literally skyrocketed in the 1970s, even surpassing the 50% mark. This spike was caused by the institution of the no-fault divorce, which made attaining one extremely easy. Prior to, a person had to prove adultery or cruelty in marriage in order to receive a divorce. Nowadays, divorce rates seem to have stabilized which is not necessarily a good thing. The only reason I say that is because people have merely replaced one bad thing with another. They're not getting married and staying married. People are opting to live together without ever getting married. Before closing out this topic, I want to share some key points to keep in mind on divorce that I learned. This is in no way meant to be a comprehensive study on the matter, so be sure to take the time to search the Scriptures to find out on your own. We need to always base our convictions from God's Word. I used to think that the matter of divorce in the Scriptures was a bit cloudy, but in reality, it's really very clear. It's a bit cloudy to us because of what we're looking at. Autonomy comes into play here. We're so focused on what we want to do instead of what's right. Here are the six key aspects on divorce to always keep in mind along with their Scripture references.

- God sees marriage as a permanent commitment (Matthew 19:4-6, Mark 10:6-9).

- There are four ways a disciple is allowed to remarry with a previous divorce: new disciple with a divorce prior to conversion (II Corinthians 5:17), death (Romans 7:2), infidelity (Matthew 5:32, 19:9), abandonment by unbelieving spouse (I Corinthians 7:15-16). The bond is broken in the eyes of God.

- Two disciples divorce for any reason other than marital unfaithfulness (irreconcilable differences, grew apart, etc.), the bond is not broken in God's eyes. Couple cannot remarry but must remain unmarried or reconcile (I Corinthians 7:10-11). Death (Romans 7:2) and infidelity (Matthew 19:9) breaks the bond.

- Two disciples divorce due to marital unfaithfulness, the partner can remarry (Matthew 19:8-9). The bond is broken in the eyes of God.

- The partner who actually divorces spouse for any reason other than marital unfaithfulness and marries another actually commits the act of adultery (Mark 10:10-12).

- Remarriage of spouse after he or she has been married to another is forbidden (Deuteronomy 24:1-4).

If you or anyone you know is going through a divorce, the first five bullets are critical to keep in mind. They are the main points of the Scriptures dealing with divorce and are a base to begin working from. You can figure out where your situation lies, then you can begin applying the specific details of your situation. With every case of divorce, I think it should be approached with much prayer, seeking the Scriptures, and consultation.

As God's Word doesn't cover every little possible detail of every situation that may occur and rightly so, as some details really don't matter, we really must allow the Spirit to guide as Paul did when advising the Corinthians in regards to a particular situation. Let's take that a little farther for our example. From I Corinthians 7:12-15, we know that a believer must not divorce his or her unbelieving spouse. What if the unbeliever leaves, but on top of that, is not responsible enough to or is concerned about filing for a divorce. They are content with just being separated from his or her spouse. Can the believer initiate and file for a divorce? How would you respond? Here's another scenario. You have two Christians who are married to each other. One of them decides to file and go through with the divorce. The spouse who was divorced from decides to marry someone else. Is the spouse who filed for divorce free to remarry? How would you respond? Unfortunately, this does happen amongst God's people. So, I talk about this simply because it does happen, not for you to premeditate your options to have in the back of your mind going into marriage. Your heart should be where Jesus took the Pharisees when they questioned Him about marriage to try and trap Him. Jesus took it back to the beginning (Matthew 19:3-6). So, do your homework while dating, get married, and stay married until death do you part.

Honored By All

An obvious problem with marriage is how it is viewed. In the eyes of men and women, it is not given its proper respect. People who have a curmudgeon of a spouse or are in difficult marriages to whatever degree usually tend to despise the institution of marriage as though it is responsible for their detriment. This is evident in their bashing of marriage, advising singles to never get married, or seeking relationships outside the marriage. The lifestyles of the rich and famous dictate that its nothing more than a mundane activity. In relation to the high standard for marriage, some seem to get in and out of marriages on a daily basis. But, despite all of this, the Scriptures are clear on how marriage was intended to be viewed.

> [4]Marriage should be honored by all, and the marriage bed kept pure, for God will judge the adulterer and all the sexually immoral.
> (Hebrews 13:4)

Marriage is to be honored as the sacred union that it was designed by God to be. It is to be highly respected, highly esteemed, highly revered, and held in high regard. This message is addressed to everyone. Whether you're married or single, it's your marriage or someone else's; you're called to honor the union of marriage.

Like Christ and the Church

As I mentioned earlier, marriage is the only relationship on Earth that draws a comparison to Christ and His relationship to His church. This relationship is extremely special and unique. It far outranks any relationship you may have with another. No matter how close you are to your twin sister/brother, any of your parents, best friends, or even that special one-of-a-kind bond you have with your furry four-legged friend. Marriage takes precedence over them all.

Jesus told a lot of parables. They are simply earthly stories with a heavenly meaning or to put it another way, it mirrors a divine truth. I believe marriage is no different. It's a reflection of something divine. So, how is marriage like Christ and His relationship with the church? Exactly what is marriage a reflection of? Let's look at some Scriptures to begin painting this picture.

> [1]Paul, a servant of God and an apostle of Jesus Christ for the faith of God's elect and the knowledge of the truth that leads to godliness – [2]a faith and knowledge resting on the hope of eternal life, which God, who does not lie, promised before the beginning of time…
> (Titus 1:1-2)

Together As One

In what appears to be just an initial greeting, the introductions to the New Testament epistles and letters are rich with little golden nuggets of information if you're paying attention. The opening of Titus has a particularly interesting nugget in its midst. I know I've glazed over this many times without paying it much thought until as of late when it pretty much leaped off the page at me. Paul opens his letter to Titus pretty much describing his mission and purpose as called by God. He was called for the faith of God's elect – a little doctrine of election here – and a knowledge of the truth that leads to godliness. He was called to preach the gospel of Jesus Christ so that those chosen by God could hear it and come to, as he says at the beginning of verse 2, "a faith and knowledge resting on the hope of eternal life." Paul says that it was promised by God who does not lie. He said this to provide reassurance of hope to his listeners. Now, here's the extremely interesting part at the end of verse 2. Paul continues saying that it was promised (by God) before the beginning of time. Wait a minute; I have to hear that again. Promised before the beginning of time. Promised to whom? I know it wasn't to me or anybody else for that matter. Humans weren't around yet as we weren't created. Phrases like before the beginning of time, before the creation of the world, and long ages past refer to a period before time as we know it began. In other words, it refers to anything happening before Genesis 1:1. Let's take a look at another Scripture to see if we can find the recipient of this promise.

> ⁴For he chose us in him before the creation of the world to be holy and blameless in his sight. In love ⁵he predestined us to be adopted as his sons through Jesus Christ, in accordance with his pleasure and will – ⁶to the praise of his glorious grace, which he has freely given us in the One he loves.
>
> (Ephesians 1:4-6)

Well, what a wonderful surprise. It appears again. The doctrine that is so hard for some people to accept as it provokes this one pressing issue. The doctrine of election – that God choses some and not others – is clearly evident here and throughout the entirety of Scripture. The issue arises out of the question most produced from this doctrine. If God is such a loving God, then how can He choose to save some people and not others resulting in them being condemned eternally in hell? Some people just can't grab a hold of this concept and accept the validity of this doctrine. This causes some to believe that God isn't who He says He is or some other blasphemy about Him. Only with a proper understanding of sin, your own wretchedness, and who God really is that question would morph into the more appropriate question of, "Why does God choose to save any of us at all?" Paul tells the Ephesian Christians that God chose them in him before the creation of the world. The "in him" is Jesus Christ. God made the promise to His Son, Jesus Christ. Here's another Scripture where Paul reiterates the exact same thing.

> ⁸So do not be ashamed to testify about our Lord, or ashamed of me his prisoner. But join with me in suffering for the gospel, by the power of God, ⁹who has saved us and called us to a holy life – not because of anything we have done but because of his own purpose and grace. This grace was given us in Christ Jesus before the beginning of time
> (II Timothy 1:8-9)

Paul writes to Timothy, who was probably ministering at the church in Ephesus at the time, that God's grace was provided because of His own purpose and not because of anything those who receive it had done. Clearly, we don't deserve God's grace, but He has a specific purpose in providing it. God's grace is given to the follower in Christ Jesus before the beginning of time. Once again, if the grace given to believers was given to them through Jesus Christ before the beginning of time, then the promise was made to Jesus Christ. But there still seems to be a piece or two missing though. Let's continue.

Remember in my initial statement in the beginning of this section, I mentioned that marriage is a little like a parable because it's a reflection of a divine truth? Well, let's look at one of Jesus' parables; the one He told in Matthew 22, the Parable of the Wedding Banquet. Although this parable is full of profound spiritual truths, I don't intend to delve into any of them, but I want to touch on something of a lighter matter, the festival itself and what it implies. Being that the setting of the parable was during the time of the banquet, there are a couple of things we know to be true. Anyone familiar with the marriage customs of that day knows that this is pretty much the final stage of the wedding process. The celebration could last up to a week in duration. Being the final stage, this means that pretty much everything else has taken place, the betrothal, the actual wedding ceremony, and the consummation of the marriage. So, who in this parable actually got married? When Jesus mentioned a king in His parables or two kings like He did when He was telling His followers the cost of being His disciple in Luke 14, rest assured the king or one of the kings represented God. Now, if God is represented by the king, then who does the king's son in the parable represent? Jesus Christ of course. So, it appears to be that Jesus Christ has a bride or at least a bride to be (Revelation 19:7, 21:9).

Let's look at this from another perspective. In Ephesians 5:22-33, Paul is seemingly providing instructions for the husband wife relationship, which I'll touch on down the road a bit later. But, there's a correlation that I'd like to point out. As you continue reading through this passage, you find out in verse 32 what Paul was actually talking about. He makes it crystal clear that he is actually talking about the relationship of Jesus and the church. This is spoken of in the context of marriage – a passage about husbands and wives. In verse 28, Paul equates a husband loving his wife to loving himself

– loving his own body. This is easily understood from the two becoming one flesh. This is analogous to Christ and the church, which it clearly says is His body. What has been a mystery in years past has been revealed – the church, the body of believers, is the bride of Jesus Christ.

I'm not trying to act as though I have a comprehensive understanding of God's purpose and plan, but what it clearly seems to me is this. A part of God's purpose in providing His grace is that in eternity past before God laid the foundation of the Earth, prior to any human existence, God made a promise to His Son. Because of His immense and inexpressible love for His Son, God promised His Son a bride, the church. When you think about the reality of the doctrine of election and cross that with the fact that in Jesus' day and in some cultures today, the parents picked the bride for their son, it kind of makes some sense. A lot of things in this life reflect a spiritual reality, hence Jesus' telling of parables. I think God is handpicking the bride for His Son. His Son's bride would adore, praise, honor, and glorify Him for all eternity. But, this would come at an exorbitant cost. The Son must go to Earth to rescue them from their sins. He will be unrecognized and not accepted by those who will have been waiting for his arrival. As a matter of fact, He will be rejected, despised, and treated like a common criminal by His very own. Many accusations will continually be brought against Him despite the numerous acts of love He will show them. He will be beaten, humiliated, and punished beyond all recognition. And, the culmination, clearly underserving of this fate, He will have to die a painful and agonizing death in their place as though He was one of them. After hearing what He would have to do to achieve this, the Son simply said, "I do."

God is weaving together a story that's far greater than us – unbeknownst to us right before our eyes and we are clueless. Essentially, we, the church – those who are truly following Jesus – have been promised to Him as a gift from His Father. I don't know about you, but when I think about who I am in and of myself before God, the only thought that comes to my mind is a sarcastic, "Some gift!" This is mind blowing. Talk about the grace of God not only to do something for me that's impossible for me to do for myself and that's save me from my sins so that I can go to heaven and be with God for eternity, but to see me in such a way as to give and receive me as a gift. Now, that's definitely a new perspective for me. What an amazing God I serve! Mankind desecrates the union of marriage. We are lightyears away from honoring or revering this union as we should. So, here's a question for thought. How does this change your perspective about marriage and your (future) spouse?

Together As One

Considering what Jesus done for us on the cross in order to be united with us like this for eternity, I have a new perspective on what husband and wife are proclaiming to each other as they become united to each other. Jesus displayed a great deal of humility to give up all He had in heaven to come and live amongst us, a bunch of good for nothing sinners. He was extremely vulnerable in that He was broken, bruised, and wrongfully disgraced in our place. Each one of us personally caused Jesus a great deal of pain for each sin we've committed and continue to commit. He did all of this so that we could be united with Him as friends, brothers, co-heirs, and ultimately as His bride, the church. So, a message reflected from the cross that soon to be husband and wife are proclaiming to each other is simply this. I am willing to be vulnerable with you, hurt by you, die for you and to myself, and give up all that I am as a single person in order to be united and one with you for the rest of our lives.

God's Expectations

Dealing with Conflict

What was once a quiet storm has now turned into a severe thunderstorm complete with dark clouds, heavy rainfall, lightning, and twisters of the inconceivable F6 magnitude. Yeah, I know you're laughing, but you know what I'm saying is true. The smooth sounds of Smokey Robinson playing in the background as the two of you huddle close together on the couch wrapped in each other's arms gazing passionately into each other's eyes have long since passed. We all have conflict, but it's a time where the most damage to your marriage can occur if you're not careful.

In August of 1983, Hurricane Alicia rose up out of the Atlantic Ocean to make her presence known and her wrath felt by the state of Texas.

Together As One

She was the costliest tropical cyclone to come from the Atlantic since Agnes in 1972. As she literally stormed northward through eastern Texas, she left a trail of devastation totaling $2.6 billion (1983 USD; $6.07 billion 2012 USD) (Wikipedia: Hurricane Alicia) in damage and was the direct cause of twenty-one fatalities during her three-day stay on land. Because of statistics like these, Alicia is one of the worst hurricanes and the first billion-dollar tropical cyclone in Texas history.

When Alicia hit, I was living in Bryan, Texas, which is approximately one hundred miles from Houston. As always, during hurricane season, you can tell when a storm is bearing down on you. You can see the aura of the day gradually fade to gloom. The darkness begins to creep in across the sky. The trees seem to bow down before you as the wind picks up in speed and intensity.

Once the storm actually arrived, an entire day of playing was lost due to the rain, wind, thunder, lighting, and all that comes with a category three hurricane. Yes, playing was the matter of importance. What else do you expect from an active thirteen-year old kid who enjoyed the outdoors? Although we got hit hard, it didn't hit us as hard as it did Houston. Neither do I recall Bryan getting any twisters like Houston did, but what we did get was more than enough.

After a considerable amount of time had passed after the storm, my mother and I traveled to Houston to visit relatives. Upon arriving at my uncle's house, I couldn't help but notice the tree that stood not more than a foot away from my uncle's house was no longer standing. It was lying down right next to the house as though it was perfectly placed. This tree was very large in diameter and it was pulled up by its roots. If it had hit the house; it would have been history. My uncle said the tree had been pulled up by Hurricane Alicia. Now, imagine the magnitude of the power of the hurricane. I couldn't help but wonder about the damage that was caused throughout the rest of the city. The flooding, which doesn't take much to happen in Houston, to the loss of homes, to the many windows that was destroyed in the skyscrapers downtown. Although, a lot of damage occurred in the wake of Ms. Alicia, the damage was repaired. Now, Houston, Galveston, and all the areas that Alicia gave the kiss of death to have flourished far beyond that disaster.

    The power to cause damage through the things we say and do or don't say and don't do in the midst of conflict can emulate what Alicia did to southeastern Texas. It can be devastating and costly. But, just as southeast Texas is not a barren wasteland today because of Alicia's visit, the same holds true for your marriage when Mr. Conflict decides to move in. Looking at the condition of some marriages, it's obvious that so much damage has been caused; you wonder how they are even still together. Many people feel that there's no hope for them to get through the dark storms of marriage. Each party retreats to the trenches either to create a marital stalemate or prepare to launch grenades. Nothing beneficial is done and they figure that the only option is to end the marriage. But, I'm here to tell you that there is always hope – no matter how bad things get. There is a God! Jesus Christ came and died on the cross, so in that fact alone, we know that wickedness does not have to prevail (Romans 6:12) unless you let it. As a matter of fact, you can endure through conflicts without causing Alicia-esque type damage, which is the far better option anyway. Causing damage is so easy to do. The slightest poorly placed word can do the trick. Repairing a badly damaged marriage is going to cost you as you must invest yourself, think about your pain less, and honor your marriage above yourself. It's difficult, but it's well worth the effort. So, if you ever find yourself heading in that direction or you may be there now, if you put in the work – and yes, it takes two – you can find yourself in a marriage that is blossoming and flourishing post Alicia-esque damage. Let's change gears slightly and talk about a few thoughts that conflicts bloom from.

Battle of the Sexes

Here's an old phrase that we ought to be familiar with – battle of the sexes. Is there a real battle going on? If so, when was the first missile fired? Or, was it just a phrase someone coined while trying to be sarcastic? I'm afraid the battle is very real and the first missile was fired by neither the man nor the woman. But, it was Satan who fired the first missile. And, men and women have been firing missiles at each other ever since. How did Satan manage to drop a bomb on us?

Traveling back to Genesis again, we see exactly what Satan did to start this on-going battle between men and women.

> [1]Now the serpent was more crafty than any of the wild animals the LORD God had made. He said to the woman, "Did God really say, 'You must not eat from any tree in the garden'?" [2]The woman said to the serpent, "We may eat fruit from the trees in the garden, [3]but God did say, 'You must not eat fruit from the tree that is in the middle of the garden, and you must not touch it, or you will die.'" [4]"You will not surely die, " the serpent said to the woman. [5]"For God knows that when you eat of it your eyes will be opened, and you will be like God, knowing good and evil." [6]When the woman saw that the fruit of the tree was good for food and pleasing to the eye, and also desirable for gaining wisdom, she took some and ate it. She also gave some to her husband, who was with her, and he ate it.
>
> (Genesis 3:1-6)

Satan got Eve to doubt and not trust God convincing her that He was withholding something from her and didn't have her best interest at heart. Can you imagine being in the Garden, with all of the beauty that surrounded her, with everything that she needed within arm's reach, she was still manipulated into thinking God wasn't on her side? Here's the start of the trend of women not trusting and respecting men.

Adam, on the other hand, passed the buck. He indirectly blamed God for his sin by stating "the woman **you** put here with me – she gave me some fruit from the tree, and I ate it" (Genesis 3:12). Thus, claiming she was the cause of his problem. Now, another trend begins, men thinking their wives are the cause of all their problems. They don't accept responsibility for the things they did wrong in their marriages. Does all of this sound familiar?

You see, what happened in the garden when Satan bamboozled Adam and Eve was a disconnection in relationship. They were disconnected from God and they were disconnected from each other. Any time there's a disconnection in a relationship, fear enters in. This leads to a lack of trust and respect. It's inevitable and it occurs in any relationship. That's an effect of sin. That's why John said there's no fear in love (I John 4:18). You absolutely can't love someone you don't know. This is why it's so important to know God, as well as your spouse.

Two Lives Joining Into One

Let me get this straight. You have this single man and woman who have made their own decisions and had no one else around that they had to truly consider. This has been the situation pretty much their entire lives. Then, you take the two and thrust them into a living situation where someone else now has a legitimate say in their life. The needs, desires, and concerns of this other person are literally pushing your life off the tracks you've been rolling on for years without the slightest interference or nudge. This is bound to cause some bumps and bruises. Wouldn't you think? Add to the mix varying personalities and the fact that men and women are different anyway and all I can say is what else would you expect? I sure wouldn't expect things to go smoothly as though they had been doing this before. Do you expect a single person to live with all of the concerns a married person does? That's preposterous! If you saw a single person living like that, tell me you wouldn't think they were absolutely crazy. Those are two completely different lifestyles on complete opposite ends of the spectrum. There need to be some time to adjust and learn with a life-long learning curve thrown in there for good measure while you get the hang of this. Hopefully, at some point, the couple does learn and get to know each other so that the drama tapers off. Things that once made the world come to a halt become less dramatic as the years go by. Progressing through the different phases of life, learning and growing with each other as you each change, and life's little challenges will always keep it interesting, hence the need for the flexibility. This is a life-long learning process and it's something we need to recognize and account for going into marriage. It took two marriages and some number of years for me to realize. Take into account the fact that we are learning is especially true for the first few years of marriage where it will be the rockiest. Trying to understand your spouse and patience should be defining characteristics during this period of time. Instead, the majority of divorces occur within the first two years of marriage. I've made my contribution to this statistic as well. I filed for divorce from my first wife only after eleven and a half months of marriage. I didn't even give us a chance to really get started.

Have you ever sat and put a puzzle together? I'm not talking about one of those wimpy puzzles with pieces the size of a gingerbread man. I'm talking about the mega puzzles with pieces numbering in the thousands. I can remember as a kid trying to put together one of those mega-sized puzzles. I can say without a shadow of a doubt that I never finished even one of those puzzles because I lacked a key ingredient for the task. It takes great patience to bring one of those together. You work on it piece by piece using trial and error because it definitely doesn't come with instructions. That would kind of defeat the purpose, wouldn't it? I've known some people who have put those sizes of puzzles together in one sitting, others over the course of days. Obviously, those puzzles consist of a multitude of pieces – each piece having its own shape, which can consist of varying shapes on each side. Every piece is designed to have a particular piece fit on each of its sides. There's no room for flexibility here. The outside pieces, which form the frame, are typically much easier to construct since you can visibly see how they line up. So, right out the box, you tend to put these pieces together first, which makes sense. It gives you something to work with as you delve deeper into constructing the bigger picture. On the contrary, as you work towards the center, those pieces aren't like the outer as they take much more work to construct – that is, until you're down to the final pieces of the puzzle. At this point in the process is where patience becomes critical. You work to construct the big picture possibly building multiple sections at a time until they merge together. Or, you expand directly from the frame that you have in place until you reach the point when the pieces come together more easily. Either way, patience is mandatory for you to reach this point where pieces come together with ease. Don't check out on me now, there is an analogy I'm trying to make between the couple in a marriage and the cycle of constructing a puzzle.

    Like a puzzle, your spouse definitely won't come with a set of instructions. So, trial and error are going to be your only option. You may like the term on the job training better, but either way, you're getting nothing to start with. In your methodology, it would be wise to ask a lot of questions. With some things, you just have to roll up your sleeves, get in there, and take a few bumps and bruises to learn what you need to know. We are a bunch of people with a multitude of attributes or shapes (pieces). When a couple decides to get married, it's a bunch of pieces coming together to form a bigger picture. During the friendship, dating, and engagement stage, the couple has seen some of the visible attributes of each other's character that they are attracted to. This forms the frame or foundation from which the relationship is built. As newlyweds, the process begins to delve deeper as they begin working towards "putting those center pieces together". They're building sections at a time and off the foundation they already have in place. More of the couples' character begins to be exposed. This is when the increase in patience is needed. As character traits, strengths, and weaknesses are revealed, it's a time when both are beginning to see how each of their attributes (shape of your pieces) are going to fit together to become one solid picture of a functioning marriage. This process unfortunately does require the production of some friction on occasion. Much like I did as a kid trying to construct those puzzles, people quit way too soon. They run off to start the process all over again with someone else who has an entirely different shape than the previous expecting different results. But, to their dismay, nothing changes. This is the process. If they would just be patient, put in the work that it takes, and be willing to change, things would come together. Over the long haul, as the puzzle becomes more defined, the pieces will come together much easier. And after it's all done and said, the puzzle is complete and you end up with a beautiful picture. In the same way, you end up with a cohesive couple in a beautiful picture of a marriage that is flourishing and has grown through the test of time.

 Consequently, there has to be some time for adjusting to this very unfamiliar lifestyle. In addition to the lifestyle change, you have to allot time for getting to know each other. In the small time you dated, you may think you know each other so well, but believe me; you probably don't have a clue. As the saying goes, "You never really know someone until you've lived with them." You are now seeing the real them in full bloom, raw and uncut. You may see things about your partner you would have never imagined. I wouldn't be surprised if some things left you in shock – jaw hanging to the ground, eyes bulging wide open. During premarital counseling of one of my marriages, we did an exercise that I thought was really helpful in preparing us for that initial shock of living together. We answered questions about our daily routine from the time we woke up until the time we went back to bed for the entire week. For most, this really isn't a lot. If you think about it, most people typically have a basic routine they follow for the week and another for the weekend. This exercise came from a premarital counseling book called *Before You Say I Do*. Some of the things discussed in this exercise were:

- When do you wake up? When do you get up? What steps do you take to get ready for the day? For example: Do you shower first or eat first? How much time do you need getting ready in the bathroom?

- What are you thinking about as you drive home from work? What do you typically do your first hour home from work?

- What do you typically do in the evening? How do you prepare for dinner?

- When do you typically go to bed? What do you do before going to bed? Do you prepare for the next day by laying your clothes out, etc.? How do you like to go to sleep? Do you listen to the radio? TV? Do you like it completely dark or a light on? Do you fall asleep where you're at then wake up in the middle of the night to go to bed?

Of course, these are only the tip of the iceberg. There are many other subjects to touch on such as money handling, spending habits, housekeeping tendencies, and the list could go on. I think the exercise is like fire prevention as it helps to keep fires from breaking out in your marriage that may result from the convergence of your two lives. What happens a lot in this temperamental period in your marriage is that one person takes something personal that the other has always done (as though they did it to them). When in reality, it was something they did because they are accustomed to doing it. It's who they are. You'd be surprised how much that happens or comes across in marriages – even in those that have some years under their belt. The exercise is in no way meant to detail everything, but it puts you in the mindset of I have to learn how to live with this other person and it gives a little glimpse of the obvious pieces that'll be merging. It helps give you an idea of who your partner is and realize that this person had a life, a routine, and things they were accustomed to doing and having before you two came together to live as one. You can deal with those matters without making a big spectacle of things. So, think about this. How does this change your perspective? What are you going to do to prepare yourself?

Environmental Products

It is absolutely crucial to understand yourself here. Some things you will learn about yourself as your marriage progresses. I'm sure your spouse will inform you of some things as well. We are the products of every day we have lived up to today. Those experiences include the victories, the trials and hardships, the environment we grew up in, the company we kept, the catastrophes and anything else we came into contact with. Those things have shaped who we are whether we are aware of it or not.

No matter how good things are going for you, how well you look, or how good you are at projecting the façade that you have your act completely together, we all are damaged goods, broken products to varying degrees of imperfection. God wants to develop us and strengthen our character, so one way He does that is by putting us in situations where we have to deal with our weaknesses and sins as that is the only way we can develop a stronger character.

> [2]Consider it pure joy, my brothers, whenever you face trials of many kinds, because you know that the testing of your faith develops perseverance. [3]Perseverance must finish its work so that you may be mature and complete, not lacking anything.
> (James 1:2-3)

Seems so logical doesn't it? Well, this warning comes from James for a specific reason. On our own, we run, we hide, we neglect to deal with, or we live in a state of denial about the reality of our character. Marriage is definitely a remedy for that. You will see and be forced to deal with things in your character or soon face a disastrous relationship destined for destruction. I became convinced of this in regards to one of my marriages. During the first three months of our separation, I was thinking about our marriage in retrospect. It suddenly became evident to me that when we were married, all we did was become the object of blame for each other for the majority of the emotional garbage, frustration, and pain that we were already suffering from before we even laid eyes on each other.

Being that I was abused by my father and had a mother who was convinced she was going to raise the perfect child, I brought a profound feeling of being disrespected and feeling as though I was never good enough into the marriage. I felt like I was just an object and I harbored a lot of anger and frustration towards my parents. My wife, on the other hand, brought living in fear to the marriage. Our marriage became nothing more than a vicious cycle – a negative action by one feeding into the pain of the other, which produced a detrimental response by that one, which fed back into the pain of the other. And, my anger didn't help that one bit. I can remember being baffled as to how she could have had so much fear of me from the onset of the marriage when we weren't married that long at all. In most cases, she exaggerated or manipulated the truth to make her look better than she was or simply to keep the focus off of herself. This didn't help me any because being lied upon only provided more fuel for my anger especially in situations when I really wasn't in the wrong. I began to realize that her fear wasn't all produced by me. She occasionally shared some things with me from her past regarding how one of her parents exaggerated the actions of the other to her and her siblings. This resulted in her being overly fearful of this particular parent. Each time she questioned why her parent would do that, I couldn't help but feel that she was doing the same thing to me. She was making me out to be the monster that I really wasn't.

This is not to say that we weren't responsible for some of those feelings we felt from each other during the marriage. It's just that when we were married, we brought all of the unresolved baggage we had been carrying around for years to the relationship. Instead of trying to understand, be a best friend – a soft place for each other to fall, and help each other through our issues, we blamed each other for it all. This has helped me to strive to confront my feelings regarding my past and the way I've been conditioned as a result of my experiences. Who we are today is a result of every single negative and positive experience we encountered prior to the present moment. We are like sponges in water; we absorb every experience we have in life. And, those experiences have conditioned the way we respond in many situations. In many instances, we respond without the depth of awareness as to what we are doing, why, and the damage we may be causing by our actions going forward. When we have conflict today, it not only involves the issue at hand, but it can involve something much more profound within us as a result of an experience from the past. As challenging as it can be, I feel like now I have more of a willingness to search my own feelings to determine if there is something there that I can change. If you can see them and are not so focused on your own hurt and placing all the blame on the other person, marriage will bring out these deeper issues within us so that we can deal with them and heal. This in no way suggests simplicity; it merely displays a willingness to grow, which is what God desires for us. This is another part of the process of being made holy – the inverse of growing in the fruit of the Spirit. We must remedy our contaminating experiences in order to be filled with the fruit of the Spirit.

Sins & Misunderstandings

If it looks like a duck, walks like a duck, and sounds like a duck, then it must be a duck. Familiar with that? If we can identify an object by its actions and appearance, let me pose a simple, inverted question to you. What should you expect from a sinner? Do I really need to say the answer? When you decide to get married, I suggest sometime before you actually do that you sit down and really let it sink in what this really means. When you get married, you are going to be sinned against by your spouse. Your spouse's sin will become a reality in your life. It's like you're inheriting someone else's sin as if it is your own. But, it won't be quite like your own because your sin is a part of who you are and it's been with you forever, so you're used to it. It doesn't really bother you. You probably hardly know it's there if at all. On the other hand, the sin of the person you're marrying is going to drive you crazy. So, take the time to prepare for this mentally. It's not some ten-step program you have to go through. Just fully know and accept this as a way of life. At this point, don't worry about the specifics of what your spouse is going to do because you can't figure that out and it really doesn't matter anyway. You'll see in due time. Just make sure you're rock solid with the idea of how your life is about to change. People, no matter who they are, will fail you, hurt you, and let you down. Sometimes, they will do it intentionally. On the other hand, people will misunderstand you, be genuinely hurt by it, and swear up and down you did it with malicious intent. In order to handle and navigate all of this conflict and misunderstanding that'll happen between the two, there's a Scripture that pretty much sums it up for me. It's a passage I merely referenced earlier, but I'll spell it out this time around. Peter instructed his audience, "Above all, love each other deeply because love covers over a multitude of sins [I Peter 4:8]." What Peter says here to the family of churches spread throughout Pontus, Galatia, Cappadocia, Asia, and Bithynia is pretty self-explanatory. True love covers over the many sins your spouse will commit against you. This means that God's love for me is larger than I can ever imagine. In the rest of this section, I want to cover three practical concepts that flows from this love that Peter is talking about. The sooner you get a grip on these, the better off you'll both be.

Communication

Did you know that it is estimated that the average person says approximately sixteen thousand words per day? Here's the real shocker. This is true for both men and women. It's generally thought of as women being more talkative than men. Well, fellas, it's time to stop ragging on your wives for talking excessively. Regardless of who speaks more, with so many words escaping from the recesses of our mouths, you'd think we'd be great communicators. Unfortunately, that's not the case. Most of us need help in this area. Communication is an art, a craft that must be honed and mastered. Here are a couple of my observations over the years where men and women can each improve in our communication towards each other. Lastly, I will share a scripture reference to help provide a little direction for improvement.

The myth that men don't talk much or are less talkative than women has been around for ages. According to the statistic above, men speak rather frequently. Truthfully, men do talk quite a bit. We talk about business, sports, cars, and the like. So, we're okay there. But, what does need to change is the lack of vulnerability and the manner in which we speak to our significant other especially in times of conflict or disagreement. Generally speaking, we need to let our wives know what we are feeling. Forget about what the world tells you. Being able to express your feelings doesn't mean you're gay or less of a man. It means you're human like I tried to get you to see earlier. God created us with emotions too and we need to be able to express them. It's healthy. That's why most of us go from zero to anger, which is a secondary emotion, at a moment's notice. We don't know how to express our feelings in a healthy manner, that is if we know how to do so at all. Address the primary emotions of fear, hurt, and frustration that causes the anger by discussing how you feel. Furthermore men, not only don't talk to their wives as they should, but also are not very good at listening either. It's viewed as being cool as it's one of the popular jokes you can hear around the office. The brother of Jesus provides some words of wisdom for men that are useful when communicating with their wives. He says in James 1:19-20, "My dear brothers, take note of this: Everyone should be quick to listen, slow to speak and slow to become angry, for man's anger does not bring about the righteous life that God desires." These are words that I feel need no further explanation.

Many women don't understand or have the slightest idea what it means to be strong. They proclaim to be a strong woman, yet they're all up in your face, head on a swivel, finger pointing, giving their husbands grief. They belittle their husbands, call him names, and say that he's weak and can't handle a strong woman. Ladies, here's something to ponder. Simply because you have the sharper tongues and possess the ability to quickly belittle and malign doesn't make you right. And, because men are not interested in hearing all of that foolishness doesn't make us weak either. Let's look at this from a perspective women may be able to grasp a lot better. God designed men physically stronger than women. Because a man can physically overpower and beat you, doesn't make it right. Likewise, because you don't want to be treated that way doesn't make you weak either. Let me continue to enlighten you. That type of behavior exhibited by women is not being strong; it's disgraceful and disrespectful. In addition, you're simply embarrassing yourself. This behavior is evidence of the fact that some man has hurt you in the past. Or, it was modeled for you and passed down to you from another woman such as your mother. Now, the women feel as though they have a right to treat every male with malice and contempt going forward. Once again, that's not strength; that's a sign of weakness because you allowed someone else to change you into something worse. Being a strong woman is a woman who has endured through many storms without losing the goodness of her character. Jesus weathered many bad situations from those around Him (the sins of the entire world – you can't get any worse than that), yet He didn't let any of it alter His good character. There's a scripture in the Bible that talks about spiritual men strengthening one another using the imagery of iron sharpening iron. Why is iron able to sharpen iron? Well, it's because in the mix of all of the friction, colliding, and abrasive rubbing against another like object, it won't relinquish or give away any of its strength, become brittle, or collapse under the pressure. In case you haven't figured it out by now. Women, you will never win your husbands over this way; you'll only push them farther away.

With all of the bad communication practices, it's no wonder we have a difficult time getting along with one another. Here is a simple concept to apply to our conversations with your spouse. "Let your conversation be always full of grace, seasoned with salt, so that you may know how to answer everyone [Colossians 4:6]." Paul offers some words of wisdom to the Christians in Colossae in regards to speaking with unbelievers. I think they are befitting no matter who we are speaking with. We should take exception to heed these words especially when speaking with our spouses during times of conflict. He advises them to let their conversation be always full of grace. In other words, he's telling them that their speech should be pleasant, delightful, kind, uplifting, and loving so that it may be received with favor.

What I really wanted to highlight is the phrase that follows – **seasoned with salt**. Salt had multiple uses in the Bible but was primarily used for seasoning and as a preservative, uses that we still benefit from today.

Have you ever sat in a restaurant at a meal ready to chow down? Upon taking your first bite; the meal tasted rather bland. It just didn't have the flavor you were expecting it to have. That can be rather disappointing especially if it was your favorite dish or you were down right hungry. Despite this letdown, all hope is not lost as you reach for the salt shaker to sprinkle just the right amount of salt over the surface. You mix it up through and through over the entire plate to make certain you worked it in. You lift up the fork and open wide. Mmm mmm! It sure tastes good, doesn't it? You've spiced up your meal, given it new life with just a little bit of salt. You don't have to send the meal back for it to be disposed of in the garbage.

In the same fashion, our conversations should have the same effect on our relationship as the salt had on the meal. Our conversations should act as a preservative and bring new flavor to the relationship. When we speak harshly during our times of conflict, we are essentially destroying the relationship, making it fit only to be thrown away in the trash. Essentially, that's what happens to a couple that continues on this path; they end up filing for a divorce. Our poorly placed words make it even harder to recover from what you're in conflict about in the first place. Speak in such a way as to preserve your bond allowing it to have new life. I am a firm believer that the hard things you have to say sometimes can definitely be said. It's just a matter of how you go about saying them (Ephesians 4:15). Remember, how good that bland meal was after you seasoned it with salt. Conversations that are full of flavor provide great experiences for the couple involved.

Now, let's look at another perspective regarding communicating positively during conflicts. Thought we were done speaking about communicating, huh? Well, not! It's such an important aspect in any relationship; it just seems imperative to discuss in more detail in relation to marriage. In an episode of Focus on the Family titled *Recognizing Your Son's Need for Respect* aired on July 20, 2017, Emerson Eggerichs made an interesting statement. Although the broadcast was geared towards mothers communicating respectfully towards their sons, it easily applies to married couples as well. Just like he mentioned in the broadcast, it's a male/female thing, so it applies to parent/child relationships, married couples, and any other cross gender relationship. Emerson said,

> "And we know in marriage, the whole joke is that women tend to be empathy-oriented, but men are solution-oriented. Men think in terms of solution. They try to help by solving it. Well, you can reverse that with your son and ask him, how is he gonna solve this problem? Appeal to him to solve the problem. 'You're an honorable young man. This is

unacceptable, I'm sure to you and to me. How can you solve this?' Rather than telling him to solve it, ask him and watch what happens."

I found this statement interesting when I heard it because it reminded me of something similar I was thinking a year earlier that I jotted down in my notes for this book. We know these simple facts about each other, men and women that is, and yet, we are unlikely to speak to each other in a way that appeals to our God-given nature; the way He designed us. Putting this into practice, I'm sure we'd get better responses from each other and connect with each other more in the process. The point Emerson was trying to get across to mothers in regards to their sons is that you respect the spirit of a man, but not the bad behavior. You can't confront your son as you would your daughter. Elsewhere, he also mentioned that women, in regards to confronting men, feel they need to talk in terms of disrespect and contempt, then up it if he's not performing as she desires. Consequently, he'll only close off, shut down, and feel shame or feel like a failure. Ultimately, you'll lose his heart. This is no more different than if a father shows harshness and anger while confronting his daughter. She'll feel he hates her. She may start performing at his desired level, but in a similar fashion, he'll lose her heart.

In times of conflict, here's what you need to remember. Words do hurt. Whoever coined the phrase sticks and stones may break my bones but words will never hurt me was smoking crack. The Bible has plenty of warnings about what we say and how we say it. Harmful words can sink deep into the depth of our being and we remember those words for a very long time. So, watch what you say especially during times of conflict. When things start to get heated, it's better to take a break, calm down, then come back later to discuss than to say something you'll both regret later. Men and women fight differently. Women fight with words and men fight physically. And I bet you'll never guess where we're most vulnerable with each other? We're most vulnerable where the other is the strongest.

With the harsh words and bad things we can say, you may get the other person to do what you want them to do, but you'll damage the relationship. People are notorious for guarding their hearts. You don't want to lose your spouse's heart. This goes hand in hand with what I was saying earlier to speak in such a way as to preserve the relationship. I'll say it again, "Don't lose his or her heart." Women, in most cases, you definitely have the upper hand in verbal warfare, not to say that men aren't verbally abusive because we are. I know I've said my fair share of things I should not have said. But, I want to leave the women with another quote from Emerson. He said, "When a wife is respectful to her husband, he softens, moves towards you, and connects. Isn't that what you want?" (Eggerichs)

And finally, something I recently realized that I think everyone should consider. As I look at the cross, I realized that people aren't motivated to change through being manipulated, belittled, or controlled, but through love, grace, patience, and compassion (Romans 2:4). If you're not familiar with the cross of Christ, this is something you don't want to miss out on.

Forgiveness

Two sinful people trying to coexist together – that's a recipe for you-know-what's about to hit the fan. Now, I'm not so naïve to think that as long as you two live together that the two of you won't say or do something to hurt each other especially during times of conflict. I'm also not so naïve to think that some of those pains inflicted on each other won't be done with explicit intent. So, I'd be remorse and have to admit this book wouldn't be worth a dollar if I didn't remind you of something we all know about and must strive to become experts in providing. What I'm referring to is forgiveness. It's one of the things that make us most like God when we do it. It's liberating for both sides especially the one who forgives. It's necessary for every relationship if the two parties are to remain close and grow closer. It is especially pertinent in a marriage because you'll have ample opportunity to put it into practice.

Together As One

To be honest, I know a thing or two about not extending forgiveness. The story that comes to my mind so vividly regarding this has to do with the relationship with my dad. Even though I wrote briefly about this in my first book, my lack of forgiveness so fits the occasion that it would seem sinful not to use it. Without going into much detail on what he did to me as it is about my side that needs emphasizing, but I do need to paint the picture sort to speak to deliver the full effect. After my ninth birthday, my dad kidnapped me from his mother's house and brought me to live with him in Las Vegas, Nevada. He abused and fought me like I was a grown man for the entire time he had me beginning with the very first day we arrived in Vegas. Instead of building me up into a confident man, he destroyed me, taking away any confidence, strength, and signs of manhood away from me. Well, after all of this was behind me and I was living back with my mother, I never forgave him. For a good portion in my early years, I began avoiding the topic altogether. I wouldn't talk about him or what he put me through. Being his namesake, I eventually dropped the Jr II suffix from my name because it reminded me of him too much. As a consequence of not dealing with the issue and forgiving him, it ate at me as the years went by. Then, by the time I reached adulthood, I had grown to hate and despise him so much. I had so much hatred for him that I had said and thought on plenty occasions that I would kill him if we ever met and he disrespected me again. The even more twisted part to it was that I wanted to choke him out eye to eye so that he knew who was killing him and the reason why. I thought shooting him or something quick was too good for him after what he had done to me. And to put the final twist on it, I felt justified in the way I felt towards him because of what he did to me as a child.

As you can see, withholding forgiveness will eat you alive and do absolutely nothing to the object you hold the grudge against. It is truly a poison to the person withholding it. When I became a disciple of Jesus in July of 2000, I realized that was the biggest issue I had to deal with in my life and the one that had affected me the most. Learning to forgive him – and forgive in general – is one of the lessons I'm most grateful to God for teaching me to this very day. It definitely wasn't something that came together instantaneously but was a long grueling process that probably took the first three years of being a Christian to get to a place where I didn't have to keep revisiting it over and over. All of those years of holding it in made it even more difficult when the time came to deal with it.

You know the truth of the matter is that people hate admitting they've been hurt by another. It means being vulnerable, which is something else that's hated. Here's an exercise for you. Mention the word in a room full of people indicating their participation and watch how fast the room clears. For the few brave souls who possess the propensity to be vulnerable in front of others, take note of all the weird looks or the subtle whispering he or she will get in response. So, when we're hurt, human nature's tendency is to avoid or deny anything ever happened. You can easily identify the mentality. Try talking to someone you know you've offended about the offense. If you get a repetitive amount of quickly spoken brushed off statements like "That's okay," "No harm done," and "It's all good." And, if his or her body language seems to communicate that they want to scamper away very quickly from the conversation, you likely have someone who doesn't want to admit being hurt.

Forgiveness is not avoidance or denial of incident. People avoid or deny because it gives the impression that the incident will go away. But when someone really hurts you, hurts you deeply, or continuously, it's not going to go away. You may try to avoid it, play it off, or act as though it didn't hurt you, but it stays with you in your heart. You may just end up avoiding the person who hurt you and that's not forgiveness at all. And, how are you going to just deny something happening that really did? That's just nuts. Acknowledge the hurt, deal with it, and extend forgiveness. Forgiveness also is not taking shots to even the playing field – to make the offender feel your pain sort to speak. This is called revenge. One of my wives swore up and down that she was so forgiving, but each time I went to her to apologize for a wrong I had done, every time she yelled at me and brought stuff up that had absolutely nothing to do with anything that occurred. She never said I forgive you not even once. And quite naturally, I never felt forgiven by her for anything. You see, when you take a shot at your offender to get even, the opportunity for true forgiveness flies out the window and it's gone forever. When you have the opportunity to get back at the offender and you don't take it, but extend forgiveness, that's true forgiveness. Just think of how God forgives Christians through Jesus Christ. He doesn't send us to hell for a week or so, pulls us out, then says, "I forgive you." We miss out on the punishment part altogether. He doesn't make us feel even a miniscule amount of the grief and pain we've made Him feel all of our lives. Even as Christians, we still cause a lot of grief in our pitiful attempts at striving to be righteous. He doesn't avoid or deny our offenses against Him. He lays everything out there bare for us to see and He even offers forgiveness before we even know it exists or we need it.

    In a marriage that's in danger, there's usually fault that's on both sides. On a less serious note, even in the individual conflicts, it's not always a one-sided affair. In marriages that are in danger, a wall has been built between the couple. This wall has been built over a long duration of time due to unresolved conflicts, which can be a continually nagging trait in the partner. You can say that each stone in the wall represents each unresolved conflict. From behind this wall is where each party stands his or her ground and wages war tossing grenades over the wall at the spouse who has now become the enemy, at least in the couple's minds. Contrary to what we may feel at times that wall can come down and be destroyed if both parties are willing participants. Sometimes the heart of one or both has become too hard and they don't want to work on it.

> [3]"Why do you look at the speck of sawdust in your brother's eye and pay no attention to the plank in your own eye? [4]How can you say to your brother, 'Let me take the speck out of your eye,' when all the time there is a plank in your own eye? [5]You hypocrite, first take the plank out of your own eye, and then you will see clearly to remove the speck from your brother's eye."
>
> (Matthew 7:3-5)

Because of human nature, our fallen human nature to be more precise, we have too much of a tendency to see what the other person is doing wrong. And, that's pretty typical of every human relationship. But Jesus clearly says in the above passage that we must start with ourselves if we want to help improve any relationship we are in. We must take a hard look at ourselves and remove the stones from our side of the wall. This is so true and obvious because the fact is --- we can only take responsibility for and change ourselves; we have no power to change the other person. Yet, this is so difficult to do. We can become so concerned about what the other person is doing on his or her side of the wall. Or, if you have an extremely self-righteous or manipulative person for a spouse, this will make it extremely tempting to not want to do anything about your side of the wall. Believe me, I know; I've been down the pit a couple times before. In an episode of Focus on the Family titled "Forgiveness," aired on March 22, 2017, Dr. Gary Chapman provided three excellent biblical principles for tearing the wall down on your side. The first of Dr. Chapman's principles comes from the following passage.

> [23]Search me, God, and know my heart; test me and know my anxious thoughts. [24]See if there is any offensive way in me, and lead me in the way everlasting.
>
> (Psalm 139:23-24)

The first principle is to **identify your own failures**. As you can see from the psalm, the psalmist asks God to search his heart as only the one, true God can. Let's not forget, He knows us far better than we know ourselves. He wanted God to search his heart due to his anxious thoughts to see if there was any fault in him. And not for God's benefit, but for his own so that he may be shown and led in the way that's right. You know, sometimes the cause of a lot of our anxiety is due to our guilty conscience because of things we've done wrong. I think identifying our own failures is an essential key to getting on the path to reconciliation. Hence, it is the first step in the process. Fallen human nature is not very good at seeing its own failures and accepting responsibility. Truth be told, we suck at it. We have multiple ways of deflecting responsibility for our failures in any situation. For example, you bring a fault committed against you to the person that's guilty in order to reconcile. Instead of simply accepting responsibility and apologizing so that the two of you can move on, he or she begins rambling on about the good he or she had done for you or even more disturbing; they point out how they aren't as bad as some other person. These tactics don't make anything better. It only adds insult to injury. When this was done to me, on a few occasions I just felt like smacking them right on the spot. The guilty never think about the fact that the good they've done or this other supposedly worse person isn't the issues at hand. We really need to get better at accepting responsibility for our own faults when necessary.

> [9]If we confess our sins, he is faithful and just and will forgive us our sins and purify us from all unrighteousness.
>
> (I John 1:9)

Dr. Chapman's second principle is to **confess your sins to God**. This step has three prongs to completing this step. We must first admit that what we identified as our failures in the incident is wrong. Dr. Chapman made a great additional point when discussing this part. I think this aspect makes it even harder for those who have been wronged initially in the incident to admit their wrong. He said that we try to excuse our sin based on the other person's sin. In other words, because they wronged me first, I have the right to wrong them, thus making me justified in anything I do in retaliation. But, this is not true. Wrong is wrong. This is so evident in arguments and fights. This is so interwoven in human nature. The second is to admit that Jesus Christ paid the penalty for my sin. And, lastly accept the forgiveness that's already been provided just for you.

> [16]So I strive always to keep my conscience clear before God and man.
> (Acts 24:16)

The last principle of tearing down the wall on your side is to **confess your sin to the other person**. In my opinion, this one is probably the most challenging one to do especially as I mentioned earlier if the other person you must confess to is of the self-righteous mindset. They'll act like they have no wrong in the matter and project this air of superiority right in front of your face. It can be very tempting to bypass this step especially if you know the other person's character and are anticipating how they'll act. I definitely have struggled with this as a couple of my ex-wives have been of the self-righteous type – one extremely self-righteous and manipulative on top of that. A particular incident recent to this writing, I had to apologize. I knew it could potentially be a disaster as I was anticipating how she may respond out of her self-righteousness as I had seen it enough times before. I knew I had a few choice morsels for her to chew on if she blasted me this time during my apology. I was ready to fire back at her and this would have resulted in nothing being accomplished and God not being glorified on my part. So, what got me through it was that I had to focus on the fact that it was between me and God. I was doing what God asked me to do. When you can really get to that point, it takes the other person out of the equation, then it really doesn't matter how the other person responds. The truth of the matter is that you don't know how the other person will respond, but that's not the point. You do your part to, in Dr. Chapman's terms; tear the wall down on your side. In doing so, you clear your conscience before God by owning your own fault in the matter and not responding negatively to the other person's negative response. Thus, you glorify God by doing what's right. However, the other person responds to your apology is not a reflection on you, but on him or her. Lastly, as I did in this particular situation, sometimes it doesn't hurt to have a little accountability on your part as in a third person, a good friend to be there to help you through just in case you're tempted to go down that wrong path.

As a final note to bring it home, Dr. Chapman noted that these three principles must be done continuously. You must become good at them because as you do, you as a couple will begin to flow seamlessly through your times of conflict. I witness this in the relationship of my married friends. This will prevent that wall from becoming too big if being built at all. Allowing that wall to become too big, apathy, callous, avoidance kicks in, thus closeness ceases to exist.

Grace & Mercy

Just as forgiveness is a necessity of marriage, grace and mercy are a necessity too. As a matter of fact, grace and mercy are running buddies to forgiveness. I mentioned earlier that some sins travel in packs. Well, the same holds true for spiritual virtues and these three definitely form a pack. So, what is grace and mercy anyway? Depending on the family you grew up in, if very religious, you may have heard your mother unexpectedly blurt out an inimitable session of praise to God for His grace after some satisfactory occurrence. If not religious, you may not have heard them much if at all. Either way, you may not know what either of the words mean. Or, you might think they are one in the same. In reality, they aren't. They're very different. On one occasion, I heard a definition that was very simplistic. The person said, "Grace means getting something we don't deserve and mercy means not getting something we do deserve." For one hearing this for the very first time and not having much knowledge about God, these would be vague because it leaves it too open for misinterpretation. For instance, when you hear that mercy is not getting something you deserve, if you're of the positive mindset, the real meaning won't come across as it should. You're liable to think "Why didn't I get what I deserved?" and be upset about it. So, let me expound on this from the perspective of what God does for believers in Jesus Christ. Mercy is the fact that God doesn't rightfully punish believers as their sins deserve. Hence, we're not getting something we deserve. Grace is the fact that God blesses believers like they were royalty. Hence, we're getting something we don't deserve. I think it's from these two qualities coming together that true forgiveness is achieved. For example, someone apologizes to you for a wrong. You relinquish all rights to get even in any way; and you follow through on that. Along the way to forgiving him or her, you may express your pain, which is fine, but you don't do it in a retaliatory way to make him or her feel your pain. That is wrong too. After you tell him or her that "I forgive you" which is good to say, you don't hold a grudge against the person. It's as though the wrong never happened. You regard that person as you would any other – with dignity and respect. This is how God wants us to treat one another especially if you're claiming to be following Jesus because this is how He treats us. It's continuous. Let's take a look at a Scripture before we go any further.

> [21]Then Peter came to Jesus and asked, "Lord, how many times shall I forgive my brother when he sins against me? Up to seven times?" [22]Jesus answered, "I tell you not seven times, but seventy-seven times."
> (Matthew 18:21-22)

What prompted Peter's question was that Jesus had just told the disciples how to handle a situation where your brother sins against you. What Peter asks, I think can be in the hearts of all of us at times. I think Peter, knowing some of his other antics throughout the Bible, was indicative of him trying to justify himself and find out the absolute minimal amount of times he had to forgive before he took things into his own hands. But, look at Jesus' response to Peter. His response comes from a heart that is full of the grace and mercy that we've been talking about. He calls Peter higher by calling him to not be so limiting in his willingness to forgive. He calls Peter to continually forgive. It's a continual cleansing modeled after the blood of the Lamb. Jesus's blood continually cleanses those who have come to Him. In marriages, I think some people get tired of forgiving; they reach a point then decide no more. They stop forgiving, that is if they were even doing it to begin with because some really don't. Just like Jesus' point to Peter, one who is full of grace and mercy will continue to forgive over and over again. I don't want to make it seem like this is going to be easy all of the time. Because it's not. Depending on how deep the offense, how long it's been carried, and how frequent the offense, you may have to work at it. You may have to forgive that same offense continually every time you want to get bitter about it until you no longer have to do it anymore. Most importantly, don't forget, you need God to get you there. So, pray. And pray some more! Grace, mercy, and forgiveness are not natural human characteristics. So, rely on God. One more thing I'd like to point out in Jesus' response to Peter, He never said anything about an apology. He just said to forgive. An apology is not a prerequisite to forgiveness. God extended the world forgiveness long before those who responded appropriately ever knew they even needed forgiveness. Anyone who's ever had to work through some deep hurts without the offender's acknowledgment knows that it takes an immense amount of grace, mercy, and God's strength to get through. And, I must point out that simply because an apology is not required for one to forgive you is not an excuse to not apologize. If you're intentionally doing that, it's a reflection of your wicked heart and that's just flat out wrong for not taking responsibility. True forgiveness extends from a heart full of grace and mercy.

God's Expectations

Roles of the Husband and Wife

An article on the Scientific American website opens up with the following paragraphs regarding train derailments. "A massive derailment of an Amtrak train in Philadelphia claimed the lives of at least six people and injured another 140 people on Tuesday night, just one of a handful of fatal train accidents this year. Derailments are by and large the leading cause of train crashes in the United States. Between 2001 and 2010, of the 58,299 train accidents that occurred, 54,889 were train derailments. That's a staggering 94 percent. Officials have not yet determined the cause of last night's Amtrak crash, but historically, broken rails and welds are the most common cause of train derailments. They account for more than 15 percent of derailments, according to data from the Federal Railroad Administration." (Tracy) The article cites that the main cause of train derailments are problems with the rails. Furthermore, the article goes on to say that they are more than twice as likely to be the reason for a derailment as any of the other causes on the list such as track geometry, bearing failure, and broken wheels. These are the only two objects that are responsible for supporting and guiding the entire train on the journey to its destination. So, obviously if anything is wrong with either of the rails, it'll have a detrimental effect on the train such as derailment. In the same regard, I believe that a marriage is synonymous to a train and its rails. Just as each of the rails has to fulfill its role of supporting its side of the train and providing a stable mechanism for the train to travel on, a marriage has roles that must be fulfilled by its respective role players. If the husband is consistently not leading and considering his wife or the wife is consistently not submitting and respecting her husband, it will derail the marriage and set it off course as the train is derailed when there's an issue with either of its rails. God in His infinite wisdom made man and woman very different. We can't help but to be as different as we are. If you think about it, it makes sense why we're so different. How did God create the two? He made the two from the one. He made Eve directly from a piece He extracted from Adam. This means that the characteristics from the one was split between the two. It's impossible for us to be similar. This also means we're really never going to completely understand each other either. This fits in perfectly with God's design for marriage of the man and woman joining together as one. He made us different so that man and woman could fulfill the roles that He designed for us in marriage and in life. Next, I would like to discuss some aspects of those roles to give an idea of some things to expect and some ways in which we struggle in fulfilling those roles.

Wives

Ladies, I'm just going to put this out here knowing that the majority of you aren't going to like this. The fact is that you were created for man. So, all of the jokes about women are better than men and God realized His mistake with Adam so He perfected it by creating Eve can stop. Neither of us is better than the other. At the fall, both Adam and Eve sinned together; therefore, they fell out of God's grace together. Remember that marriage reflects the relationship that Christ has with the church. The role modeled after Christ has already been taken, so there's only one vacancy left – the church. And, I'm sure I don't have to tell you that the church was created for Christ and not the other way around. So, if anything, you came second because you were created for man as his help mate (Genesis 2:18).

Now, I know there are many of you out there who are extremely successful in your careers even reaching the ranks of top executives in high profile corporations. Women who are highly intelligent, determined, strong-willed, motivated, accustomed to calling their own shots, have single-handedly raised kids while holding down a nine to five, and those who have been around the block with the best of them and have held their own. And, that's great. I commend you from the bottom of my heart. But, if you get married, you are no longer calling the shots. You are to be submissive to your husband. He is your leader and you are the subordinate. It doesn't matter how smart you are or think you are over him. It doesn't matter if you're bringing home more money than him. It doesn't matter how well you was doing before you met him. It's his God-given right that he has authority over you just like parents have a God-given authority over their children. And, this doesn't mean that you idly and passively sit by watching him until he makes a mistake, then you're all in his face spitefully saying, "Well, you're the man!" Leadership does not mean that your husband is responsible for doing everything. Please refer back to Genesis 2:18 and study out what *helper suitable for him* means. You are an equal participant and you are to help and support him in order for the both of you to be successful.

Roles of the Husband and Wife

> ¹Wives, in the same way be submissive to your husbands so that, if any of them do not believe the word, they may be won over without words by the behavior of their wives, ²when they see the purity and reverence of your lives. ³Your beauty should not come from outward adornment, such as braided hair and the wearing of gold jewelry and fine clothes. ⁴Instead, it should be that of your inner self, the unfading beauty of a gentle and quiet spirit, which is of great worth in God's sight. ⁵For this is the way the holy women of the past who put their hope in God used to make themselves beautiful. They were submissive to their own husbands, ⁶like Sarah, who obeyed Abraham and called him her master. You are her daughters if you do what is right and do not give way to fear.
>
> (I Peter 3:1-6)

In Peter's admonishing the wives to submit to their husbands, he provides a model for them to do so. He says, "…in the same way," which points back to his discussion in chapter two verses 13 through 25 where he commands everyone to submit yourselves to every authority and slaves to masters. The Greek word for submissive, transliterated *upotassomenai*, means to place or rank under, to subject, to obey. This meaning gives the impression that it is something you continuously decide to do. It involves the active surrendering of the will. You yield your will to that of another. In this case, wives yield to your husbands. Now, this doesn't mean that you don't share your input, thoughts, or ideas. This is contradicting to human nature. It's totally contradictory to this women's liberation, women empowerment, I don't need a man movement you see in today's time. For disciples of Jesus, this is synonymous with becoming a part of the church. You either subject yourself to Jesus – make Him Lord of your life – or you're not a part of the church or have any part of Him no matter what you do. And, don't look to Him to be your Savior either. Now, those living in contrast to God will ridicule this as though it's absolute absurdity and will heavily contend with this teaching of submitting to your husband to the ends of the Earth. But on the contrary, they teach and encourage women to engage in submitting their bodies to any man outside of the marital context to have authority over their bodies for the momentary pleasures of sex. They do this willingly without any lasting commitment or any responsibility to them whatsoever for what happens afterwards. Women come up pregnant from random sexual encounters, diseases are transmitted, and this continues to encourage men to treat and view you as mere objects. And, women are applauding this as some kind of women empowerment or form of discovery of themselves. Now, you tell me, which teaching is absolute absurdity. This sentiment towards this teaching is not a recent ordeal. Feminists of the 1970s criticized the Donna Reed Show arguing that the show promoted submissiveness among housewives. In other words, they felt it made women look weak. An excerpt from an article puts it this way. "Feminists criticized the show for its perpetuation of the image of the subservient, content-to-stay-home wife, although Reed, a working mother of four who became associated with her housewife character, took umbrage during a 1979 interview with the

Associated Press: 'I played a strong woman who could manage her family. That was offensive to a lot of people.'" (Gilbert)

Along with his command for wives to submit to their husbands, Peter provides some insight into what's considered true beauty – the secret to really winning a man's heart. Being that there were Christian women who were married to men who weren't followers of Jesus, the way Peter advised them to win their husbands over to Jesus was through the purity and dignity of their lives. This is a very powerful statement. This is what's attractive to an unbelieving world. It gets their attention because it is so abstract and different from what they're used to. Your external beauty may catch our eyes, but it is your internal beauty that'll capture our hearts. Too many women put entirely too much work on beautifying the outside and pay no attention to the inside – the most valuable part. They decorate and embellish themselves outwardly to make themselves more attractive. They adorn themselves with extravagant jewelry and fine clothing. They religiously maintain biweekly appointments to keep their hair tight and their nails in pristine condition. They even beautify themselves with manufactured items that they can't grow naturally on their own resulting in an industry where billions of dollars a year is spent on hair weaves, fake eyelashes, and press-on fingernails. Some women think that their man is so blessed solely because she is considered to be beautiful while they're overall character is rude, disdainful, loud, disrespectful, contemptuous, cynical, overly critical, bitter, domineering, head on a swivel all up in your man's face out of control. If any combination of these terms or any like them describes your primary persona towards your husband, then you are pretty much a nightmare and a pain in your husband's behind to deal with (Proverbs 12:4; 21:9, 19; 27:15-16). I'll tell you one thing, that thick mascara, those expensive hair extensions, and those high hills you're wearing don't mean a thing to your husband when you're verbally assaulting him. And, I'm willing to bet that he wishes that part of you would come to a quick demise, that is, if he hasn't lost all respect for you altogether. Over the course of my life, I personally have seen extremely gorgeous women but would steer clear of because they were so foul personality wise. And, it's not because I'm weak; it's because I don't want to deal with all of that drama when I come home. A woman should bring her husband peace. It's a war out in the world and I don't want to come home to fight another battle for little to no reason at all. The world glorifies these obnoxious drama-riddled women. They exalt them and give them a platform to perform on in shows like Bridezillas and those Real Housewives series. I have found women who wasn't probably the most attractive who possessed a genuine demeanor that exudes peace, honor, and self-respect to be very attractive than someone who is drop-dead gorgeous and totally out of control.

A good man – he wants to be your hero, your king. And, women you do play a big role in that too. Do you make him feel like he's your hero, your king? I've heard my share of sayings from women that it takes a real man to handle a real woman to there's not a lot of good men out there. Well, it takes a real woman to make a real man feel like a king. And from my perspective, real women are pretty doggone scarce too. Are you his biggest supporter, the CEO of his fan club? When he falls off the tracks, do you criticize, scold, and point out everything he's done wrong? Or, do you encourage him, lift him up, and help him get back on track? Do you provide constructive criticism and challenge him genuinely with his best interest at heart in order to help him be the best he can be? Do you inspire and dream with him? Do you pursue him intimately in the bedroom or are you one of those who only provide sex out of duty? That is, if you even provide it at all. Yes, wives, your husbands love it when you pursue him sexually. Want to really make him feel kingly, that's one way to do it. The out of duty loving just isn't quite the same. We'll take it, but it doesn't quite make us feel like your hero or that you have a desire for us. It doesn't reach our hearts. Yes, I know some of you have past trauma that hinders you in this area, but just like a husband who doesn't connect with his wife emotionally, you have to realize that this is a problem and seek help to resolve this issue for the benefit of your marriage and you too.

Women, we aren't quite finished talking about submission to your husbands just yet. There's another aspect of it that we're missing and it's just as important. "Wives, submit to your husbands, as is fitting in the Lord [Colossians 3:18]." Paul wrote the same thing to the church in Colossae as Peter did to his audience, but with a noticeably added stipulation. As fitting in the Lord is what Paul notes to his female audience. The Greek word for the phrase "as is fitting" means to be fit, be proper, suitable, becoming. Quite naturally, this means that you are to follow, submit to your husband in as much as he is following Jesus Christ. You see, your ultimate allegiance is to the Lord and you never disobey Him to follow your husband. You are not called to blindly follow your husband, especially into sin. That's foolishness. But, I think that some women think that's the case or they haven't figured out how to appropriately deal with the circumstances when they arise. I was reading a post a user submitted to an article about this very topic we're discussing. She clearly thought that women submitting to their husbands was foolish and unreasonable and said that she couldn't support a God who would set up such an imbalance in a relationship. Her basis for such was due to the fact that her father continuously made poor decisions which led to horrendous consequences. Her mother, who was intellectually superior and a better decision maker, in the name of submission to her husband continually bit her tongue and never challenged her husband on his poor decisions. Another scenario she brought up was when a man decides to be incestuous and forbids his wife to tell anyone. In the former case, her mother should have respectfully challenged her husband on the decisions he was making. In the latter, you just have to call sin for what it is and let someone know. I know most times things are easier said than done. I say that because I don't know the character of each of these men and how hard it was to approach them. I have my ideas, but for each of these women to submit to each of these circumstances without as much as a challenge, they are falling short on other aspects of Scripture that they shouldn't. There are clearly examples of this in the Bible as well. Abraham and Sarah quickly come to mind. Upon becoming fearful for his life due to the beauty of his wife Sarah, he trusted in himself instead of God and lied twice, once in Egypt and the other in the Gerar (Genesis 12:10-13; 20:1-3). He instructed her to tell the kings there that she was his sister instead of his wife, which wasn't totally untrue. By doing so, he ended up endangering his wife by putting her in a situation to be defiled. God had to personally step in both times to rescue her. Another example that comes to mind is that of another lying couple, Ananias and Sapphira (Acts 5:1-10). They lied about the amount of money they received from the sale of their land. It was contribution time and they sold some of their property to give. They acted as though they gave all of the money from the sale when in reality they held some of the money back. God killed them both for their pride and deceitfulness. Had Sapphira spoken up and refused to go along with the lie, she may have very well not only saved her life, but her husband's as well. In both situations, the women should have spoken up and clearly refused to go along with their husband's plan; they knew it was clearly wrong, a disobedience to God.

Even though husbands are designated by God as the leaders of their wives and households, we are still human just like you. Like you, we are still sinners and still prone to sin. Just because we are appointed as the leader doesn't mean we are perfect and you shouldn't expect us to be or hold us to a standard that you can't attain to yourself. The way I see it, this is the way God deemed for you to help keep us spiritually accountable. We're still tempted to do wrong and we make mistakes. And, notice the correlation between what Paul and Peter wrote in their respective letters. Peter explicitly emphasized behavior of the wife towards her husband, which was especially powerful in the conversion of unbelieving husbands. It's not a guarantee of a conversion, but it would be the key to a conversion. Although Paul doesn't make any particular distinctions between a believing and unbelieving husband or delves into any specific details or examples, in that one sentence, he still alludes to the wife's behavior towards her husband. She is to submit to her husband as he is appropriately following the Lord Jesus. The commonality between the two passages is the wife's behavior. What was the key ingredient for these women whether submitting to an unbelieving or a believing husband? Those women ultimately submitted themselves and hoped in God. In other words, women who trust God trust Him ultimately to meet their needs. This is what alleviates their fear. The more they trusted God directly correlated to the loss of fear. It was through their submission and reverence for Him that they could exude those same qualities towards their husbands and respectfully oppose when being led from the way of the Lord. This is what made them beautiful.

Let's change direction here for a moment to take a look at a woman who embodied a subservient behavior while acting with diligence, intellect, and honor even towards her foolish husband. The person I'm referring to is Abigail from the historical account of David, Nabal, and Abigail from I Samuel 25:1-44. For the sake of brevity, I won't include the entire story here, but you're welcome to take a break now to read it in its entirety or you can

Together As One

do so later. We will learn a little bit about the nature of men too as we observe David's initial reaction as the situation begins to unfold. In the beginning, we quickly find out that Nabal was a curmudgeon of a man. He was very wealthy, yet foolish and unruly, thus very hard to deal with. His wife Abigail was beautiful and intelligent. You see, Abigail had it going on. She was beautiful. She was smarter than her husband; yet unlike some modern women, she didn't try to supersede her husband by trying to take his God-given role.

> [4]While David was in the desert, he heard that Nabal was shearing sheep. [5]So he sent ten young men and said to them, "Go up to Nabal at Carmel and greet him in my name. [6]Say to him: 'Long life to you! Good health to you and your household! And good health to all that is yours! [7]Now I hear that it is sheep-shearing time. When your shepherds were with us, we did not mistreat them, and the whole time they were at Carmel nothing of theirs was missing. [8]Ask your own servants and they will tell you. Therefore be favorable toward my young men, since we come at a festive time. Please give your servants and your son David whatever you can find for them.'" [9]When David's men arrived, they gave Nabal this message in David's name. Then they waited. [10]Nabal answered David's servants, "Who is this David? Who is this son of Jesse? Many servants are breaking away from their masters these days. [11]Why should I take my bread and water, and the meat I have slaughtered for my shearers, and give it to men coming from who knows where?"
>
> (I Samuel 25:4-11)

While hiding out from Saul, David heard that Nabal was shearing sheep. He sent some men to Nabal to ask for rations for him and his company as a show of favor. Previously, David and his men had done likewise by protecting Nabal's shepherds and sheep from raiders while they were grazing in nearby fields. Like your typical ingrate, Nabal flat out declined to provide David any assistance. He even went so far as to act as though he didn't even know who David was. Upon hearing Nabal's response, immediately, "David said to his men, 'Put on your swords (v13).'" I wonder what David was feeling at this point in time. More than likely, David was feeling very disrespected by Nabal. So much so that he was greatly moved to vengeance. He was going to kill Nabal and every male in his entire household. Here's a tidbit about men. Respect is monumental for men to live out our God-given roles. Disrespect is like our kryptonite; it drives us crazy mad whether it's real or perceived. You see how David responded at the lack of respect shown him by Nabal? Another thing that's probably not so obvious that may be affecting David as well is that his mentor Samuel just died (v1). Samuel was someone who believed in David and was someone who kept him spiritually-focused. With this lost, David may be feeling lost himself, unfocused, stuck, and unsure of any appropriate direction. Here's another tidbit about men. God made men passionate, with a need to conquer something significant, and a need to have someone to believe in them. That last one is especially an important one coming from the wife. Those qualities need to be driven in a godly way; otherwise, they'll be crippling to any man and especially hard to deal with in life. Men can become susceptible to bitterness, frustrations, and addictions when those characteristics aren't driven in a way God intended. Essentially, this is what keeps men from leading. Now, you may be wondering every man is definitely not passionate about conquering anything. I see the proof everyday as I have the luxury of coming home to see mine with his feet propped up on the coffee table playing video games instead of finding a job to help me with some bills. I know ladies that that kind of man does exist and it really is a crying shame. Remember, I just said those qualities need to be driven in a godly way or else. Also, I did say that God "made" men passionate. That's the key word there. He made men to rule over His entire creation (Genesis 1:26) so you better believe that takes passion. But, think about King David; he was a very passionate man. Better yet, think about Jesus. He is a passionate man. Not to mention, he is the mold from which all men were created. So, what happened you ask. That's simple. It's the work of sin. Sin degrades the quality of human nature as time continues. Some men may have had their spirit broken, let's say for example, by being abused as a child or being continually disrespected and degraded in his early years. On the other hand, some men may be enjoying their sin like the one who seem to can't get his feet off the coffee table to go find a job. Other men may be passive out of ignorance; they just don't realize it. More food for thought is the difference in personality types. A man can be passionate but it doesn't manifest itself in an aggressive way whereas in another, it might. This is no different than women who don't support and respect their husbands like they should. Surely God "made" women to do so, but many don't for some of the same reasons I mentioned above.

Now, let's center our attention on Abigail to see how the beauty of a woman manifests itself.

> [18]Abigail lost no time. She took two hundred loaves of bread, two skins of wine, five dressed sheep, five seahs of roasted grain, a hundred cakes of raisins and two hundred cakes of pressed figs, and loaded them on donkeys. [19]Then she told her servants, "Go on ahead; I'll follow you." But she did not tell her husband Nabal.
> (I Samuel 25:18-19)

Many people when they hear the word submissive, they think it means being passive or even that the submissive person is weak. But nothing could be farther from the truth. Upon hearing the deadly dilemma imputed to her household by her husband and understanding the consequences, Abigail displayed some serious assertiveness. She clearly knew her husband was wrong, so she quickly jumped to rectify the situation. She wasted no time loading up enough food to send out to David and his men. Without informing her husband, she sent the food on ahead and went out to meet David and his men.

> [23] When Abigail saw David, she quickly got off her donkey and bowed down before David with her face to the ground. [24] She fell at his feet and said: "My lord, let the blame be on me alone. Please let your servant speak to you; hear what your servant has to say. [25] May my lord pay no attention to that wicked man Nabal. He is just like his name – his name is Fool, and folly goes with him. But as for me, your servant, I did not see the men my master sent. [26] Now since the LORD has kept you, my master, from bloodshed and from avenging yourself with your own hands, as surely as the LORD lives and as you live, may your enemies and all who intend to harm my master be like Nabal. [27] And let this gift, which your servant has brought to my master, be given to the men who follow you. [28] Please forgive your servant's offense, for the LORD will certainly make a lasting dynasty for my master, because he fights the LORD's battles. Let no wrongdoing be found in you as long as you live.
>
> (I Samuel 25:23-28)

Upon meeting David, Abigail continues to display the beauty of a submissive woman. She approached David with a gentle and respectful demeanor that was sandwiched between a great deal of humility. She deflected the attention from her husband and took the blame for everything herself (v24, 25). In doing so, this was the first step in diffusing David's anger as it turned his attention away from the object of his anger. Using her intelligence and assertiveness, she avoided a devastating situation. She agreed with David that he was gravely disrespected all the while showing him the respect that he deserved. She averted David's anger even more and consequentially prevented him from using his power to take personal revenge (v32-34). In everything she did, Abigail embraced her God-given role. She didn't sit back and wait, gossip, go into hiding, nor criticize her husband. She displayed a great deal of discernment and acumen. She was nurturing, aggressive yet gentle, and very humble. After the disaster was avoided, she returned home and informed her husband of everything. And in that, she displayed patience and respect because she waited until the morning to tell him because when she arrived home he was in the middle of throwing a banquet and was drunk. So, the message wouldn't have set in at the time anyway. There was absolutely nothing passive about what Abigail did. Her actions captured David's heart hook line and sinker; and melted it completely. She has become one of my favorite women in the Bible and I completely understand why David sent for her to be his wife after he found out her husband had died (v39). I think I would have done the same. Spiritual men adore this kind of woman and will bend over backwards and go to the ends of the Earth for this type of woman. Women who constantly criticize, take control, and think they know it all aren't what godly men find attractive. Those types of women tend to be corrupt and very insecure.

God has provided an exceptional portrait of what a beautiful, submissive woman looks like in Proverbs 31:10-31. In her character, there aren't any signs of weaknesses or even a hint of the degradation of women. As a matter of fact, it's the polar opposite. She is honored, highly exalted, and shown for what she truly is – a pillar of strength and extremely invaluable. Here are some of the qualities that I see in this woman that makes her so noble and worthy of praise. She is reliable and trustworthy (v11). She is respectful and supportive of her husband and brings him peace (v12). Additionally, she is responsible (v14-15), shrewd and resourceful (v16), diligent (v17-18, 27), generous (v20), prepared (v21), wise and discerning (v26). Also, she's organized as she effectively manages the affairs of her home (v27), handles herself with dignity and self-respect (v25), and most importantly, she fears God (v30). Without this type of woman by his side, her husband would not have the respect of his peers (v23). And, he is fully aware of this fact and doesn't hesitate to take the opportunity to praise her and let her know her worth to him (v29). As I mentioned earlier, there's no mention of Eve's time with God in the creation account, but I like to think that this is what she looked like characteristically by the time she was brought to Adam.

In closing, the thing with marriage is that the more you get to know your spouse and can put yourself in the other person's shoes the better you'll be able to understand where they're coming from. In essence, it'll help you get through conflicts smoother and quicker. Like many other things in marriage, it's easier said than done. When you have two people adamantly determined to get their point across, it takes a conscious effort to step outside of yourself and leave your wants for a while to actively listen to the other person to try to understand his or her perspective. It takes practice. And, of course, some are better at this than others. I personally probably fit more in the "than others" category although I can probably say that I've grown in that area some over the years; and I can definitely say that I've turned to head in the right direction. So, that's what I want to do now – just a little bit – help you start down that path.

> [17]Obey your leaders and submit to their authority. They keep watch over you as men who must give an account. Obey them so that their work will be a joy, not a burden, for that would be of no advantage to you.
> (Hebrews 13:17)

This Scripture is most often thought of from the perspective of leadership in the church and rightly so because that's the context that it is written in. Over the years as a Christian, I began to see that it is applicable to marriages as well. Ladies, your husbands are your leaders. And God holds them accountable for you and the entire household. Can you imagine the potential for burden to not only be responsible for oneself, but for your wife and family too? There can be an extreme amount of pressure on a man's shoulders when facing critical decisions from the curve balls that life has a tendency of throwing one's way that will affect his entire family. Trying to think through multiple critical paths to determine outcomes and potential pitfalls to determine the best way to go for everyone can be strenuous at times. God designed us to be able to handle situations like that but it doesn't mean it's easy. This passage says that you should not add any extra burden to your husband, but you should be a joy for him to lead. And what I mean by this is your overall relationship with him. It's like I said earlier, a wife should bring her husband peace. Doing otherwise wouldn't be a benefit to you at all.

Husbands

Gentlemen, I want you to know this right off the bat because it's imperative that you get this. I don't want it to get lost amongst the other verbiage. Being that your role as the man in the marriage is modeled after that of Christ means that you're the head of the household, the leader. Here's what's important for you to know. In the relationship, the husband is called to sacrifice (die to self) more for the wife – like Christ did for the church or to make it more personal, for you. It's not that it doesn't go both ways in a marriage, the husband for the wife and the wife for the husband. That's the nature of the relationship. All of us Christians – men and women alike – died to ourselves when we came to Christ. But, the husband is called to the level of Christ, which means that the greater burden to love is on you (Ephesians 5:25-29). Think about it. Your role is modeled after Christ and

He gave up far more establishing the church than we did in converting to the church. He gave up the riches of being in heaven. He chose to be physically away from the Father. He gave up His glory to be found in the likeness of a lowly human being. He gave up His life and died. Not only did He die, but He died the most disgraceful death anyone could have died in His day and time. And because of that, He paid the ultimate sacrifice. He was completely separated from God in hell for three days because of our sin. In coming to the church, all we gave up was the sin that enslaved us and brought us death. So, what does that mean for you? Specifically, I have no idea, but it won't be without its challenges. It all depends on who you're married to and how bad Leah is when she shows up. This also means that some situations will probably arise and lean to your wife's favor that clearly should sway to yours. Yes, this will be totally and completely unfair. But that's the way it's designed. Once again, remember who your role is modeled after and what He did for you. He paid the price for your sins to keep you from being separated from God and burning for eternity. And, that wasn't fair to Him. I'm sharing this with you so you will know this up front and won't have to learn it the hard way – blindsided through trial and error until it finally clicks. And, to be honest with you, it may not really click until somebody either takes you aside to tell you after you've had a few quarrels with your spouse or it comes out as a reminder in the middle of a couples counseling session.

Leadership is not something to be reminiscent of a dictatorship, a hostile take-over, or a situation of a domineering, oppressive exertion of force where you've taken absolute control over someone's life. It's not to be characterized anything like the previously mentioned. That's how leadership in the world is characterized – forceful manipulation, my way or the highway, I'm the one in charge type of patronization. It wasn't until I came into contact with the Lord Jesus that I realized what leadership really was. He clearly refuted the above type of leadership methodology when teaching the Twelve (Matthew 20:25-28; Mark 10:42-45). Then, I also understood what was really meant by the expression, "You must learn to follow before you can lead." As a young adult, before I came to Christ, I probably wasn't trying to figure out stuff like that anyway. The qualities that it takes to follow are much more magnified and even more significant in a leadership role as it has a greater impact and a much farther reach than a subordinate role. A leader is responsible for the overall success and direction of the entity he is overseeing and each of his subordinates. I think there are three key characteristics that are imperative to changing your perspective on what a leader is – especially leading your wife and family. If you find yourself stuck thinking like the aforementioned characteristics, we're going to take a look at the life of Jesus Christ as He is the ultimate leader and He exemplified leadership qualities His entire life.

> ¹It was just before the Passover Feast. Jesus knew that the time had come for him to leave this world and go to the Father. Having loved his own who were in the world, he now showed them the full extent of his love. ²The evening meal was being served, and the devil had already prompted Judas Iscariot, son of Simon, to betray Jesus. ³Jesus knew that the Father had put all things under his power, and that he had come from God and was returning to God; ⁴so he got up from the meal, took off his outer clothing, and wrapped a towel around his waist. ⁵After that, he poured water into a basin and began to wash his disciples' feet, drying them with the towel that was wrapped around him.
>
> (John 13:1-5)

Now, let me take a brief moment to set the scene here. It was customary in those days to have one's feet washed upon arrival as a guest at one's home especially for a dinner. In those days, it was necessary because they didn't have the vast array of expensive footwear we possess today. All they had were sandals and those were some dusty roads they travelled mostly by foot. So, you can imagine how one would have looked arriving for dinner – clean from head to ankles, nothing but dust down below. Being that the dinner was already in the process of being served and their feet still needed washing, it's safe to assume that there wasn't a servant available for the evening and no one else was about to volunteer for the task. Now, I don't know about you but I couldn't imagine that their feet were the most pleasant things to wash. Shoot, I wouldn't wash many people's feet today outside of my own. With their meager footwear and those roads traversing across fields, down into valleys, and up mountainsides, I can only imagine they had some pretty rough looking feet. But, that could be just my imagination. Anyway, Jesus saw the need and took it upon Himself to meet the need before dinner was served. And, this leads me to the first of the three characteristics I was referring to.

As I read this passage, I can't help but be mesmerized by the humility of Jesus, the exact representation of God in the flesh. Not only was He humble enough to step way down from His lofty position of honor, prestige, and majesty far above the Earth in the Third Heaven to be found in the likeness of man, but to stoop even farther down to perform the lowly menial task of washing the feet of those who clearly should have been not only washing but kissing His feet. Mind you, this included the feet of Judas Iscariot who He knew was to betray Him soon thereafter. As the leader of an organization, he has no chance of success without being humble enough to know that he can't do it all by himself. He needs every person on every level beneath him – even the bottom dwellers – to do their part. So, leading your wife, it's imperative to your relationship to have the humility to know that you need her in order to be successful. You are no longer a solo act anymore; you are now a duet. Being the leader, you must realize that she has talents and abilities that you don't possess and some things she's better at than you. You must seek to find these things out about your spouse. Also, she can see things that you won't be able to see and will be able to bring a new perspective to things you do see. It doesn't mean that it'll be right all of the time, but it is right for you to consider them as much as possible. And, the things that she's better at than you, you would be considered a wise man to surrender your way to hers in order that the both of you can effectively partner and be better together than you were as singles.

The second of these key characteristics is that a leader must be an example, a model of what he believes. There's no sure-fire quicker way for a leader to lose the heart and respect of his followers than to talk the talk but not walk the walk. It's just like parents who constantly tell their children to do as I say and not as I do all the while they're doing as they told the children not to. That's not the kind of example to set for your children. That's called being a hypocrite. Even if they've only said the phrase, it's not a good one because it communicates a bad message to the children. They may do as you say of course to keep from getting punished, but you could possibly be losing some of their respect in the process and making them angry. No one talked the talk and walked the walk better than Jesus. He is the absolute truth so He couldn't do otherwise. His performing of this lowly menial task really set an example for them they'd never forget. He made sure that they got this message after He finished washing their feet.

> [13]"You call me 'Teacher' and 'Lord,' and rightly so, for that is what I am. [14]Now that I, your Lord and Teacher, have washed your feet, you also should wash one another's feet. [15]I have set you an example that you should do as I have done for you. [16]I tell you the truth, no servant is greater than his master, nor is a messenger greater than the one who sent him. [17]Now that you know these things, you will be blessed if you do them.
>
> (John 13:13-17)

As I mentioned earlier, such a task was usually reserved for a servant. With human nature being so full of pride, I'm sure that no one volunteered to perform the task because they thought it was beneath them. But Jesus took the initiative to perform the task for them all. Afterwards, He directly told them, as He had to do on so many occasions, that if He could do such a menial task, your Teacher, your Lord, then surely you guys can. He emphasized His role in contrast to theirs to bring home His point. Jesus set such a great example for these guys throughout His time with them that – with the exception of Judas – those ordinary men were transformed and were willing to give up their lives for Him literally and figuratively. What kind of example do you want to leave behind for your wife and family?

The third and final of these key characteristics is that a leader must be a servant. It is without a shadow of a doubt that Jesus came to Earth the first time to serve. Granted, the next time will be way different though. His servitude to mankind stretches far beyond the mere washing of His disciples' feet in this passage. As a matter of fact, the washing serves as an illustration of what He ultimately does spiritually for those who accepts His gift. Jesus' washing of His disciples' feet symbolized the cleansing of sin that Jesus provided on the cross (John 13:6-8). Jesus served His disciples by teaching them throughout the time He was with them. That's no different than what he was doing here. He was teaching them here about humility, love, servitude, taking the initiative to meet the need, Christ's spiritual cleansing, submission, and leading by example. In teaching His disciples, Jesus empowered these men with truth and knowledge. They became better than they would have ever been without Him. These ordinary men (minus Judas Iscariot of course) went on to turn the world upside down and inside out for Jesus Christ. Jesus is still doing the same thing today for His disciples. He's teaching us and as we follow, He empowers and strengthens us. Now, let's revisit the example of the organizational leader again. He now knows he needs his team to be successful in order to be successful. He has to empower his subordinates. He has to listen to constructive criticism, meet their needs, and put them in positions where they will be most effective so they can grow to be better than they are now. The more his people beneath him grow the more effective they'll become. The more they feel empowered to do what needs to be done without supervision, the better they function together. Overall, the more successful his organization will be. As a leader of an organization, you have to be genuinely concerned about your subordinates in their respective roles and any obstacles they have performing their duties. The leader must be involved and know what's going on in the realm beneath him. Now, as a husband, the leader of your wife, family, and household, if this is the way it is for a company or organization, how much more should you want this for your own family? If you desire this for your family, then it's going to take your complete devotion in order to attain. Do I mean for you to run your family like a Fortune 500 company? Absolutely not! If you had to ask that question in all seriousness, you've totally missed the point. So, let me spell it out for you. If you're one of those bread winner husbands meaning you've done your part for the family and earned the mighty dollar for today. Now, it's time to go home, sit down, relax, and read the paper in the lazy boy with no disturbances. You need to undergo a major attitude adjustment. I know it can be hard and challenging at times, but you need to come home and get really involved with your wife and kids. Serve them, lead (teach) them, and be an example. Help your family be the best that it can be. I don't care what kind of success you're having in the office. You can be working with billion-dollar clients bringing in billions of dollars into the company, but if you're not getting it done on the home front, you're failing as a man. Your family is your most valuable asset. I look at it this way. When you're on your death bed, who's going to be there by your side? Who do you think you'll be calling for? Is it your job or your family? As far as I can remember throughout my adult life, one of the biggest things that I see that encourages my heart is seeing a father outside spending time with his son whether it be throwing the ball around, riding bikes, or whatever. That's something you don't really see much of these days. It's like an epidemic in our society. Many children are growing up without their fathers being there or at least having a male role model in the home. Some men have too many children by too many different women to get around to all of their children if he is even trying to do so. This is damaging each successive generation of kids – boys and girls alike. They are missing out on what fathers bring to the table. And, this is sad. God designed the family to have mothers and fathers in the home rearing the children. Any other way, there are consequences to suffer.

Alright gentlemen, things are about to get a little uncomfortable for you. And, you might be tempted to put the book down now. But don't! This is an area where I feel men are missing the boat whether they simply refuse to get on it, they're lost and don't know where the boat is, or they're running too far behind to catch it. Judging from what I hear around the office and many other places, I'll bet it's due to refusal. Either way, it causes dark clouds to blow in over your marriage. The more it persists, those dark clouds begin to produce rain, then lightning, thunder, hail, and strong gusts of wind. Pretty soon, you'll find yourself sitting in every abnormal disturbance of the atmosphere known to mankind. If you haven't figured out what I'm talking about by now, let me introduce this to you with a passage of Scripture.

> [7]Husbands, in the same way be considerate as you live with your wives, and treat them with respect as the weaker partner and as heirs with you of the gracious gift of life, so that nothing will hinder your prayers.
> (I Peter 3:7)

Men do you realize that you are required to be submissive to your wives too? The passage opens up saying, "…in the same way." What is Peter referring to when he says that? Well, you should know what he's talking about unless you skipped the section immediately before this one where I talk about the wives' roles. But, I seriously doubt that. I'm sure curiosity of what your wife should be doing would have drawn you into reading it. Then, soon as you found out I was talking about wives being submissive to their husbands, I'm sure you were a fish on the hook – couldn't get away from it if you wanted to. So, yes that's what Paul is talking about now. You see, being considerate is an act of submission. And here's what this is calling men to and where we miss the boat so badly. It's calling husbands to show a high regard for the feelings, thoughts, and emotions of your wives. Most men have a propensity to completely ignore his wife's feelings and thoughts. Or, he may hold onto them long enough to use them as an object of ridicule and scornful jokes with his colleagues in the office, on the golf course, in the locker room, or any other place where men congregate to engage in banter and foolish mockery amongst themselves. Let's face the truth plain and simple, we fail miserably at this and we miss out on knowing our wives, connecting with them, encouraging them, and meeting their needs to the degree that we could. We are to treat them with the proper respect that they deserve. Gentlemen, I'm a fellow male, so don't think that I'm weird or something. I'm telling you this for your own good. I do know that God didn't design us in a way to take in a lot of information like that especially if it's trivial to us. Let's face it, everything has meaning to women and everything is connected to everything else. Ladies, this isn't a knock against you, so stay with me here. For us men, we compartmentalize everything meaning everything isn't connected to everything else, that is, unless it's really connected. And worse yet, we have this nothing box right in the middle of everything that women just cannot wrap their minds around. They can't believe we can think about absolutely nothing. The first time your wife asks you what you're thinking about and you say, "Nothing honey," watch her facial expression and don't be surprised if you see smoke rising out of her ears. God knows, we'd spend all of our time in that box if we could. Continuing with the point I was expressing, we become overwhelmed and shutdown with too much information that we may consider trivial. But you have to work towards connecting to your wife. Your marriage depends on it. I mean it! You will have problems and you won't have a clue as to what's going on. So, start small and work your way up. On the other side of the coin, she has to understand that you as a man is not wired the way she is and meet you half way. If you're not meeting her need in that area, she has to tell you in a way that you understand the severity and not assume that you're deliberately shunning her. Essentially, you two have to work together in this process to determine what works for the both of you so that you're not shutting down on her and her needs are being met with flying colors. You'll find that the both of you are much happier and fulfilled in your marriage.

We are to treat them with due respect because of two primary reasons. First, it says that they are the weaker partner. What exactly does Peter mean when he says **weaker** partner? Well, I'm going to start off by telling you exactly what that doesn't mean. Weakness doesn't mean that they are any less than we are as far as intellect, talent, strength of character, or abilities are concerned. We all have varying degrees of those anyway. There are some women that are top executives in or running big corporations or their own businesses and bringing home their own bacon and cooking it too. There are women raising multiple kids alone, working a fulltime job, if not multiple jobs, and just flat out holding it down. And this, a lot of times is because a man simply refused to be a man. The proof is there; it's been there all along. They are not inferior. It's ridiculous to think such a thing. So, what's the problem? Society has dealt them some hard blows that just aren't fair just like it's dealt us men some too that aren't fair. That's just the way it's been all these years since Genesis 3. But, here's the kicker. What exactly is society? What am I referring to when I say society? Society is us – men and women alike. It's the people. We don't see each other in the true light of what we are because we aren't looking at each other through the eyes of God and what He created us to be. So, we are the ones who are exacting those blows to one another that are unfair. The solution – get connected to God and look at each other through His eyes and help each other be what He created us to be. So, back to weakness and what does it mean? First, I personally do think it refers to physical strength. Men are physically stronger than women, which goes without saying. And, that calls husbands to be the protector of their wives. This is especially true spiritually. Here's something to think about. In the beginning, Satan didn't attack Adam; he went after Eve and got them both. Why? I don't quite have a definitive answer to that but I do have a thought or two of my own. Anyway, I'll leave it for you to ponder. But, the lesson to learn from this is husbands, make sure your wives are doing well – especially spiritually and emotionally. How many marriages have ended or suffered because the woman didn't feel secure and connected with her husband? He wasn't available to her. Being secure comes from a sense of protection and it's not always a physical thing. Lastly, when I think of weakness in this context, it goes to something a little deeper. When I think of weaker in this context, I don't think of something along the lines of being so brittle, but something more along the lines of being so precious. It's something so precious, like fine china, that you treat it with special care and attention. And, there is an area that husbands must be mindful of or you can poison your wife against you. Paul captures this perfectly in his letter to the Colossians. He says, "Husbands, love your wives and do not be harsh with them (Colossians 3:19)." Some men tend to be very harsh with their wives. A lot of women aren't able to take what we can in the area of emotions. They have far more than we do and they run deep, so we are not as sensitive to that because we simply don't know. So, husbands have to be mindful how you come across because you can literally be destroying your wife emotionally and have no idea the damage you're causing.

The second reason we are to treat them with the utmost of respect is because they are co-heirs with you in the precious gift of eternal life. If this isn't proof enough that your wife is your equal partner, I don't think there's anything that can convince you. If you and your wife are disciples of Jesus, she experiences God's saving grace on equal terms with you. God has equally given her His saving grace. God does not make any distinction between men and women in terms of His gift of life through Jesus Christ. Now back to what Peter was saying, if you aren't treating your wife the way God desires, you will not have the fellowship with God you desire because your prayers will be hindered as well as you will not have as good a connection with your wife as you should. Don't believe me? Take a look at all of the bad marriages across this country. And, what was the divorce rate statistic I mentioned earlier in this book? This applies to whether you're a disciple of Jesus or not – whether you believe in God or not. God is the one who designed us as well as life itself. He has consequences woven into life and everything He created. If you aren't doing right, you are suffering the consequences.

If you don't want to take it from me how important it is for husbands to get on the boat with considering your wives, then take it from the very first man who became a husband.

> [23]The man said, "This is now bone of my bones and flesh of my flesh; she shall be called woman for she was taken out of man."
>
> (Genesis 2:23)

As we were created in the image of God, God duplicated that process in the creation of Eve from Adam. Remember, Adam and Eve's relationship is to be especially unique to one another like mankind's relationship to God is unique and supersedes any of God's other creatures. You see, as the man, the leader, Adam realized the oneness and the unity he now had with Eve. He realized that this woman was now a part of his identity. It was no longer Adam, but Adam **and** Eve. Notice the conjunction? For the rest of his life, he had to take her into consideration as though he was caring for the very parts of his own body. If he didn't, it would have a profoundly negative impact on his life. Adam got this right out the box, but men, we've lost this somewhere over the many years. We desperately need to get this kind of heart back towards our wives as soon as possible. It's imperative; your marriage depends on it.

Being that we are designated by God as the leaders of our wives and our households, the church has taken that to mean something that God didn't intend for it to mean. I have experienced this to an extensive degree where I attend and I know that some other men have experienced the same as well. What I'm referring to is placing the blame on the husbands for everything that goes wrong in the marriage. Essentially, what happens is that you end up beating up the husbands for every single thing expecting the marriage to improve. With no counseling for the wife, she ends up getting off scot-free, her self-righteousness takes off, and she wants to get counseling all the time as she knows what it's going to turn into. You expect a man to lead his wife and his household, but he can't do that when he's continuously being emasculated over and over again as though everything he does is wrong. During my first Christian marriage, I began to wonder how so many people could be so doggone stupid. Here you have two sinful people in a marriage; to the neglect of one, you continuously beat up on the other in expectations of their marriage getting better. In my case, it did not matter what I said my wife was doing wrong; it was as though I was speaking Greek or something. It never got addressed. You would think that there would have been a readiness to try to find out both sides but that wasn't the case. It's like they took what she said as the gospel. Despite how hard I tried, I could not lead the marriage because the role was given to my wife at the onset of the marriage. What killed me at times when I thought about it was that this abuse was coming from fellow men. I could understand if it was coming from an all-woman regime or something. But from men, some of which I overheard talking about their own wives' misbehavior. So, I wondered how they could think that mine was perfect. Something else I wondered is how can you expect to help and counsel a couple's marriage when you're really not taking the time to get to know who they really are. Thirty minutes a week or every other week just doesn't get it. At the meeting with church leadership where it was decided that she and I should separate for a while to work on our own characters, one of the elders at the time admitted that it was unfortunate that that's the way problems were handled in a marriage by beating up on the husband. Honestly, I had had enough. Something that was seemingly not taken into consideration is the fact that women have a will and sinful nature of their own too. That's why God commanded them to respect their husbands. I always felt that my church was counseling marriages as though Ephesians 5:33 said, "…husbands must love their wives, **then** wives will respect their husbands." It's as if the husband must get in line and then the wife will automatically fall into place and do what she should. That's not the conjunction that joins those two sides and it does make a difference. Remember, Eve accepted Satan's offer without consulting her husband first.

Several years ago, before this book was even a thought in my mind, I was at work perusing the Internet looking at some spiritual articles and ran across an article in particular on the Crosswalk website that caught my attention. It was an article about the same thing I'm talking about – beating up on Christian husbands. I was like this seems to be a universal thing. The author used the terms prejudice against the male nature and bigotry to describe it. I'd say I have to agree with those terms. Some of the things those Christian men were told in that article are just flat out wicked and depraved as that's the only thing I can think of to describe it because those things are so unbiblical. You will find no such things in God's holy word. Some of those same things were going on in the church where I attend. Now, I must say that some of those things were not verbally said like in the article, but by the actions we have boldly shown where we stood on the matter. Remember, our actions are very powerful and speak louder than words to what we believe. Our actions reveal our beliefs to things we have not spoken to and it confirms or denies things that we have spoken to. The article tells various ways some of those men have been harmed. I see those ways in which some of those men have been treated resulting from three false messages that are propagated to Christian men. Those messages are one, "If there is a major problem in a couple's marriage, whether or not it leads to divorce, it is ultimately the husband's fault." (Coughlin) Two, that is that women are more moral, spiritual, and sensitive to the Holy Spirit than men. Third, a good Christian man does not confront his wife about her sinful behavior. With these types of messages being conveyed to men, no wonder there are so little of them sitting in the church pews. Messages like these and the treatment that follows have embittered, angered, and have made some Christian men stop going to church altogether. It has made others reluctant, ambivalent, and insecure in their leading and even though they may continue to go to church, they go out of duty, not for inspiration to be the faithful men and leaders that God desires. I'm sure you can tell by reading the previous paragraph that I definitely relate to some of those same feelings those guys felt. Let's take a minute to talk about some of these misconceptions.

    The Bible teaches us to lovingly confront one another regarding our sins. That's one of the major differences that make Jesus' church different from the rest of the world; it deals with sin and holds each member accountable. This is an essential part of God's plan in order for His people to live holy and righteous lives in this present life. We need the accountability. We are our brothers' keeper. God gave no distinctions in who could confront who. If you love your fellow brothers and sisters and want to see them get to heaven, then you'll lovingly confront them. If this is truly the case, then why would anyone think that's different with a husband confronting his wife? Now, I know there are some Christian men who do this. But, there's this seemingly universal concept implicitly taught in some church (explicitly in the article) about husbands not confronting their wives about their sinful behavior or anything they're doing that isn't right. Where did this come from? Remember the husband who needed to leave immediately after church, but his wife was holding him up fellowshipping and he wouldn't confront her. What do you think that is? That isn't the first time I've heard a husband say something like that when his wife was doing something inconsiderate to him but he better not do the exact same thing to her. Where's the mutual respect? There are wives who are literally assassinating their husbands verbally and no one confronts her about it or they tie the husband's hands by saying "that a 'good Christian man' does not confront his wife about her behavior." (Coughlin) Let's look at a familiar passage.

> [25]Husbands, love your wives, just as Christ loved the church and gave himself up for her [26]to make her holy, cleansing her by the washing with water through the word, [27]and to present her to himself as a radiant church, without stain or wrinkle or any other blemish, but holy and blameless.
>
> (Ephesians 5:25-27)

Husbands are charged to love their wives with nothing less than a sacrificial love the way Christ loved the church. Husbands should love their wives literally to the point of death. But, there's a bit of a transition that I still consider being an aspect of love. The husbands are given responsibility for how their wives turn out. In other words, he is responsible for her Christlikeness. Now, do I believe that the husband will be eternally condemned for his wife's sin? No, that's not what that's saying and we know that the soul that sins is the soul that dies. He is responsible for presenting her as a radiant church, without stain, wrinkle, or blemish. Now, if God holds a husband responsible for this, then tell me how do you accomplish this without correcting bad behavior? She is to be cleansed through the word by her husband (v26). Women are to help their husbands when they go astray as they are charged only to follow their husbands as they follow Christ (Colossians 3:18) as this should convict them of their sinfulness. Surely, you would think this is a mutual responsibility. As I mentioned earlier, your spouse is your twenty-four by seven discipleship partner. Your ultimate goal is to help each other follow Jesus right into heaven. Husbands are to correct their wives, firm and lovingly, and as with us, sometimes you need to get a little help in there by pulling in another woman.

There is something critical missing that I realized some years ago around the demise of my first Christian marriage. At the moment I noticed it, it was so glaringly obvious that is was missing and I want to lead into this one with a Scripture.

> ³Likewise, teach the older women to be reverent in the way they live, not to be slanderers or addicted to much wine, but to teach what is good. ⁴Then they can train the younger women to love their husbands and children, ⁵to be self-controlled and pure, to be busy at home, to be kind, and to be subject to their husbands, so that no one will malign the word of God.
>
> (Titus 2:3-5)

Is it obvious what I saw that was missing? What I don't see enough in the church is the older women teaching the younger women how to love and respect their husbands. To be completely honest with you, it's almost scarce. Why is this not happening more in the church when it is right here in the black and white text of God's Word? I don't know how it is elsewhere, but I know where I attend, if a husband needed to have something in his wife's character dealt with, it was pretty much one couple whose name that I typically heard come up. But, in reality, I do know there's probably about a handful of other couples who's in that mix as well. That's not enough. I think it's a shame that you have to seek a specific couple out and it's not a general practice across God's kingdom. Why? Once again, it is plain biblical instruction in God's Word. Husbands and wives should receive instruction and correction simultaneously where needed as needed. This is precisely why I opened up this chapter with the train analogy because I felt that it was so fitting to illustrate this. I can only imagine that this prejudice towards

Christian husbands has caused some of their hearts to become hardened over the long haul.

Here's a thought I think is worth pondering. There isn't a Scripture anywhere in the Bible that reciprocates the sentiment in Titus 2:3-5 for husbands. Don't take what I'm saying to the extreme. Husbands need spiritual counseling too. We all do no matter our status in life. What I'm pointing out is that God in His infinite wisdom found it necessary to put this passage in His Word about women being taught how to love and respect their husbands. Why? Well, outside this happening on the island of Crete, I haven't the slightest idea specifically why but I do know that it's there and it's there for a reason. You see, the thing is this prejudice, this beating up of Christian husbands is worldly. It's from men. Anything from man is not pleasing to God. As a matter of fact, that negative handling of husbands reminds me of a group of bitter women who come together to bash men and their masculinity without even much of a hint of awareness of their own faults in the situation.

The claim that men are to blame for everything major that goes wrong in their marriage no matter the outcome is so asinine that I really don't feel compelled enough to address it because it's not worth the time or effort. What I do want to touch on a bit is the women being more moral, spiritual, and in touch with the Holy Spirit than men. I do not believe this because the Bible doesn't even remotely teach anything close to this. As a matter of fact, I see just the opposite in the Scriptures. Although there are distinct groups of people, I Corinthians 12:13 and Galatians 3:28 reminds us that we are all equal before God. On the other hand, Romans 3:23 reminds us that we all are just as depraved before God. First Peter 3:7 reminds husbands to treat their wives with respect because they are their co-heirs of God's gracious gift. We all are on an equal playing field or as I like to say – in the same boat. I made the remark earlier that I agreed with the article's terminology of calling this treatment of Christian husbands a prejudice and bigotry because that's exactly what that is. And yes, I do know it goes both ways, otherwise husbands would not have needed to be reminded by Peter that their wives are co-heirs with them. But this really reminds me of the prejudice that's magnified in society – that's of whites against blacks. And yes, I know this goes the other way too. Prejudice is interwoven in society in multiple ways; some are just magnified and more visible than others. This is simply the concept of raising the value of one group over another in order to create a favorable position over the devalued group by exacting limitations in order to gain advantages or privileges. The article, which was talking about professional Christian counselors at the time, presents a perspective in light of this. It states, "I also point out that beating up on Christian men in church is good business in Christian media. The Apostle Paul wrote about this tendency in his second letter to the church in Corinth. 'For we are not, like so many, peddlers of God's word' (II Cor 2:17). Some Christian authors and speakers know that they can malign men and get away with it because guys will 'suck it up' and keep coming to church. They know that their message plays well with some women. It's hard to get a person like this to understand the problem when their paycheck depends upon them not understanding the problem." (Coughlin)

I think that this idea that women are more spiritual, more moral than men, more sensitive to the Holy Spirit than men may arise out of the fact that women are more emotional and relational than men. This is absolutely true. As surely as I'm a black man, I'm in agreeance with this. But, when I think of emotions, feelings come to mind and my first thought is, "Be careful." We know the bankability of feelings. Men and women relate differently to God because he designed us differently and we do so with the tools we've been given. There are ways we need to grow in order to relate to Him better. Now, do we need emotions to relate to God? Of course, we do! And, you better believe that we need to get in touch with them in order to relate to God. He no doubt wants our hearts. No robots allowed. Do I believe that a woman can be more spiritual than a man? Of course, I do! I also know that there are some very spiritual men out there. And, some are even in touch with their emotions too. I know that there are some out there that are more spiritual than some women. So, I don't think you can or should take a whole group when there are individuals within that group at varying levels – some below members of the opposing group – and say that the one group is better than the other. It seems like this is a case of comparing apples and oranges and saying that one is better than the other.

Furthermore, emotions are just one aspect used in spirituality or relating to God. In Romans 7, Paul unleashes this tongue twister of a description regarding the internal battle he has as one belonging to Jesus. He explicitly said that he was unspiritual. In context, he was talking about God's law, which is spiritual, and the battle he had doing what he wanted to do in his human nature versus the good that God wanted him to do. In other words, he was saying that despite his desire to do good and please God, he has a strong inclination to be disobedient to God; this is what he keeps on doing. If in his disobedience he is unspiritual, quite naturally, obedience then is being spiritual. Now, which of us is exempt from having that problem? I think that being spiritual is comprised of not just one component, but multiple spiritual components coming together in conjunction with each other to make an individual noteworthy in spirituality.

On a personal note, as I wrote about this topic and reminisced about some of those experiences, I still remembered some of the strong emotions I felt during that time probably as a result of some scars that may have been left behind. Those scars definitely aren't fresh or open wounds by any stretch of the imagination as they took place several years ago and I have healed to some extent. They remind me of where I've been, but don't dictate where I'm going. God has allowed me to endure through some things for whatever reason He has deemed necessary in His infinite wisdom. Because those scars are there is why I believe I have now become more vocal about these things because they will bring about more of a healing in me if any is still necessary as well as others who have experienced something similar. Also, vocalizing it will help to bring about a change to reduce the chances of someone else unnecessarily experiencing this because it is flat out wrong and something needs to be done about it. That's the only way it'll change.

Husbands and Wives

As we know by now, one aspect of marriage is that it's a partnership. One is not superior over the other in terms of being superior or more valuable. The two are different for different reasons. Each one has a role to fulfill which is integral to the overall success and functioning of the marriage. One is designated as the leader and designed to do so. The other is to follow and has been equipped for that purpose. This is a must otherwise without those designations; it would make for a chaotic relationship. Either way, it's not by God's original design and doesn't glorify Him. Depending on the combination of personality traits between the husband and wife, you'll have a few variations. In marriages where you have a more domineering, independent type of woman, she may be trying to lead with her husband; that is if he is fulfilling his role. If not, she'll be more than happy to do so. In marriages where you have an extremely passive man, the woman may be forced to lead as he may not have a single care in the world. This may cause the woman to become frustrated. In others, there may be a complete role reversal where the wife willingly leads and the husband simply follows. Neither of these situations is of God's design for marriage.

So, I'm curious about what your expectations were going into the chapter about the roles of the husband and wife. Were you expecting a long laundry list of duties to perform itemized out into two columns one labeled for the husband and the other for the wife? I'm sure you noticed quickly that I didn't do anything remotely close to that. I didn't do that because God doesn't get into specifics like that either. I think it's this way for at least two reasons that I can think of. First, I believe it helps eliminate the legalism. We would be so much more like the Pharisees in our marriages; it would be a crying shame. Sinful human nature doesn't need any more help being legalistic. Give us an itemized list of things to do. We'll go down that list checking off each item upon completion and feel that there's absolutely no one better. But, there aren't many things out there that'll kill a relationship faster than legalism. This is the thing that crippled the Pharisees and kept them from having a relationship with God and Jesus wasn't shy about letting them know about it. The second reason is of extreme importance because it has the opposite effect of the first reason. Although I haven't been married long enough to have experienced this to any significant degree, my recommendation of this comes purely from my observation of couples that I'm close to. Also, being that marriages do reflect our relationship with God, I've seen this in my walk with God over the eighteen years I've been a disciple of Jesus. As I've grown to know God over those eighteen years as a disciple, I've come to see that with God most everything is a process. Of course, there are reasons for that. That is something that has taken me some time to realize and will definitely take me even more time to grow substantially in that area. You know, human nature is all about instant gratification. That's a big part of our struggle in relating to God. Anyway, in light of this fact, you as a couple have to work through your struggles and figure each other out. Your goal is to have true intimacy. It's through this process of working together and learning about each other that creates true intimacy. It's not something you can just add water and presto, now you have intimacy. Let's detour back to the original model here for a minute. Marriage is like the relationship Christ has with His church. As his disciples, we struggle in our relationship with God to know Him. He knows us perfectly inside and out, the good (what little there is), the bad, and the despicable. But, we struggle in our relationship to know Him and allow that knowledge of Him to affect our walk and lives. The more intimately we know Him and hold consistently to that intimacy, it impacts our life in a major way. For example, you come to have an unexplainable level of peace and joy in your life even through some of the most difficult of circumstances. He makes your paths straight and I think that comes from just knowing Him intimately because it's not that life gets any easier as a disciple, but you know who you're walking with and that's what makes all of the difference. And consequently, this intimate knowledge of Him essentially allows you to trust Him. And this is the exact process that carries over into a marriage. With the intimacy comes that trust in one another because you each know who you're walking with. Your times of conflict will decrease and you and your spouse will experience peace and joy within your marriage. Now, as disciples in our walk with Jesus, we can lose sight or our grasp of that intimacy we have with God no matter how long we've been His disciples or mature we've become. This does happen and that can put the person back on a bad path; one that's in conflict with God. It may take a bit for the person to get back in line with God if he or she doesn't leave Him altogether. Well, the same can happen with couples too. Sometimes it can be some long enduring pain or suffering that can disrupt the intimacy or it can be a dramatic life changing event that happens. I know a good friend of mine who's enduring through something like this in his marriage. It takes some work to get through these kinds of situations and sometimes a couple rebounds from it to be even stronger than they were in the beginning. And unfortunately, sometimes couples don't rebound and the marriage is dissolved. So, remember! True intimacy is one of your goals of marriage.

This shouldn't be a secret at all, but I think in order to build trust in a marriage, it's very important for both parties to have a willingness to be vulnerable and honest with one another. Being transparent is a term that I like to use that encompasses both vulnerability and honesty. Trust is a critical aspect of marriage. This is your partner for life; you ride or die with this person. If you can't trust your partner, then what do you have? I can tell you from personal experiences that that's not a good feeling. Human nature truly has a hard time with both of these concepts. I think this transparency is best starting back in the early stages of your relationship during your dating period. I'm pretty sure it was back in 2010 when I began a long-distance friendship with a single woman from a sister church located in Toronto, Canada. She initially reached out to me through a website that belonged to our family of churches. I don't recall if I ever knew why she chose me to send an email to but it was definitely random from what I recall. One day I saw that I had an email from someone that I didn't know. It was a short introductory email that was akin to an initial face to face meeting. It was something along the lines of, "Hello. How are you doing?" It was a little unusual for me but I decided to respond. Our primary mode of communication began with some long emails back and forth. After a couple of months or so, we transitioned into phone calls. We actually built a great friendship over the next year and a half. We laughed a lot. We talked about our victories, weaknesses, and our struggles. As time passed by, an opportunity where we might get a chance to meet approached. In July 2012, the discipleship conference I mentioned earlier was approaching. At the conference, we met and had the chance to hang out two or three times. As a matter of fact, she was the last person I hung out with right before hitting the road to return home. Although it was our first time meeting face to face, it didn't feel that way to me. Well, after returning home during maybe our first or second conversation, she springs this question on me, "Where do you see our relationship going?" I definitely wasn't expecting that. But, after briefly thinking about it, I responded that I see us just being friends and that I really wasn't looking for anything serious. Now, common sense tells you that a question like that, something must be going on. This is typically not a question you just ask for the sake of asking. So, I questioned her as to why she was asking. I specifically asked her, "Was she acquiring any feelings?" She responded that she wasn't and she was asking because she was just curious. At that point, I was tempted to question her again to make sure, but I went on and took her at her word as I thought it was possible that was the case. Well, we probably had maybe a couple of conversations after that. Then, I get a phone call from her and she just lays into me right off the bat. She was angry because she thought that I was taunting her, playing with her emotions because I had left a voicemail referring to her as either baby girl or sweetheart. I can't remember exactly the term it was. Now, anybody who knows me knows that I use terms of endearment all the time and I had done so with her as well. I even had her laughing with one of the terms I used when we first started talking on the phone because she had never heard it before. So, I politely brought these facts to her attention. After she confirmed, I asked her what the problem was. Then she explained that she thought I was taunting her because of the question she asked me about our relationship and assumed that I would know that she did like me. I then confirmed that yes, that was the natural assumption, but that's why I asked her the follow up question because I wanted to know for sure. I don't read minds and I'm not going to try. I wanted to know so that we could discuss how we needed to progress in our friendship. If she couldn't handle it, then maybe we needed to stop. Or, if she could, then I would have to be mindful of what I said in an effort to be sensitive to her feelings. I reminded her of the fact that she told me no, so as far as I was concerned things were normal. So, how could I be playing with her feelings when in my mind there were none to play with? Then, I told her that she couldn't be honest with me, but she was quick to blast me for something she thought I was intentionally doing wrong to her. So, why would I want to date someone who couldn't be open and honest with me? After a moment of silence, I gave her a little more food for thought. I then asked her why would she want to date someone she didn't trust enough that she could be vulnerable with. I must admit though after talking to her for a year and a half and all we talked about, I felt a little wronged that she didn't trust me enough to be open with me.

After discussing this a bit, we got on the same page and I think she understood where I was coming from. Don't get me wrong. I understand having feelings of not wanting to be rejected. I've been in those same shoes a number of occasions myself so I know how it feels. But when we're not transparent, things like this and worse can happen. The truth is eventually going to come out one way or another. Looking back, this was probably a growing experience for the both of us. This is one reason why I believe as singles we need those cross-gender relationships; it helps us learn how to interact with each other without any expectations. It helps us mature in our relationships with each other.

Marriage is also a mutual submission of both partners to one another. Paul tells the Ephesians, "Submit to one another out of reverence for Christ" (Ephesians 5:21). This was a great summation statement to close out the preceding section to the general population. On the other hand, it was an excellent statement to open up his next topic of discussion specifically for the wives and husbands of the church. Although this is a mutual submission of each spouse to one another, it's not in the same fashion on equal terms as some feminists would be too quick to argue. The submission of one calls for an obedience and a constant submission of ones will to the other whereas the submission of the other calls for a taking the other into account in every aspect of life as though one was considering oneself.

Another statement Paul said to the Ephesians, "However, each one of you also must love his wife as he loves himself and the wife must respect her husband" (Ephesians 5:33). This statement is the crowning point of this entire section Paul was addressing to the married couples in Ephesus. Likewise, I think this is the single most important thing for a successful marriage. There's an entire book written on the topic simply called *Love & Respect* by Dr. Emerson Eggerichs. This is a book that I have in my collection of books but haven't gotten a chance to read yet. Through the apostle Paul, God provided the command for husbands to love their wives and wives to respect their husbands. It's an imperative command and take notice of the conjunction that joins the two. That means that they both are required simultaneously. I can see a reason why God would command us to just flat out do this. Love and respect are women's and men's language respectively. We typically don't do the other naturally, so we will naturally relate to the other with what we've been equipped with. Not knowing what the other needs, what happens when we come at each other with our language is that misinterpretations can occur. A wife who has an issue with something may approach her husband to discuss but may communicate her message in such a way that it is disrespectful to him. As a result, he may shut down and retreat without showing concern for her issue as he doesn't want to be bothered with the lack of respect. As I mentioned earlier that this was like kryptonite to men and like Superman, we retreat to get away from it. This may not have been her intentions and she may not be aware of how she came across. On the other hand, his response feels unloving to her. These are the automatic responses. So, husbands and wives must be careful how they communicate with each other. Wives need love from their husbands; husbands need respect from their wives. No matter where the cycle begins if the husband initiates an unloving interaction, he'll eventually get a disrespectful response in return. Likewise, if a wife constantly initiates a disrespectful interaction, she'll eventually get an unloving response in return. Love and respect are the bloodline to a successful marriage.

Now, you know I have to go there, don't you? I'd be doing you a big disservice if I didn't. And, how could I say with good conscience that I was trying to help prepare you if I didn't? What I'm talking about is your roles and what happens when either of you flat out rebel – you don't feel like fulfilling your God-given role in marriage or the moment you realize you two aren't as similar as you thought. It's going to happen whether you believe it or not and probably will happen much sooner than you'd expect. Here are some scenarios to help you consider these situations a little now than being shocked by them later when they happen. This will hopefully prevent you from questioning who is this person and did you marry the right one. Here are a few samples for you to chew on.

- Wife's sinful nature kicks in and she absolutely refuses to be submissive.
- Husband is being passive and wishy-washy and doesn't lead like he should.
- Husband doesn't like wife's cooking.
- You realize your perspective of something about your spouse was way off.

Think some of these are just silly scenarios? Well, they're not. They do occur and they turn some couples' world upside down. For those that are more serious character issues, how are you going to deal with those situations when they arise? If it's an issue in your character, what is it going to take for you to change for your marriage? These are things for you to consider because it's a part of the realities of marriage?

Because Satan instigated Adam and Eve's separation from God and started the battle of the sexes I mentioned earlier, here's one way that has played out in our relating to one another. We are so adept at putting each other's gender down in order to make our own look important. It's so interwoven in our relationships; it's done all of the time. Women make men look incapable to show their importance; men minimize women in order to make us look stronger. Wrong! So wrong! Men and women are all equal before God (Galatians 3:28). We were designed and created by Him and we need each other. How many times have I heard a woman act like she doesn't need a man or a man act like women are worthless other than for one thing? Too many times to count! But the truth is this. The humility of man is that he needs a woman (a partner), and the humility of woman is that she needs a man (an authority figure/security).

In light of Ephesians 5:21-33 and what was just discussed in the roles, what parts are the most difficult for you to understand or put into practice? And why? Next, what can you now do to strive towards incorporating this into your life going forward?

Personal Expectations

Having Realistic Expectations

Now that we've ironed out some of the expectations that are important in marriage, we can briefly discuss your personal expectations for marriage. Don't fool yourself! We all have expectations for things we engage in. No matter how simple or complex the expectation may be, we expect to receive something in return for our participation. And, that makes perfect sense. If we don't have expectations for something we engage in, then it makes no sense for you to participate. Otherwise, we typically have no interest at all. Human nature is so what's in it for me. If we do engage in something without having any expectations, then you can pretty much know that we're not going to give our hearts and simply go through the motions in order to get through it.

Marriage is no exception. So, what are your expectations for marriage? I touched on it a bit earlier when I talked about finding someone who complements you. I applied it in the context of character traits, but it works in other contexts too. If you plan to own a business, you may want someone who has the same desire and possess entrepreneurial skills. This could be a legitimate expectation for you. What your expectations are is an important question to consider. You'll again be taking a look at your future spouse, yourself, and your marriage overall. It's important because it'll help you decipher which of your expectations are realistic and unrealistic. Some expectations that'll probably come to mind initially are faithfulness, companionship, loving spouse, and support. These are definitely realistic expectations, but they also are common characteristics of marriage. So, everyone should expect those and the others when they get married. From this point, you need to dig a little deeper to draw out those that are more specific to you than to marriage. These will be the ones you need to be concerned about and inspect them a little further. They can be noble and honorable expectations, but in some cases, they can be extremely unrealistic or even worse – more like they're from a fairy tale. Many of these fairytale-like expectations can be unspoken, hidden ones that lurk just below the surface in our subconscious. How can we identify them if they're just beneath the surface? What is it that you dream or secretly fantasize about your future spouse doing or being for you? Some women are notorious for this. They'll fantasize things like he'll always come to my rescue whenever I need him; he'll be the perfect hero, he'll be in tune with my emotions and always know exactly what I need, he'll always be interested in what I'm doing and eager to join me, and he'll always bring me flowers just because. Yikes! That's scary. Keep her away from me. I don't want to get involved with a woman like that. Hold on a minute fellas. We're not exempt from this type of behavior. In our own masculine sort of way, we do the same thing. Some of us think that we'll always be able to keep our spouse in a state of blissful happiness. Any guy who thinks that is no doubt living in a fairy tale. Or, smoking weed. Maybe both. Women have emotions that run so deep that you won't be able to understand your wife at times, and you shouldn't expect to. We're not built that way. Those emotions at times are going to drive you insane because nothing you do will please her. Then, you'll probably just want to go away for a while. Another fairytale-like expectation some men may have is that there will be sex all of the time. Well, you'll figure this one out the first time you realize you can't always make her happy all the time.

These fairy tale expectations are so dangerous because they are all about self and assume that your spouse was designed to meet all of your needs.

> [25] Whom have I in heaven but you? And earth has nothing I desire besides you. [26] My flesh and my heart may fail, but God is the strength of my heart and my portion forever.
> (Psalm 73:25-26)

This is from one of my favorite Psalms – a psalm of Asaph. Asaph was struggling with living righteously amongst the wicked because they seemed to be so much more prosperous than he. It was like they were being rewarded for their wickedness. He was doing what's right and they were getting away with murder. He almost forsook his righteous life to live as they were. But, he remembered who his source was and the end that befalls the wicked. Asaph remembers that God is his source and he fulfills his every desire even on Earth. The same is true for marriage. God must be your source, your everything in your marriage. Otherwise, like those who live in opposition to Him, your marriage will come to utter ruin with all of the burdens and expectations you'll put on one another. Instead of being a parasite to each other, you have to, as I've heard it phrased so cleverly, outdo each other in love. Other expectations that may lurk below the surface, but not be so fairytale-like, but still unrealistic are: things will be no different than when I was single, I'll be hanging out with my friends the same amount of time after

I'm married, I'm going to change my spouse into the perfect spouse for me, and we are so much alike. On the other hand, sometimes expectations aren't met for understandable reasons. In a worst-case scenario, your spouse may become incapacitated and unable to perform many, if any, of his or her previous duties. Situations like this will be extremely rough and hard to deal with. There will be no simple way to adjust to this. A couple of things still hold true no matter the severity of the unmet expectation. You must work through them and remember that God works for the good of those who love Him (Romans 8:28).

Here's a bit of a warning about your expectations. Be careful that those expectations, no matter how shallow or noble they are, don't turn into selfish desires, otherwise known as idols. I mentioned earlier that I had idolatry in my heart at the inception of a recent relationship. As a result of a previous marriage, something that became important to me was to have a woman who truly respected me and had my back. Well, there's nothing wrong with that at all. That's a fairly noble and legitimate desire to have. The problem is that I put way too much emphasis on that – so much that it dethroned God in my heart. That's what idolatry is, right? Anything that takes the place of God. Therefore, I bought a lie and abandoned all sensible reasoning, which is why I became so oblivious to the blatant wrong she was doing that spoke otherwise. Idolatry will make you see things that aren't even there. What you end up seeing is from your false perception that's driven from the strong desires that are in your heart. Just think about Samson again for a moment. Samson had a penchant, a weakness for beautiful women. He knew Delilah was trying to set him up and hand him over to the Philistines, but yet he had such an emotional affair with her that he stayed with her even making playful banter about her trying to entrap him. You think, what is wrong with this guy? Is he crazy or something? No. No one is exempt from this type of behavior. You see it all the time. Although, I think there are other things going on in his heart, one of the things going on with him is that I believe he's struggling with idolatry. In his case, he had to have every beautiful woman he saw and it was hard for him to disconnect from that. With idolatry, your desires own you. He lost sight of what's true and abandoned all sensible reasoning. If he hadn't, he would not have stayed with Delilah soon as he realized what she was up to. But, he didn't and it led to his downfall. What about the Israelites? God performed many miraculous feats to rescue them out of Egypt. They walked through the Red Sea on dry ground as the LORD held back the water and destroyed the Egyptians as they tried to go through. God fed them with food that literally fell from heaven and provided water for them to drink from rocks. God showed them convincingly that He was with them all the way. Yet, the moment Moses went up on the mountain to visit with God, the Israelites became impatient, figured they were abandoned by God and decided to build a golden calf to be their god. Once again, another example of the loss of what's true and sensible reasoning despite all of the visible proof they had seen and known. Idols in our hearts are absolutely no good for us. Now, I know that we aren't going to do everything perfectly. Sometimes, we just have to make those mistakes in order for us to wake up. Hopefully, the difference is that we learn from them early on so that they don't ultimately become our downfall as it was for Samson.

Finally, once you establish which of your expectations are legitimate, discuss them with your spouse as soon as possible – preferably before you are married and continue until each of you are on the same page. This will prevent some issues and misunderstandings. We all have certain expectations when we enter marriage – the husband is expected to do this and the wife is expected to do that. Our expectations come from a variety of sources like our parents' marriage, books, other people, and our own ideas. Do you see how this can cause some problems if you don't discuss and work them out as you progress? No two persons will have all of the same expectations if any at all. Without openly discussing, expectations will unintentionally go unmet. An unmet expectation is a disappointment. This may not come out immediately. Hopefully, it won't cause a major conflict but will cause some degree of hurt. You'll have more than enough conflict and issues to deal with in your marriage. Do a little fire prevention early on…talk about your expectations up front.

Conclusion of the Matter

Practical Application

So finally, you've reached the end. I'm not sure what you're feeling or thinking right now. You may be wondering what to make of it all. You may be feeling a little intimidated. Or, you may feel enlightened or encouraged. Hopefully, the latter is the case and you haven't been deterred from journeying down that path. But, if you do decide to venture down this path, I think the following passage of Scripture has a few take-a-way points that would be good for you to keep at the forefront of your mind.

> [1]Guard your steps when you go to the house of God. Go near to listen rather than to offer the sacrifice of fools, who do not know that they do wrong. [2]Do not be quick with your mouth, do not be hasty in your heart to utter anything before God. God is in heaven and you are on earth, so let your words be few. [3]As a dream comes when there are many cares, so the speech of a fool when there are many words. [4]When you make a vow

to God, do not delay in fulfilling it. He has no pleasure in fools; fulfill your vow. ⁵It is better not to vow than to make a vow and not fulfill it. ⁶Do not let your mouth lead you into sin. And do not protest to the temple messenger, "My vow was a mistake." Why should God be angry at what you say and destroy the work of your hands? ⁷Much dreaming and many words are meaningless. Therefore stand in awe of God.

(Ecclesiastes 5:1-7)

King Solomon is credited with authorship of the book of Ecclesiastes. He succeeded his father David as king over Israel. Shortly after his throne was established, God came to Solomon in a dream and questioned the desire of his heart; He would give him whatever he wanted. Solomon replied, "Now, O Lord my God, you have made your servant king in place of my father David. But I am only a little child and do not know how to carry out my duties. Your servant is here among the people you have chosen, a great people, too numerous to count or number. So give your servant a discerning heart to govern your people and to distinguish between right and wrong. For who is able to govern this great people of yours?" Wow, what an amazing response, laced with so much humility. Consequently, God responded by giving Solomon so much wisdom that there had never been or will ever be anyone wiser, so you would do well to pay attention.

In the passage, Solomon is providing some strict warnings when going to the house of God to worship. There are three main concepts that I see to be of great value when considering marriage as well. The first, be prepared, comes directly from verse one. He says, "Guard your steps when you go to the house of God." You're not even there yet and you should begin preparation long before you get to the altar. And, not to mention, the initial part of it is a warning. When you're told to guard or watch your steps, you're being told to be careful because there's danger involved. So, before you actually cross the threshold, you should beware some of the pitfalls like the ones we discussed earlier such as impurity and your selfish desires. Each can ensnare you, be a distraction and an obstacle to overcome, and can ruin your relationship. A second part of preparation is that of knowing your responsibilities and what's expected of you in regards to your role. The second part of verse one seems to be information more for when you're participating in worship told to you prior to getting to the temple. It's no different for marriage. You need to know or have some idea of what your role and responsibilities are. Entering into marriage unarmed and unequipped would mean not getting off to a good start and certain disaster. You're not going to know every detail or how it's going to play out. Everyone's journey is going to be different, but the concepts are the same. Getting to know your partner's character can give you an initial idea of how you might have to fulfill your role in your partner's life as you two become joined together.

Secondly, take it seriously. I can't express this enough. Take it seriously. I don't want you to be so serious that you suck all of the fun and joy out of the occasion, but this is not something to be taken lightly. Marriage is a sacred institution, a union between man and woman before God. This is a vow that you're making and vows are made to be fulfilled without delay. There will be no acceptable excuses for not fulfilling. Simply put, it's sin.

Finally, realize who has authority. God is the ultimate authority whom we all have to give an account to. He is the designer and creator of marriage. The vow you make in marriage, you really make it to Him. So, this is between you and God. So, don't be too hasty or make under false pretenses, then decide to back out after it's too late. God's anger will be aroused by your reneging and it could mean disastrous consequences for you.

In closing, people put so much energy and time into planning the wedding day. They spend thousands upon thousands of dollars on the wedding. A lot of women, since they were little girls, have been dreaming about that day and can probably envision every detail of the wedding in their minds. They, including men, want to make sure that day is absolutely perfect. And, they expend a substantial amount of energy in an effort to make sure it is perfect. When things don't go as they planned, they can skyrocket to extreme levels of stress and lose control. People plan and exert so much effort into their wedding day – we're talking about just one day – and show little to no concern for their marriage, which is the rest of their lives. There's so much more to marriage than the wedding day. Have you prepared yourself more for the wedding day than the marriage afterwards? Don't put too much emphasis on the wrong thing. That one day is not going to define the rest of your lives together.

About the Author

A Jet Tour Through the Author's Life

The only child born to his parents, Clarence Benoit was born in Novato, California on June 8, 1970. His father was an officer in the United States Air Force stationed at the now-defunct Hamilton Air Force Base once located on the western shore of San Pablo Bay while his mother was a stay-at-home mom. After their separation and eventual divorce, Clarence lived the majority of his childhood with his mother, who had sole legal custody of him. The two lived with his maternal grandmother in Jennings, LA for a few weeks after the separation just until his mother secured a job and a place to stay. This led them to Lake Charles, LA where they lived for several years and his mother worked as a cook at a local

Piccadilly restaurant. As a young child, Clarence knew he was going to college probably before he really knew what college was all about. He remembers sitting on the floor watching television one day when an advertisement for a university came on the screen. He was so intrigued and captivated by what he saw that he knew he wanted to go there someday. Initially, he aspired to be a police officer when he grew up. Soon after, as his athleticism and love for playing sports began to manifest. He dreamt of becoming a professional athlete someday. He couldn't make up his mind whether he wanted to play football or basketball professionally. So, he decided to keep his options open since there really wasn't much of a rush to make a decision right away.

Late in the summer of 1979, Clarence was kidnapped by his father from his paternal grandmother's house in Huntsville, TX and taken to live in Las Vegas, NV where his father was stationed at Nellis Air Force Base and lived with his wife and infant daughter. For the entire duration, Clarence was abused and mistreated by his father; he slept on the floor because his father never bought him a bed to sleep in, and his father frequently fought him as though he was fighting a grown man. Although you could always tell he would be athletic and play sports, it was during this time that his love for playing sports really grew. Back to his days with his mother, he went from occasionally playing a little baseball in the yard with her to now playing football and basketball regularly with the neighborhood kids. In Vegas, he once played on a co-ed little league baseball team where he led the team in home runs with two. The team was at the bottom of the league and couldn't find a way to win their first game until the last game of the season. They were so excited, jumping, and hollering, and carrying on, you would have thought they'd won the championship. Most often though, he could be found playing football or basketball at the neighborhood hotspots. Or, playing basketball during recess on the grounds of Rose Warren Middle School where he frequently had some intense battles with the likes of Donald Seaton and Mike Rasmussen. Over the years, his mother worked with a lawyer and made painstaking attempts to retrieve Clarence from his father. Clarence was fortunate enough to maintain consistent contact with his mother throughout those years. Just when it seemed that he would be stuck there for the duration of his childhood, things took a turn for the better. In April of 1982, while attending Jim Bridger Jr. High School, Clarence's mother secretly came into town to take him back home with her where he belonged. To this day, he still hasn't found the words to capture the magnitude of joy he felt in being reunited with his mother and freed from his abuser.

Now, back with his mother, living in Bryan, Texas, Clarence finished his last two months of the 6th grade. Then, he attended Anson Jones Middle School, an all 7th grade school, where he began playing organized football and basketball for the first time. This late start fits perfectly with Clarence's description of his days growing up. He considers himself a late bloomer due to his seemingly perpetual knack for getting involved in activities behind everyone else. Because of a friend who attended the university, on occasion, you could find him playing football with some of the college students at Texas A&M. The football was entirely too big for him to grasp with his small hands, so he couldn't grip the football to make a decent throw. But it was perfectly suited for catching on the run, which is all he seemed to be concerned about anyway. Continued from his days in Vegas, he also participated in the band playing the tuba, the sousaphone, and the cornet. Another activity he started behind in. By the time he started band in the 6th grade, the students had already learned how to read music. So, he had to compensate somehow to keep up with his fellow classmates. The instrument he really had a passion for learning to play was the alto saxophone. He performed at concerts with the school's band over the course of the year. Although he liked playing in the school band, his days of being a band member was short-lived. He figured out that it just wasn't for him. He added ROTC to his list of activities when he entered the 8th grade at Stephen F. Austin Middle School. Midway through his first semester, his mother decided to move to Houston, TX. This move proved to be more detrimental than beneficial. Hard times hit the two pretty hard for the first couple of years or so. Things were somewhat unstable and his mother at times struggled to make ends meet. They moved frequently and, on a few occasions, they had to live with relatives for a while. Due to these circumstances, Clarence changed schools pretty often and had to miss playing organized sports. Their situation seemed a bit more promising when Clarence began his freshman year at Sam Houston Senior High School in 1984. He was determined to get back into playing sports before it was too late. After arriving on campus the first day and seeing some of the seemingly monstrous football players, he became very intimidated. Being a rather small guy, he thought to himself that nobody that size was ever going to hit him. So, shooting jump shots became the viable option and his dilemma of playing professional football or basketball had suddenly been resolved. Unfortunately, it would be a couple of more years before he would participate in anything because midway through his first semester at Sam Houston; they had to move again. At Sam Houston, Clarence seemed to begin to flourish more socially than he had at any other time in his life. He had built a good rapport with his teachers and was building good friendships with some of his fellow classmates. Leaving Sam Houston seemed to propel him backwards into being more reserved and withdrawn. After moving, he ended up at E. L. Furr Senior High School, which is where he would eventually graduate from in 1988. It was in his junior year when he began playing basketball again and he would play in his senior year as well. He also served as manager of the track team as a junior. Then, as a senior, was a distance runner competing in the mile and two-mile events, which he absolutely did not like but got stuck in them. In his first meet, coach tossed him in the two-mile event to see how he would do. Clarence, not too fond of having to run for so long, kicked the last two hundred meters to hurry up and get the race over. To his detriment, he ended up impressing the coach and sealing his fate as a distance runner. This wasn't quite the outcome he was hoping for.

In the fall of 1988, he ventured off to college where he attended Ottawa University in Ottawa, KS. At first, it was a bit of a culture shock going from a major metropolitan area such as Houston to a seemingly one-horse town as Ottawa. But, his flexibility and ability to adapt to unfavorable circumstances proved valuable in getting him through. While at Ottawa University, Clarence majored in Computer Information Systems and continued his career in playing basketball and running track. His collegiate basketball career started off a little rough; and he only ran track for his freshman and sophomore years. In track, he participated in the 400m, 4 x 100m relay, and the 4 x 400m relay events. As you can tell, he stayed far away from distance. Before hanging up his spikes, he earned two varsity letters and made All-KCAC Conference Third Team his sophomore year. Basketball was always his passion and under a new coach, he would get to experience some degree of success. He earned two varsity letters and in his senior year, the Braves secured a berth in the NAIA Division II National Basketball Tournament held in Nampa, ID. This was the school's first tournament appearance in forty-two years. In the summer of 1993, he went on to graduate and earn his Bachelor of Arts degree.

After college, he moved up the road to Lawrence, KS. As with most, finding a job in his field didn't occur immediately. So, he worked at UPS, a job he had while in college, as a part-time supervisor as his main job in hopes of advancing there. Along with that job, he worked various other jobs off and on for the next three years. After two years, he moved away to Kansas City, MO in June 1995 in hopes of finding a job where he could put his degree to use. He struggled to find a job in his field of study. Being that he didn't consider Kansas City a place he desired to make his home, he took the difficulty of finding a job as a sign that maybe it was time to move on. He decided to look elsewhere for job opportunities primarily on the west coast. No sooner than he made that decision, in February 1996, he received a call back from a job he applied to earlier. He ended up working as a Programmer Trainee for the City of Kansas City, MO in the payroll department. Then, eight months later, he was hired on at DST Systems as an Analyst Programmer. He remained employed there for the next thirteen and a half years until February 2010 where he was a casualty of a series of layoffs due to the bad economic downturn. The fall after moving away from Lawrence, KS, Clarence met his first wife while she was a foreign exchange student at the University of Kansas. After she completed her year at KU, she returned to France to finish her last year of school and would return back to the States afterwards. Clarence waited for her return and the two were married on May 24, 1997. Unfortunately, this union would not last long as the two were separated eleven and a half months later with her returning to France and the divorce finalized only two months later. In February 1999, Clarence began attending Keller Graduate School of Management in pursuit of his Master's in Business Administration and a Graduate Certificate in Information Systems Management. He graduated from Keller in June of 2004. He was again wed in December 2001. The two separated in June 2006 and divorced in April 2008. Throughout all of the trials and life's so-called successes, his greatest blessing came on July 16, 2000 when he decided to follow Jesus by proclaiming Jesus as Lord of his life and became a baptized disciple (Christian) of Jesus Christ. Currently, Clarence is still living in Kansas City, MO.

About the Author

Keeping Tabs on the Author

Website:	www.ClarenceBenoit3.com
Facebook:	www.facebook.com/BenoitClarence3
Twitter:	www.twitter.com/BenoitClarence3
Email:	clarence@clarencebenoit3.com
Blog:	Walk According to the Savior (WAttS)
	www.clarencebenoit3.com/blog
Previous Book(s):	Enduring Through the Storms
Coming up Next:	Lord, What Have I Done?

Bibliography

Chamie, Joseph. "Out of Wedlock Births Rise Worldwide." 16 March 2017. *YaleGlobal Online*. <https://yaleglobal.yale.edu/content/out-wedlock-births-rise-worldwide>.

Coughlin, Paul. "Pain and Prejudice." 5 July 2011. *Crosswalk*. <www.crosswalk.com/faith/men/pain-and-prejudice-11536448.html>.

DiDonato, Ph.D., Theresa E. "Should You Move-in Together, or Not?" 25 July 2014. *Psychology Today*. <https://www.psychologytoday.com/us/blog/meet-catch-and-keep/201407/should-you-move-in-together-or-not>.

Eggerichs, Emerson. "Recognizing Your Son's Need for Respect (Parts 1 & 2)" with Jim Daly. *Focus on the Family*. Bott Radio Network. KCCV, Kansas City. 20 July 2017. <http://www.focusonthefamily.com>.

Fertel, Mort. "Rachel and Leah." 15 October 2010. *Marriage Fitness*. <www.marriagemax.com/blog/rachel-leah>.

Gilbert, Tom. "Donna Reed's Show Reflects an Era When Mother, Too, Knew Best." 27 December 2011. *Pittsburg Post-Gazette*. <http://www.post-gazette.com/tv-radio/2011/12/27/Donna-Reed-s-show-reflects-an-era-when-mother-too-knew-best/stories/201112270205>.

Ingram, Chip. "Love, Sex, and Lasting Relationships (Parts 1 & 2)." 23-24 August 2012. *Living on the Edge*. <www.livingontheedge.org>.

Kimball, Spencer W. "Oneness in Marriage." March 1977. *Church of Jesus Christ of Latter-Day Saints*. <https://www.lds.org/ensign/1977/03/oneness-in-marriage?lang=eng>.

Stoeker, Fred. "Men: Maintaining Sexual Purity (Part 1)" with Jim Daly. *Focus on the Family*. Bott Radio Network. KCCV, Kansas City. 21 February 2017. <http://www.focusonthefamily.com>.

Tracy, Abigail. "Broken Rails Are Leading Cause of Train Derailments." 13 May 2015. *Scientific American.* <www.scientificamerican.com/article/broken-rails-are-leading-cause-of-train-derailment>.

Walsh, Matt. "Matt Walsh: 5 Reasons Why Living Together Before Marriage Will Kill Your Relationship." 6 September 2017. *The Blaze.* <https://www.theblaze.com/contributions/5-reasons-why-living-together-before-marriage-will-kill-your-relationship>.

Wikipedia: Hurricane Alicia. n.d. <https://en.wikipedia.org/wiki/Hurricane_Alicia>.

Wright, Jennifer. "How to Decrease Your Risk of Divorce." 3 May 2011. *The Gloss.* <http://www.thegloss.com/sex-and-dating/how-to-decrease-your-risk-of-divorce/>.